THE COMMON LAW LIBRARY

MCGREGOR ON DAMAGES

SECOND CUMULATIVE SUPPLEMENT TO THE TWENTY-FIRST EDITION

Up to date until August 2022 with additional amendments incorporated

By

JAMES EDELMAN

A Justice of the High Court of Australia

SWEET & MAXWELL

THOMSON REUTERS

Published in 2022 by Thomson Reuters,
trading as Sweet & Maxwell.
Thomson Reuters is registered in England & Wales,
Company No.1679046.
Registered office and address for Service:
5 Canada Square, Canary Wharf, London, E14 5AQ.

For further information on our products and services, visit *http://
www.sweetandmaxwell.co.uk.*

Computerset by Sweet & Maxwell.
Printed and bound by CPI Group (UK) Ltd, Croydon, CR0 4YY.
A CIP catalogue record for this book is available from the British Library.

ISBN (print): 978-0-414-10427-3

ISBN (e-book): 978-0-414-10429-7

ISBN (print and e-book): 978-0-414-10428-0

Thomson Reuters, the Thomson Reuters Logo and Sweet & Maxwell ® are
trademarks of Thomson Reuters.

Crown copyright material is reproduced with the permission of the
Controller of HMSO and the King's Printer for Scotland.

THE COMMON LAW LIBRARY

McGregor on Damages

VOLUMES IN THE COMMON LAW LIBRARY

Arlidge, Eady & Smith on Contempt
Benjamin's Sale of Goods
Bowstead & Reynolds on Agency
Bullen & Leake & Jacob's Precedents of Pleadings
Charlesworth & Percy on Negligence
Chitty on Contracts
Clerk & Lindsell on Torts
Gatley on Libel and Slander
Goff & Jones on Unjust Enrichment
Jackson & Powell on Professional Liability
McGregor on Damages
Phipson on Evidence

HOW TO USE THIS SUPPLEMENT

This is the Second Cumulative Supplement to the Twenty-First Edition of *McGregor on Damages*, and has been compiled according to the structure of the main volume.

At the beginning of each chapter of this Supplement, a mini table of contents of the sections in the main volume has been included. Where a heading in this table of contents has been marked with a square pointer, this indicates that there is relevant information in this Supplement to which the reader should refer. Material that is new to the Cumulative Supplement is indicated by the symbol ■. Material that has been included from the previous supplement is indicated by the symbol □.

Within each chapter, updating information is referenced to the relevant paragraph in the main volume.

TABLE OF CONTENTS

How To Use This Supplement v
Table of Cases ix
Table of Statutes xix
Table of Statutory Instruments xxi

1. THE MEANING OF DAMAGES AND COMPENSATION AT COMMON LAW AND IN
   EQUITY 1

2. THE OBJECT OF AN AWARD OF COMPENSATORY DAMAGES 5

3. THE TERMINOLOGY IN COMPENSATORY DAMAGES AND IN CONSEQUENTIAL
   LOSS CLAUSES 9

5. NON-PECUNIARY LOSSES 13

6. THE GENERAL PROBLEM OF LIMITS 19

7. REDUCTION OF DAMAGES FOR CONTRIBUTORY NEGLIGENCE 21

8. CAUSATION OF DAMAGE, SCOPE OF DUTY, AND REMOTENESS OF DAMAGE 25

9. MITIGATION OF DAMAGE 41

10. CERTAINTY OF DAMAGE, PRESUMPTIONS OF DAMAGE, AND LOSS OF
    CHANCE 47

12. NOMINAL DAMAGES 59

13. EXEMPLARY DAMAGES 61

14. LICENCE FEE (NEGOTIATING AND USER) DAMAGES 65

15. ACCOUNT AND DISGORGEMENT OF PROFITS 69

16. LIQUIDATED DAMAGES AND PENALTIES 73

18. THE INCIDENCE OF TAXATION 85

19. THE AWARDING OF INTEREST 89

22. BREACH OF UNDERTAKINGS AS TO DAMAGES 95

25. SALE OF GOODS 99

28. LEASE OF LAND 105

29. SALE OF SHARES AND LOAN OF STOCK 109

34. CONTRACTS FOR PROFESSIONAL AND OTHER SERVICES 111

37. Torts Affecting Goods: Damage and Destruction 119

38. Torts Affecting Goods: Misappropriation 123

39. Torts Affecting Land 127

40. Torts Causing Personal Injury 133

41. Torts Causing Death 143

42. Assault and False Imprisonment 153

43. Statutory Torts: Discrimination and Harassment 155

44. Malicious Institution of Legal Proceedings 159

46. Defamation 161

47. Privacy, Confidence and Private Information 169

48. Economic Torts and Intellectual Property Wrongs 173

49. Misrepresentation 177

50. Damages under the Human Rights Act 181

TABLE OF CASES

Abbey Forwarding Ltd v Hone (No.3). *See* Hone v Abbey Forwarding Ltd (In Liquidation) 22-002A, 22-006A

Adan v Securicor Custodial Services Ltd [2004] EWHC 394 (QB); [2004] 2 WLUK 596; [2004] C.P. Rep. 33; [2005] P.I.Q.R. P6 .... 40-007A

Adelfa, The. *See* Adelfamar SA v Silos e Mangimi Martini SpA (The Adelfa) 16-027A

Adelfamar SA v Silos e Mangimi Martini SpA (The Adelfa); Adelfa, The [1988] 2 Lloyd's Rep. 466; [1988] 2 WLUK 212 QBD (Comm Ct). 16-027A

AerCap Partners 1 Ltd v Avia Asset Management AB [2010] EWHC 2431 (Comm); [2010] 10 WLUK 107; [2010] 2 C.L.C. 578; [2011] Bus. L.R. D85 .... 10-065, 10-068

AI Giorgis Oil Trading Ltd v AG Shipping and Energy Pte Ltd; MT Marquessa [2021] EWHC 2319 (Comm); [2021] 8 WLUK 115. .... 16-066A

Aktieselskabet Reidar v Arcos Ltd; sub nom. Reidar A/S v Acros Ltd [1927] 1 K.B. 352; (1926) 25 Ll. L. Rep. 513; [1926] 7 WLUK 94 CA. 16-027, 16-027A

Al-Rawas v Pegasus Energy Ltd [2008] EWHC 617 (QB); [2009] 1 All E.R. 346; [2009] 1 All E.R. (Comm) 393; [2008] 4 WLUK 191. .... 22-006A

Alta Trading UK Ltd (formerly Arcadia Petroleum Ltd) v Bosworth [2021] EWHC 1126 (Comm); [2021] 4 W.L.R. 72; [2021] 4 WLUK 400 22-006

Andrews v Australia and New Zealand Banking Group Ltd (2012) 247 C.L.R. 205 16-002

Antuzis v DJ Houghton Catching Services Ltd [2021] EWHC 971 (QB); [2021] 4 WLUK 249. 48-008

Argos Pereira Espana SL v Athenian Marine Ltd [2021] EWHC 554 (Comm); [2021] Bus. L.R. 866; [2021] 3 WLUK 135. 2-010

Armstead v Royal and Sun Alliance Insurance Co Ltd [2022] EWCA Civ 497; [2022] 4 WLUK 243; [2022] R.T.R. 23. .... 8-093A, 37-028A

Arsalan v Rixon [2021] HCA 40; (2021) 96 ALJR 1 .... 9-068, 37-016A

Aslani v Sobierajska [2021] EWHC 2127 (QB); [2021] 7 WLUK 445 46-030

AssetCo Plc v Grant Thornton UK LLP [2020] EWCA Civ 1151; [2021] 3 All E.R. 517; [2021] Bus. L.R. 142; [2020] 8 WLUK 227; [2021] 2 B.C.L.C. 227; [2021] P.N.L.R. 1 .... 10-044, 34-089, 34-089A

Attorney General of the Virgin Islands v Global Water Associates Ltd [2020] UKPC 18; [2021] A.C. 23; [2020] 3 W.L.R. 584; [2021] 2 All E.R. (Comm) 1; [2020] 7 WLUK 169 .... 6-010A

Attorney General v Observer Ltd; Attorney General v Guardian Newspapers Ltd (No.2); Attorney General v Times Newspapers Ltd (No.2) [1990] 1 A.C. 109; [1988] 3 W.L.R. 776; [1988] 3 All E.R. 545; [1988] 10 WLUK 130; [1989] 2 F.S.R. 181; (1988) 85(42) L.S.G. 45; (1988) 138 N.L.J. Rep. 296; (1988) 132 S.J. 1496 HL 15-049B

AXD v Home Office [2016] EWHC 1617 (QB); [2016] 7 WLUK 73 44-005

Axnoller Events Ltd v Brake [2022] EWHC 1162 (Ch); [2022] 5 WLUK 306 ..... 14-014, 14-028

B Lawrence & Associates v Intercommercial Bank Ltd [2021] UKPC 30; [2021] 11 WLUK 291; [2022] P.N.L.R. 7 .... 8-052A

B v Cager [2021] EWHC 540 (QB); [2021] 3 WLUK 99 42-004

Balogh v Hick Lane Bedding Ltd [2021] EWHC 1140 (QB); [2021] 3 WLUK 749 ...... 48-008C

Barron v Collins [2017] EWHC 162 (QB); [2017] 2 WLUK 136 46-075

Barrowfen Properties Ltd v Patel [2021] EWHC 2055 (Ch); [2021] 7 WLUK 338 10-068

Barrowfen Properties Ltd v Patel [2022] EWHC 1601 (Ch); [2022] 6 WLUK 254 .. 19-042, 34-080

Bath and North East Somerset DC v Mowlem Plc [2004] EWCA Civ 115; [2015] 1 W.L.R. 785; [2004] 2 WLUK 586; [2004] B.L.R. 153; 100 Con. L.R. 1; (2004) 148 S.J.L.B. 265 .... 16-027B

BDW Trading Ltd v URS Corp Ltd [2021] EWHC 2796 (TCC); [2021] 10 WLUK 324; 200 Con. L.R. 192. 8-043

Beattie Passive Norse Ltd v Canham Consulting Ltd [2021] EWHC 1116 (TCC); [2021] 4 WLUK 386; [2021] T.C.L.R. 5; 196 Con. L.R. 85; [2021] P.N.L.R. 22 12-008

Blackledge v Person(s) Unknown [2021] EWHC 1994 (QB); [2021] 7 WLUK 179 43-019

Blizzard Entertainment SAS v Bossland GmbH [2019] EWHC 1665 (Ch); [2019] 7 WLUK 62 .... 15-049A, 18-041A

Bloomberg LP v ZXC; sub nom. ZXC v Bloomberg LP [2022] UKSC 5; [2022] 2 W.L.R. 424; [2022] 3 All E.R. 1; [2022] 2 WLUK 191; [2022] 2 Cr. App. R. 2; [2022] E.M.L.R. 15; [2022] H.R.L.R. 8; 52 B.H.R.C. 708; [2022] Crim. L.R. 500. .... 47-010A

Bockenfield Aerodrome Ltd v Clarehugh [2021] EWHC 848 (Ch); [2020] 12 WLUK 622 . . 39-026
Bonde, The. *See* Richco International Ltd v Alfred C Toepfer International GmbH (The
 Bonde) 16-027A
Booth v White [2003] EWCA Civ 1708; [2003] 11 WLUK 437; (2003) 147 S.J.L.B. 1367 . . . 7-011
BP Oil International Ltd v Glencore Energy UK Ltd [2022] EWHC 499 (Comm); [2022] 3
 WLUK 104 . . . . 25-062, 25-065
BPE Solicitors v Hughes-Holland. *See* Gabriel v Little 6-005, 34-089
Brain v Yorkshire Rider Ltd [2007] 3 WLUK 668; [2007] Lloyd's Rep. I.R. 564 CC
 (Leeds) 37-016
Brearley v Higgs & Sons (A Firm) [2021] EWHC 2635 (Ch); [2021] 10 WLUK 78 . . . . 8-005A
Breslin v Loughrey [2020] NICA 39; [2020] 9 WLUK 485; [2021] I.R.L.R. 320 43-007
British Gas Trading Ltd v Shell UK Ltd [2020] EWCA Civ 2349; [2020] 12 WLUK 62 . . . 8-142A,
 10-117A
British Transport Commission v Gourley [1956] A.C. 185; [1956] 2 W.L.R. 41; [1955] 3
 All E.R. 796; [1955] 2 Lloyd's Rep. 475; [1955] 12 WLUK 31; 49 R. & I.T. 11; (1955)
 34 A.T.C. 305; [1955] T.R. 303; (1956) 100 S.J. 12 HL. 18-078
Brooke Homes (Bicester) Ltd v Portfolio Property Partners Ltd [2021] EWHC 3015 (Ch);
 [2021] 11 WLUK 162. 10-068
Broome v Cassell & Co Ltd [1972] A.C. 1027; [1972] 2 W.L.R. 645; [1972] 1 All E.R.
 801; [1972] 2 WLUK 97; (1972) 116 S.J. 199 HL 15-049A, 15-049B
Brown v KMR Services Ltd (formerly HG Poland (Agencies) Ltd); Sword Daniels v Pitel
 [1995] 4 All E.R. 598; [1995] 2 Lloyd's Rep. 513; [1995] 7 WLUK 153; [1995] C.L.C.
 1418; [1995] 4 Re. L.R. 241 CA (Civ Div) 1-021B
Cairns v Modi; KC v MGN Ltd; sub nom. C v MGN Ltd [2012] EWCA Civ 1382; [2013]
 1 W.L.R. 1015; [2012] 10 WLUK 957; [2013] E.M.L.R. 8 46-075
Campbell v Advantage Insurance Co Ltd [2021] EWCA Civ 1698; [2022] Q.B. 354;
 [2022] 2 W.L.R. 246; [2021] 11 WLUK 188; [2022] R.T.R. 8; [2022] P.I.Q.R. P6. 7-011
Carnes v Nesbitt 158 E.R. 682; (1862) 7 Hurl. & N. 778; [1862] 1 WLUK 382 Ex Ct 16-027B
Cash v Chief Constable of Lancashire [2008] EWHC 396 (Ch); [2008] 2 WLUK 72;
 [2008] Po. L.R. 182 . . . . 5-013, 38-074A
Cavendish Square Holdings v Makdessi. *See* Makdessi v Cavendish Square Holdings BV . 16-029
Central Bank of Ecuador v Conticorp SA [2015] UKPC 11; [2015] 3 WLUK 617; [2016]
 1 B.C.L.C. 26; [2015] Bus. L.R. D7. 19-068
Chandris v Isbrandtsen Moller Co Inc [1951] 1 K.B. 240; [1950] 2 All E.R. 618; (1950) 84
 Ll. L. Rep. 347; 66 T.L.R. (Pt. 2) 358; [1950] 7 WLUK 61; (1950) 94 S.J. 534 CA 16-027A
Charles B Lawrence & Associates v Intercommercial Bank Ltd [2021] UKPC 30; [2021]
 11 WLUK 291; [2022] P.N.L.R. 7 34-078
Charles Villeneuve Kyoto Securities Ltd v Joel Gaillard H Holdings Ltd. *See* Villeneuve v
 Gaillard 1-021B
Checkprice (UK) Ltd v Revenue and Customs Commissioners. *See* R. (on the application
 of Checkprice (UK) Ltd (In Administration)) v Revenue and Customs Commissioners 12-008
Chouza v Martins [2021] EWHC 1669 (QB); [2021] 6 WLUK 305 . . . . 41-027, 41-105, 41-108
Chouza v Martins; sub nom. Rodriguez (Deceased), Re [2021] EWHC 1669 (QB); [2021]
 6 WLUK 305; [2021] P.I.Q.R. Q4; [2021] Med. L.R. 546. 41-131
Coldunell Ltd v Hotel Management International Ltd [2022] EWHC 1290 (TCC); [2022]
 5 WLUK 531 . . . . 28-057A, 28-068
Coles v Sims 43 E.R. 768; (1854) 5 De G.M. & G. 1; [1854] 1 WLUK 120 Ct of Chancery . . . .
 16-027B
Columbia Pictures Industries v Robinson [1987] Ch. 38; [1986] 3 W.L.R. 542; [1986] 3
 All E.R. 338; [1985] 12 WLUK 221; [1986] F.S.R. 367; (1986) 83 L.S.G. 3424; (1986)
 130 S.J. 766 Ch D 22-006A
Comberg v Vivopower International Services Ltd [2020] EWHC 2787 (QB); [2020] 10
 WLUK 241; [2020] Costs L.R. 1655. . . . . 18-059A
Constantine v Imperial Hotels Ltd [1944] K.B. 693; [1944] 2 All E.R. 171; [1944] 6
 WLUK 30 KBD 12-008
Corr v IBC Vehicles Ltd [2006] EWCA Civ 331; [2007] Q.B. 46; [2006] 3 W.L.R. 395;
 [2006] 2 All E.R. 929; [2006] 3 WLUK 889; [2006] I.C.R. 1138; (2006) 103(16) L.S.G.
 24. 8-117
Daily Office Cleaning Contractors v Shefford [1977] 4 WLUK 63; [1977] R.T.R. 361 DC . . 37-016
Davies v Carter [2021] EWHC 3021 (QB); [2021] 11 WLUK 193 43-019
Davies v Ford [2021] EWHC 2550 (Ch); [2021] 9 WLUK 226 . . . . 1-021A, 15-055, 15-058

Davies v Frimley Health NHS Foundation Trust; sub nom. Davies (Deceased), Re [2021]
EWHC 169 (QB); [2021] 1 WLUK 445; [2021] P.I.Q.R. P14; [2021] Med. L.R. 294;
(2021) 180 B.M.L.R. 56 8-018
De Havilland Aircraft of Canada Ltd v Spicejet Ltd [2021] EWHC 362 (Comm); [2021] 2
WLUK 334. . . . . 16-029A
Deutsche Bank AG v Total Global Steel Ltd [2012] EWHC 1201 (Comm); [2012] 5
WLUK 359; [2012] Env. L.R. D7. 9-079
Douglas v Hello! Ltd [2003] EWHC 2629 (Ch); [2003] 11 WLUK 178; [2004] E.M.L.R. 2 . 12-008
Douglas v Hello! Ltd *Also see* OBG Ltd v Allan 12-008
Doyle v Smith [2018] EWHC 2935 (QB); [2018] 11 WLUK 27; [2019] E.M.L.R. 15 46-030
Dr Reddy's Laboratories (UK) Ltd v Warner-Lambert Co LLC [2021] EWHC 2182 (Ch);
[2021] Bus. L.R. 1496; [2021] 7 WLUK 551 . . . . 22-008A
Dudley v Phillips [2022] EWHC 930 (QB); [2022] 4 WLUK 171 46-030
Durham Tees Valley Airport Ltd v bmibaby Ltd; sub nom. Durham Tees Valley Airport
Ltd v BMI Baby Ltd [2010] EWCA Civ 485; [2011] 1 All E.R. (Comm) 731; [2011] 1
Lloyd's Rep. 68; [2010] 5 WLUK 49; (2010) 154(18) S.J.L.B. 28 . . . . 10-117B
Durkin v DSG Retail Ltd and HFS Bank Plc [2008] GCCG 3651 10-012
Eco World - Ballymore Embassy Gardens Co Ltd v Dobler UK Ltd [2021] EWHC 2207
(TCC); [2021] 8 WLUK 5; [2021] T.C.L.R. 7; 197 Con. L.R. 108 . 16-029, 16-061, 16-093, 16-107
Elliott v Hattens Solicitors [2021] EWCA Civ 720; [2021] 5 WLUK 185 34-009
Ennismore Fund Management Ltd v Fenris Consulting Ltd [2022] UKPC 27; [2022] 6
WLUK 311. . . . . 22-007A, 22-010A
ERG Raffinerie Mediterranee SpA v Chevron USA Inc (t/a Chevron Texaco Global
Trading); Luxmar, The [2006] EWHC 1322 (Comm); [2006] 2 All E.R. (Comm) 913;
[2006] 2 Lloyd's Rep. 543; [2006] 6 WLUK 138 . . . . 16-027A
F&T Terrix Ltd v CBT Global Ltd [2021] EWHC 3379 (Comm); [2021] 12 WLUK 181 . . . 25-030
FBT Productions LLC v Let Them Eat Vinyl Distribution Ltd [2021] EWHC 932 (IPEC);
[2021] 4 WLUK 186. 14-044
Fentiman v Marsh [2019] EWHC 2099 (QB); [2019] 7 WLUK 535 46-071
Financial Conduct Authority v Arch Insurance (UK) Ltd; Hiscox Action Group v Arch
Insurance (UK) Ltd; Argenta Syndicate Management Ltd v Financial Conduct
Authority; Royal & Sun Alliance Insurance Plc v Financial Conduct Authority; MS
Amlin Underwriting Ltd v Financial Conduct Authority; Hiscox Insurance Co Ltd v
Financial Conduct Authority; QBE UK Ltd v Financial Conduct Authority; Arch
Insurance (UK) Ltd v Financial Conduct Authority [2021] UKSC 1; [2021] A.C. 649;
[2021] 2 W.L.R. 123; [2021] 3 All E.R. 1077; [2021] 1 WLUK 101; [2021] Lloyd's
Rep. I.R. 63 . . . . 8-013A
Fittschen v Chief Constable of Dorset [2022] EWHC 399 (QB); [2022] 2 WLUK 380 8-005
FM Capital Partners Ltd v Marino. *See* Marino v FM Capital Partners Ltd 15-046
Foreman v Williams [2017] EWHC 3370 (QB); [2017] 12 WLUK 649 40-269
FP McCann Ltd v Department for Regional Development [2020] NIQB 51; [2020] 6
WLUK 537 10-048
FS Cairo (Nile Plaza) LLC v Lady Brownlie; sub nom. Brownlie v FS Cairo (Nile Plaza)
LLC [2021] UKSC 45; [2021] 3 W.L.R. 1011; [2022] 3 All E.R. 207; [2022] 2 All E.R.
(Comm) 1; [2021] 10 WLUK 231 8-057
Gabb v Farrokhzad [2022] EWHC 212 (Ch); [2022] 1 W.L.R. 2842; [2022] 2 WLUK 61;
[2022] L. & T.R. 16; [2022] 2 P. & C.R. DG10. . . . . 13-025A
Gabriel v Little; Hughes-Holland v BPE Solicitors; Gabriel v Little (t/a High Tech Design
& Build Ltd); BPE Solicitors v Gabriel [2017] UKSC 21; [2018] A.C. 599; [2017] 2
W.L.R. 1029; [2017] 3 All E.R. 969; [2017] 3 WLUK 531; 171 Con. L.R. 46; [2017]
P.N.L.R. 23 . . . . 6-005, 34-089
Gale v Scannella [2021] EWHC 1225 (QB); [2021] 5 WLUK 97 46-038
General Accident Assurance Corp v Noel [1902] 1 K.B. 377; [1901] 12 WLUK 41 KBD . 16-027B
Ghannouchi v Middle East Online Ltd [2020] EWHC 1992 (QB); [2020] 7 WLUK 391 46-071
Gilham v MGN Ltd [2020] EWHC 2217 (QB); [2020] 8 WLUK 87 . . . . 46-070, 46-075
Glenn v Kline [2021] EWHC 468 (QB); [2021] 3 WLUK 73 . . . . 43-019, 43-020, 46-038
Glenn v Watson [2018] EWHC 2016 (Ch); [2018] 7 WLUK 750 19-068
Glenn v Watson [2018] EWHC 2483 (Ch); [2018] 9 WLUK 293 19-068
Global Display Solutions Ltd v NCR Financial Solutions Group Ltd [2021] EWHC 1119
(Comm); [2021] 4 WLUK 367 . . . . 13-013, 13-043
Glossop Cartons and Print Ltd v Contact (Print and Packaging) Ltd [2021] EWCA Civ
639; [2021] 1 W.L.R. 4297; [2021] 5 WLUK 54. . . . . 49-028A

Godwin v Uzoigwe [1992] 6 WLUK 233; [1993] Fam. Law 65; (1992) 136 S.J.L.B. 205;
[1992] T.L.R. 300 CA (Civ Div) 48-008C
Google LLC v Lloyd; sub nom. Lloyd v Google LLC [2021] UKSC 50; [2021] 3 W.L.R.
1268; [2022] 2 All E.R. 209; [2022] 1 All E.R. (Comm) 1107; [2021] 11 WLUK 95;
[2022] E.M.L.R. 6; [2022] H.R.L.R. 1 . . . . 14-037, 47-015
Gosden v Halliwell Landau [2021] EWHC 159 (Comm); [2021] 2 WLUK 42; [2021]
P.N.L.R. 14; [2021] W.T.L.R. 205 . . . . 18-078, 34-035
Gray v Global Energy Horizons Corp [2020] EWCA Civ 1668; [2021] 1 W.L.R. 2264;
[2020] 12 WLUK 115 15-051
Gray v Thames Trains Ltd [2009] UKHL 33; [2009] 1 A.C. 1339; [2009] 3 W.L.R. 167;
[2009] 4 All E.R. 81; [2009] 6 WLUK 456; [2009] P.I.Q.R. P22; [2009] LS Law
Medical 409; (2009) 108 B.M.L.R. 205; [2009] M.H.L.R. 73; [2009] Po. L.R. 229;
(2009) 159 N.L.J. 925; (2009) 153(24) S.J.L.B. 33 8-117
Greatship (India) Ltd v Oceanografia SA de CV; Greatship Dhriti, The [2012] EWHC
3468 (Comm); [2013] 1 All E.R. (Comm) 1244; [2013] 2 Lloyd's Rep. 359; [2012] 12
WLUK 87; (2012) 162 N.L.J. 1563 . . . . 16-066A
Grieves v FT Everard & Sons Ltd; Quinn v George Clark & Nem Ltd; Mears v RG Carter
Ltd; Jackson v Brock Plc; Rothwell v Chemical & Insulating Co Ltd; Downey v
Charles Evans Shopfitters Ltd; Storey v Clellands Shipbuilders Ltd; Topping v
Benchtown Ltd (formerly Jones Bros (Preston) Ltd); Johnston v NEI International
Combustion Ltd; Hindson v Pipe House Wharf (Swansea) Ltd [2007] UKHL 39; [2008]
1 A.C. 281; [2007] 3 W.L.R. 876; [2007] 4 All E.R. 1047; [2007] 10 WLUK 411;
[2007] I.C.R. 1745; [2008] P.I.Q.R. P6; [2008] LS Law Medical 1; (2008) 99 B.M.L.R.
139; (2007) 104(42) L.S.G. 34; (2007) 157 N.L.J. 1542; (2007) 151 S.J.L.B. 1366. . . . . . 40-007B
Groom v Selby [2001] EWCA Civ 1522; [2001] 10 WLUK 513; [2002] P.I.Q.R. P18;
[2002] Lloyd's Rep. Med. 1; (2002) 64 B.M.L.R. 47 . . . . 8-050A
Gul v McDonagh [2021] EWCA Civ 1503; [2021] 10 WLUK 204; [2022] R.T.R. 9 7-007
Gulati v MGN Ltd; Taggart v MGN Ltd; Yentob v MGN Ltd; Alcorn v MGN Ltd; Roche
v MGN Ltd; Gascoigne v MGN Ltd; Ashworth v MGN Ltd; Frost v MGN Ltd; sub
nom. Representative Claimants v MGN Ltd [2015] EWCA Civ 1291; [2017] Q.B. 149;
[2016] 2 W.L.R. 1217; [2016] 3 All E.R. 799; [2015] 12 WLUK 608; [2016] E.M.L.R.
9; [2016] F.S.R. 13 47-015
Hamilton v NG Bailey Ltd [2020] EWHC 2910 (QB); [2020] 10 WLUK 400; [2021]
P.I.Q.R. P8 . . . . 40-007B
Hayden v Duckworth [2020] EWHC 1033 (QB); [2021] 3 WLUK 251 . . . . 8-044, 47-010A
Head v Culver Heating Co Ltd [2021] EWCA Civ 34; [2021] 1 WLUK 129; [2021]
P.I.Q.R. Q2 . . . . 40-064, 41-082A
Hedley Byrne & Co Ltd v Heller & Partners Ltd [1964] A.C. 465; [1963] 3 W.L.R. 101;
[1963] 2 All E.R. 575; [1963] 1 Lloyd's Rep. 485; [1963] 5 WLUK 95; (1963) 107 S.J.
454 HL 2-010
Henderson v Dorset Healthcare University NHS Foundation Trust [2020] UKSC 43;
[2021] A.C. 563; [2020] 3 W.L.R. 1124; [2021] 2 All E.R. 257; [2020] 10 WLUK 386;
[2021] P.I.Q.R. P7; [2021] Med. L.R. 26; (2021) 177 B.M.L.R. 1; [2021] P.N.L.R. 7 8-117
Hijazi v Yaxley-Lennon [2021] EWHC 2008 (QB); [2021] 7 WLUK 369 . . . . 46-036, 46-038A
Hills v Tabe (aka Mateke) [2022] EWHC 316 (QB); [2022] 2 WLUK 245 . . . . 43-019, 46-030
Hirtenstein v Hill Dickinson LLP [2014] EWHC 2711 (Comm); [2014] 7 WLUK 1118 10-065
HL Motorworks (Willesden) v Alwahbi [1977] 2 WLUK 16; [1977] R.T.R. 276 CA (Civ
Div) 37-016
Holtham v Commissioner of Police for the Metropolis [1987] 11 WLUK 282; [1987]
C.L.Y. 1154 CA (Civ Div) 19-053
Hone v Abbey Forwarding Ltd (In Liquidation); sub nom. Abbey Forwarding Ltd (In
Liquidation) v Hone [2014] EWCA Civ 711; [2015] Ch. 309; [2014] 3 W.L.R. 1676;
[2014] 5 WLUK 836 . . . . 22-002A, 22-006A
Hotel Portfolio II UK Ltd (In Liquidation) v Ruhan [2022] EWHC 383 (Comm); [2022] 2
WLUK 307 . . . . 1-021B, 15-049B
Howard v Woodward (1864) 34 L.J. Ch. 47 . . . . 16-027B
Hunter v Canary Wharf Ltd; sub nom. Hunter v London Docklands Development Corp
[1997] A.C. 655; [1997] 2 W.L.R. 684; [1997] 2 All E.R. 426; [1997] 4 WLUK 366;
[1997] C.L.C. 1045; 84 B.L.R. 1; 54 Con. L.R. 12; [1997] Env. L.R. 488; [1997] 2
F.L.R. 342; (1998) 30 H.L.R. 409; [1997] Fam. Law 601; [1997] E.G. 59 (C.S.); (1997)
94(19) L.S.G. 25; (1997) 147 N.L.J. 634; (1997) 141 S.J.L.B. 108; [1997] N.P.C. 64 HL. . . 39-020,
39-022A
Hussain v EUI Ltd [2019] EWHC 2647 (QB); [2019] 10 WLUK 152; [2020] R.T.R. 7 . . . 37-016A

Imageview Management Ltd v Jack [2009] EWCA Civ 63; [2009] 2 All E.R. 666; [2009] 1 All E.R. (Comm) 921; [2009] Bus. L.R. 1034; [2009] 1 Lloyd's Rep. 436; [2009] 2 WLUK 374; [2009] 1 B.C.L.C. 724. . . . . 15-049B
Imperial Tobacco Co v Parsley [1936] 2 All E.R. 515 CA 16-027B
Jackman v Harold Firth and Son Ltd [2021] EWHC 1461 (QB); [2021] 5 WLUK 479 41-108
James v White Lion Hotel. *See* White Lion Hotel (A Partnership) v James 8-121
Johnson v Agnew [1980] A.C. 367; [1979] 2 W.L.R. 487; [1979] 1 All E.R. 883; [1979] 3 WLUK 74; (1979) 38 P. & C.R. 424; (1979) 251 E.G. 1167; (1979) 123 S.J. 217 HL. 3-012A
Johnson v King, The [1904] A.C. 817; [1904] 7 WLUK 89 PC 19-068
Jon Richard Ltd v Gornall [2013] EWHC 1357 (QB); [2013] 5 WLUK 406 46-030
Jones v Heavens (1877) 4 Ch. D. 636; [1877] 2 WLUK 36 Ch D 16-027B
Joyner v Weeks [1891] 2 Q.B. 31; [1891] 5 WLUK 10 CA 28-057A, 28-068, 28-090
K Line PTE Ltd v Priminds Shipping (HK) Co Ltd; sub nom. "Eternal Bliss" [2021] EWCA Civ 1712; [2022] 3 All E.R. 396; [2022] Bus. L.R. 67; [2021] 11 WLUK 24 . . . . . 16-027A
KC v MGN. *See* Cairns v Modi 46-075
Kerrigan v Elevate Credit International Ltd (t/a Sunny) (In Administration) [2020] EWHC 2169 (Comm); [2020] 8 WLUK 186; [2020] C.T.L.C. 161 10-012
Khan v Meadows; sub nom. Meadows v Khan [2021] UKSC 21; [2021] 3 W.L.R. 147; [2021] 6 WLUK 253 . . . . 6-005, 6-010A, 8-033, 8-047, 8-050A
Khan v Mehmood [2022] EWCA Civ 791; [2022] 6 WLUK 507 . . . . 28-033, 40-285
Khuja v Times Newspapers Ltd. *See* PNM v Times Newspapers Ltd 8-044
Kotula v EDF Energy Networks (EPN) Plc [2011] EWHC 1546 (QB); [2011] 6 WLUK 374 . . . . 40-007A
Kuchenmeister v Home Office [1958] 1 Q.B. 496; [1958] 2 W.L.R. 453; [1958] 1 All E.R. 485; [1958] 1 WLUK 708; (1958) 122 J.P. 160; (1958) 102 S.J. 196 QBD. 8-005
Lakatamia Shipping Co Ltd v Su [2021] EWHC 1907 (Comm); [2021] 7 WLUK 95 . 8-007, 13-008
Large v Hart; sub nom. Hart v Large [2021] EWCA Civ 24; [2021] 1 WLUK 97; [2021] B.L.R. 189; [2021] T.C.L.R. 2; [2021] P.N.L.R. 13. . . . . 8-049, 8-052, 34-064
Leeds Industrial Co-operative Society Ltd v Slack. *See* Slack v Leeds Industrial Cooperative Society Ltd (No.1) 3-012A
Lewis v Australian Capital Territory (2020) 271 C.L.R. 192 8-005
Lifestyle Equities CV v Ahmed; sub nom. Lifestyle Equities CV v Santa Monica Polo Club Ltd [2021] EWCA Civ 675; [2021] Bus. L.R. 1020; [2021] 5 WLUK 55; [2021] F.S.R. 31. . . . . 15-046, 15-049A, 18-041A
LIV Bridging Finance Ltd v EAD Solicitors LLP (In Administration) [2020] EWHC 1590 (Ch); [2020] 6 WLUK 251; [2020] P.N.L.R. 24. 34-089
Lloyd v Google LLC. *See* Google LLC v Lloyd 14-037, 47-015
Loughlin v Singh; sub nom. Loughlin v Dal Singh [2013] EWHC 1641 (QB); [2013] 6 WLUK 494; [2013] Med. L.R. 513. . . . . 40-007A
LP v Wye Valley NHS Trust [2018] EWHC 3039 (QB); [2018] 11 WLUK 428 40-211
Luxmar, The. *See* ERG Raffinerie Mediterranee SpA v Chevron USA Inc (t/a Chevron Texaco Global Trading) 16-027A
MacMahon v Grant Thornton UK LLP. *See* McMahon v Grant Thornton UK LLP 9-079
MAD Atelier International BV v Manes [2021] EWHC 3335 (Comm); [2021] 12 WLUK 143. . . . . 10-006, 10-015
Maharaj v Johnson [2015] UKPC 28; [2015] 6 WLUK 458; [2015] P.N.L.R. 27 34-009
Main v Giambrone. *See* Various Claimants v Giambrone and Law (A Firm) 8-050
Maisto v Kyrgiannakis [2012] EWHC 4084 (QB); [2012] 11 WLUK 815 43-019
Makdessi v Cavendish Square Holding BV; ParkingEye Ltd v Beavis; sub nom. Cavendish Square Holding BV v Makdessi, El Makdessi v Cavendish Square Holdings BV [2015] UKSC 67; [2016] A.C. 1172; [2015] 3 W.L.R. 1373; [2016] 2 All E.R. 519; [2016] 2 All E.R. (Comm) 1; [2016] 1 Lloyd's Rep. 55; [2015] 11 WLUK 78; [2015] 2 C.L.C. 686; [2016] B.L.R. 1; 162 Con. L.R. 1; [2016] R.T.R. 8; [2016] C.I.L.L. 3769 16-029
Mallino Development Ltd v Essex Demolition Contractors Ltd [2022] EWHC 1418 (TCC); [2022] 6 WLUK 229 . . . . 10-117B
Maloney v Mundays LLP [2021] EWHC 1324 (Ch); [2021] 5 WLUK 241 19-113
Malyon v Plummer [1964] 1 Q.B. 330; [1963] 2 W.L.R. 1213; [1963] 2 All E.R. 344; [1963] 3 WLUK 100; (1963) 107 S.J. 270 CA 41-082A
Manchester Building Society v Grant Thornton UK LLP [2021] UKSC 20; [2021] 3 W.L.R. 81; [2021] 6 WLUK 246 . . . . . 6-005, 6-010A, 7-012, 8-033, 8-047, 8-047, 8-050, 8-050A, 8-055, 34-089, 34-089A
Manson-Smith v Arthurworrey [2021] EWHC 2137 (QB); [2021] 7 WLUK 469 . . . . 39-022A, 43-020A

Marathon Asset Management LLP v Seddon [2017] EWHC 300 (Comm); [2017] 2
WLUK 594; [2017] 2 C.L.C. 182; [2017] I.C.R. 791; [2017] I.R.L.R. 503; [2017]
F.S.R. 36 10-001
Marino v FM Capital Partners Ltd; sub nom. FM Capital Partners Ltd v Marino [2020]
EWCA Civ 245; [2021] Q.B. 1; [2020] 3 W.L.R. 109; [2020] 2 WLUK 331; [2020] 1
C.L.C. 319. 15-046
Mathieu v Hinds [2022] EWHC 924 (QB); [2022] 4 WLUK 164 . . . . 9-088A, 18-057, 40-007A
McFarlane v Tayside Health Board; sub nom. Macfarlane v Tayside Health Board [2000]
2 A.C. 59; [1999] 3 W.L.R. 1301; [1999] 4 All E.R. 961; 2000 S.C. (H.L.) 1; 2000
S.L.T. 154; 2000 S.C.L.R. 105; [1999] 11 WLUK 846; [2000] 1 F.C.R. 102; [2000]
P.I.Q.R. Q101; [2000] Lloyd's Rep. Med. 1; (2000) 52 B.M.L.R. 1; (1999) 149 N.L.J.
1868; 1999 G.W.D. 39-1888 HL 8-050A
McKibbin v UK Insurance Ltd [2021] NIQB 27; [2021] 3 WLUK 740 37-017
McMahon v Grant Thornton UK LLP [2020] CSOH 50; [2020] S.T.C. 1732; 2020 S.L.T.
908; [2020] 5 WLUK 338; [2020] B.T.C. 16; [2020] S.T.I. 1388; 2020 G.W.D. 19-269 9-079
Medsted Associates Ltd v Canaccord Genuity Wealth (International) Ltd [2020] EWHC
2952 (Comm); [2020] 11 WLUK 53 . . . . 8-142A
Mirza v Ali [2021] EWHC 1494 (QB); [2021] 6 WLUK 71 46-038
Mirza v Farooqui [2021] EWHC 532 (QB); [2021] 3 WLUK 107 46-038
Mitchell v Royal Liverpool and Broadgreen University Hospitals NHS Trust [2006] 7
WLUK 481; 17 July 2006 . . . . 40-007A
Monroe v Hopkins [2017] EWHC 433 (QB); [2017] 4 W.L.R. 68; [2017] 3 WLUK 289;
[2017] E.M.L.R. 16; [2017] Info. T.L.R. 101 46-038
Morgan v Fry [1968] 1 Q.B. 521; [1967] 3 W.L.R. 65; [1967] 2 All E.R. 386; [1967] 1
Lloyd's Rep. 471; [1967] 3 WLUK 69; 2 K.I.R. 264; (1967) 111 S.J. 397 QBD 48-008B
Morris-Garner v One Step (Support) Ltd; sub nom. One Step (Support) Ltd v
Morris-Garner [2018] UKSC 20; [2019] A.C. 649; [2018] 2 W.L.R. 1353; [2018] 3 All
E.R. 659; [2018] 2 All E.R. (Comm) 769; [2018] 1 Lloyd's Rep. 495; [2018] 4 WLUK
243; [2018] 1 C.L.C. 778; [2018] I.R.L.R. 661 . . . . 3-012A, 14-028
National Provincial Bank of England v Marshall (1888) 40 Ch. D. 112; [1888] 11 WLUK
50 CA 16-027B
Nautica Marine Ltd v Trafigura Trading LLC; Leonidas, The [2020] EWHC 1986
(Comm); [2021] 1 All E.R. (Comm) 1157; [2021] 2 Lloyd's Rep. 165; [2020] 7 WLUK
407. 10-098
Nocton v Lord Ashburton [1914] A.C. 932; [1914-15] All E.R. Rep. 45; [1914] 6 WLUK
60 HL 2-010
O'Loughlin v Cape Distribution Ltd; sub nom. Cape Distribution Ltd v O'Loughlin
[2001] EWCA Civ 178; [2001] 2 WLUK 214; [2001] P.I.Q.R. Q8. . . . . 41-082A
OBG Ltd v Allan; Mainstream Properties Ltd v Young; Douglas v Hello! Ltd; sub nom.
OBG Ltd v Allen [2007] UKHL 21; [2008] 1 A.C. 1; [2007] 2 W.L.R. 920; [2007] 4 All
E.R. 545; [2008] 1 All E.R. (Comm) 1; [2007] Bus. L.R. 1600; [2007] 5 WLUK 21;
[2007] I.R.L.R. 608; [2007] E.M.L.R. 12; [2007] B.P.I.R. 746; (2007) 30(6) I.P.D.
30037; [2007] 19 E.G. 165 (C.S.); (2007) 151 S.J.L.B. 674 12-008
One Step (Support) Ltd v Morris-Garner. See Morris-Garner v One Step (Support) Ltd . . . 3-012A,
14-028
Original Beauty Technology Co Ltd v G4K Fashion Ltd [2021] EWHC 3439 (Ch); [2021]
12 WLUK 271; [2022] E.C.D.R. 18; [2022] F.S.R. 11 . . . . 48-070A
Owners of the Sakizaya Kalon v Owners of the Panamax Alexander; Owners of the Osios
David v Owners of the Panamax Alexander; Owners of the Osios David v Owners of
the Sakizaya Kalon; Sakizaya Kalon, The; Panamax Alexander, The; Osios David, The
[2020] EWHC 2604 (Admlty); [2021] 2 Lloyd's Rep. 70; [2020] 10 WLUK 39 8-109
PAL (A Child) v Davison [2021] EWHC 1108 (QB); [2021] 4 WLUK 319 . . . . . . 40-006, 40-007B
Palmali Shipping SA v Litasco SA [2020] EWHC 2581 (Comm); [2020] 9 WLUK 350 2-008,
10-031
Paramount Shopfitting Co Ltd v Rix; sub nom. Rix v Paramount Shopfitting Co Ltd
[2021] EWCA Civ 1172; [2021] 4 W.L.R. 109; [2021] 7 WLUK 443 . . . . 41-082A, 41-082B
Parker v Chief Constable of Essex [2018] EWCA Civ 2788; [2019] 1 W.L.R. 2238; [2019]
3 All E.R. 399; [2018] 12 WLUK 154 8-005
Parkinson v St James and Seacroft University Hospital NHS Trust [2001] EWCA Civ 530;
[2002] Q.B. 266; [2001] 3 W.L.R. 376; [2001] 3 All E.R. 97; [2001] 4 WLUK 343;
[2001] 2 F.L.R. 401; [2002] 2 F.C.R. 65; [2001] P.I.Q.R. Q12; [2001] Lloyd's Rep.
Med. 309; (2001) 61 B.M.L.R. 100; [2001] P.N.L.R. 43; [2001] Fam. Law 592; (2001)
98(22) L.S.G. 35; (2001) 145 S.J.L.B. 118 . . . . 8-050A

Patterson v Ministry of Defence [1987] CLY 1194; [1986] 7 WLUK 264 . . . . 40-007A
Paul v Royal Wolverhampton NHS Trust; sub nom. Polmear v Royal Cornwall Hospital
  NHS Trust, Purchase v Ahmed [2022] EWCA Civ 12; [2022] 2 W.L.R. 917; [2022] 1
  WLUK 49; [2022] P.I.Q.R. P8; (2022) 184 B.M.L.R. 20. 8-077
PCP Capital Partners LLP v Barclays Bank Plc [2021] EWHC 307 (Comm); [2021] 2
  WLUK 413. . . . . 10-052, 10-065, 10-068
Permavent Ltd v Makin [2021] EWHC 467 (Ch); [2021] 3 WLUK 18; [2021] F.S.R. 26 . . 16-018A,
    16-033
Philips Hong Kong Ltd v Attorney General of Hong Kong [1993] 2 WLUK 128; 61
  B.L.R. 41; (1993) 9 Const. L.J. 202 PC (HK) 16-033
Phoenicks Ltd v Bellrock Property & Facilities Management Ltd [2021] EWHC 2639
  (Comm); [2021] 9 WLUK 359 . . . . 10-044, 10-065
PJSC National Bank Trust v Mints [2021] EWHC 1089 (Comm); [2021] 4 WLUK 405 . . 22-002A,
    22-006A
PNM v Times Newspapers Ltd; sub nom. M v Times Newspapers Ltd, Khuja v Times
  Newspapers Ltd [2017] UKSC 49; [2019] A.C. 161; [2017] 3 W.L.R. 351; [2017] 7
  WLUK 430; [2018] 1 Cr. App. R. 1; [2017] E.M.L.R. 29; [2017] Crim. L.R. 998 8-044
Power v Bernard Hastie & Co Ltd [2022] EWHC 1927 (QB); [2022] 7 WLUK 289 40-007
Pullman Foods Ltd v Welsh Ministers [2020] EWHC 2521 (TCC); [2020] 9 WLUK 277 . . . 3-019,
    28-055
R. (on the application of Abulbakr) v Secretary of State for the Home Department [2022]
  EWHC 1183 (Admin); [2022] 5 WLUK 554 42-021
R. (on the application of Checkprice (UK) Ltd (In Administration)) v Revenue and
  Customs Commissioners; sub nom. Checkprice (UK) Ltd (In Administration) v
  Revenue and Customs Commissioners [2010] EWHC 682 (Admin); [2010] S.T.C.
  1153; [2010] 3 WLUK 860; [2010] A.C.D. 67. 12-008
R. (on the application of Hemmati) v Secretary of State for the Home Department; sub
  nom. R. (on the application of Khalili) v Secretary of State for the Home Department,
  R. (on the application of Abdulkadir) v Secretary of State for the Home Department, R.
  (on the application of Mohammed) v Secretary of State for the Home Department, R.
  (on the application of S) v Secretary of State for the Home Department [2019] UKSC
  56; [2021] A.C. 143; [2019] 3 W.L.R. 1156; [2020] 1 All E.R. 669; [2019] 11 WLUK
  422; [2020] H.R.L.R. 4; 47 B.H.R.C. 600; [2020] I.N.L.R. 260 8-005
R. (on the application of Linse) v Chief Constable of North Wales [2020] EWHC 3403
  (Admin); [2020] 12 WLUK 214 . . . . 5-013, 38-071, 38-074A, 38-083
Radia v Marks [2022] EWHC 145 (QB); [2022] 1 WLUK 287; [2022] P.N.L.R. 12 . . . . 8-052B
Rahman v Rahman [2020] EWHC 2392 (Ch); [2020] 9 WLUK 159 . . . . 3-012A, 29-005
Raymond v Young [2015] EWCA Civ 456; [2015] 5 WLUK 359; [2015] H.L.R. 41 . . . . . 39-022A
Recorded Picture Co Ltd v Alfama Films Production [2020] EWHC 3481 (Ch); [2020] 12
  WLUK 304 10-052
Recovery Partners GP Ltd v Rukhadze [2022] EWHC 690 (Comm); [2022] 3 WLUK 405 . . . .
    15-049A, 15-051
Rees v Commissioner of Police of the Metropolis [2021] EWCA Civ 49; [2021] 1 WLUK
  159. . . . . 19-053, 44-016
Richco International Ltd v Alfred C Toepfer International GmbH (The Bonde); Bonde,
  The [1991] 1 Lloyd's Rep. 136; [1990] 5 WLUK 296 QBD (Comm Ct) 16-027A
Riley v Murray [2021] EWHC 3437 (QB); [2021] 12 WLUK 273; [2022] E.M.L.R. 8 46-038
Rix v Paramount Shopfitting Co Ltd [2020] EWHC 2398 (QB); [2020] 4 W.L.R. 123;
  [2021] 2 All E.R. 844; [2020] 9 WLUK 48; [2021] P.I.Q.R. Q1 . . . . 41-082A
Roberts v Johnstone [1989] Q.B. 878; [1988] 3 W.L.R. 1247; [1988] 3 WLUK 229; (1989)
  86(5) L.S.G. 44; (1989) 132 S.J. 1672 CA (Civ Div). 40-212
Rookes v Barnard (No.1) [1964] A.C. 1129; [1964] 2 W.L.R. 269; [1964] 1 All E.R. 367;
  [1964] 1 Lloyd's Rep. 28; [1964] 1 WLUK 887; (1964) 108 S.J. 93 HL 13-008, 13-025A,
    48-008A
Rothwell v Chemical & Insulating Co Ltd. See Grieves v FT Everard & Sons Ltd 40-007B
Ruxley Electronics v Forsyth; Laddingford Enclosures Ltd v Forsyth [1996] A.C. 344;
  [1995] 3 W.L.R. 118; [1995] 3 All E.R. 268; [1995] 6 WLUK 384; [1995] C.L.C. 905;
  73 B.L.R. 1; 45 Con. L.R. 61; (1995) 14 Tr. L.R. 541; (1995) 11 Const. L.J. 381; [1995]
  E.G. 11 (C.S.); (1995) 145 N.L.J. 996; (1995) 139 S.J.L.B. 163 HL 28-057A
SAAMCO. See South Australia Asset Management Corp v York Montague Ltd . . . 6-005, 8-052A,
    34-009, 34-064, 34-078
Sahota v Middlesex Broadcasting Corp Ltd [2021] EWHC 3363 (QB); [2021] 12 WLUK
  159. 46-038

Sainter v Ferguson 137 E.R. 283; (1849) 7 C.B. 716; (1849) 1 Mac. & G. 286; [1849] 1
WLUK 28 CCP 16-027B
Salt Ship Design AS v Prysmian Powerlink Srl [2021] EWHC 2633 (Comm); [2021] 9
WLUK 356; [2022] F.S.R. 16 13-011
Salwin v Shahed [2022] EWHC 1440 (QB); [2022] 6 WLUK 94 40-006
Sarwar v Ali [2007] EWHC 1255 (QB); [2007] 5 WLUK 674; [2007] LS Law Medical
375 . . . . 40-007A
Saunders v Edwards [1987] 1 W.L.R. 1116; [1987] 2 All E.R. 651; [1987] 3 WLUK 166;
[2008] B.T.C. 7119; (1987) 137 N.L.J. 389; (1987) 131 S.J. 1039 CA (Civ Div) 19-053
Schembri v Marshall [2020] EWCA Civ 358; [2020] 3 WLUK 102; [2020] P.I.Q.R. P16;
[2020] Med. L.R. 240; (2020) 175 B.M.L.R. 14; [2020] Inquest L.R. 66. . . . . 10-057A
Sicri v Associated Newspapers Ltd [2020] EWHC 3541 (QB); [2021] 4 W.L.R. 9; [2020]
12 WLUK 391; [2021] E.M.L.R. 10. . . . . 8-044, 47-010A
Sigma Pharmaceuticals (Australia) Pty Ltd v Wyeth [2018] FCA 1556 . . . . 22-008A
Simmons v Castle [2012] EWCA Civ 1288; [2013] 1 W.L.R. 1239; [2013] 1 All E.R. 334;
[2012] 10 WLUK 326; [2013] C.P. Rep. 3; [2012] 6 Costs L.R. 1150; [2013] E.M.L.R.
4; [2013] P.I.Q.R. P2; [2013] Med. L.R. 4; (2012) 162 N.L.J. 1324; (2012) 156(39)
S.J.L.B. 31 . . . . 28-033, 40-285
Singh v Yaqubi [2013] EWCA Civ 23; [2013] 1 WLUK 551; [2013] C.P. Rep. 22; [2013]
R.T.R. 15; [2013] Lloyd's Rep. I.R. 398; (2013) 157(5) S.J.L.B. 31 . . . . 37-016A
Slack v Leeds Industrial Cooperative Society Ltd (No.1); sub nom. Leeds Industrial
Cooperative Society Ltd v Slack [1924] A.C. 851; [1924] All E.R. Rep. 264; [1924] 5
WLUK 110 HL 3-012A
Smith v Lancashire Teaching Hospitals NHS Foundation Trust; sub nom. Bulloch
(Deceased), Re [2017] EWCA Civ 1916; [2018] Q.B. 804; [2018] 2 W.L.R. 1063;
[2017] 11 WLUK 606; [2018] P.I.Q.R. P5; (2018) 162 B.M.L.R. 1; [2017] W.T.L.R.
1469. 41-019
Soteria Insurance Ltd (formerly CIS General Insurance Limited) v IBM United Kingdom
Ltd [2022] EWCA Civ 440; [2022] 4 WLUK 1; 202 Con. L.R. 1 . . . . 3-018A, 25-107
South Australia Asset Management Corp v York Montague Ltd; Nykredit Mortgage Bank
Plc v Edward Erdman Group Ltd; United Bank of Kuwait Plc v Prudential Property
Services Ltd [1997] A.C. 191; [1996] 3 W.L.R. 87; [1996] 3 All E.R. 365; [1996] 6
WLUK 227; [1996] 5 Bank. L.R. 211; [1996] C.L.C. 1179; 80 B.L.R. 1; 50 Con. L.R.
153; [1996] P.N.L.R. 455; [1996] 2 E.G.L.R. 93; [1996] 27 E.G. 125; [1996] E.G. 107
(C.S.); (1996) 93(32) L.S.G. 33; (1996) 146 N.L.J. 956; (1996) 140 S.J.L.B. 156;
[1996] N.P.C. 100 HL. 6-005, 8-052A, 34-009, 34-064, 34-078
Space Shipping Ltd v ST Shipping and Transport Pte Ltd [2021] EWHC 2288 (Comm);
[2021] 8 WLUK 89 . . . . 9-142A
Stansfield v BBC [2021] EWHC 2638 (QB); [2021] 9 WLUK 360 40-269
Steve Hill Ltd v Witham [2021] EWCA Civ 1312; [2021] 8 WLUK 176; [2022] P.I.Q.R.
P2 41-026
Stone Heritage Developments Ltd v Davis Blank Furniss [2007] EWCA Civ 765; [2007] 7
WLUK 679; [2007] 31 E.G. 80 (C.S.). 10-068A
Suisse Atlantique Societe d'Armement SA v NV Rotterdamsche Kolen Centrale [1965] 1
Lloyd's Rep. 533; [1965] 3 WLUK 50 CA 16-027, 16-027A
Summerfield Browne Ltd v Waymouth [2021] EWHC 85 (QB); [2021] 1 WLUK 183 46-030
Suttle v Walker [2019] EWHC 396 (QB); [2019] 1 WLUK 449 . . . . 43-019, 46-038
Swift v Carpenter [2020] EWCA Civ 1295; [2021] Q.B. 339; [2021] 2 W.L.R. 248; [2021]
3 All E.R. 827; [2020] 10 WLUK 74; [2021] P.I.Q.R. P3; [2020] Med. L.R. 527; (2021)
179 B.M.L.R. 1 . . . . 40-211, 40-212
Tharros Shipping Co Ltd v Bias Shipping Ltd (The Griparion) (No.1); Griparion, The
(No.1) [1994] 1 Lloyd's Rep. 577; [1993] 7 WLUK 355 QBD (Comm Ct) 22-006A
The Kennel Club Ltd v Micro-ID Ltd [2019] EWHC 1639 (IPEC); [2019] 6 WLUK 401 . . . 14-037
Toombes v Mitchell [2020] EWHC 3506 (QB); [2021] Q.B. 622; [2021] 2 W.L.R. 661;
[2020] 12 WLUK 377; [2021] P.I.Q.R. P10; [2021] Med. L.R. 220; (2021) 180
B.M.L.R. 38 40-289
Toombes v Mitchell [2021] EWHC 3234 (QB); [2021] 12 WLUK 18 40-289
Total Transport Corp of Panama v Amoco Transport Co (The Altus); Altus, The [1985] 1
Lloyd's Rep. 423; [1985] 1 WLUK 921 QBD (Comm Ct) 16-027, 16-027A
Total Transport Corp v Arcadia Petroleum Ltd (The Eurus); Eurus, The [1996] 2 Lloyd's
Rep. 408; [1996] 2 WLUK 88; [1996] C.L.C. 1084 QBD (Comm Ct) 3-019
Triad Group Plc v Makar [2020] EWHC 306 (QB); [2020] 2 WLUK 217 43-019

Triple Point Technology Inc v PTT Public Co Ltd [2021] UKSC 29; [2021] 3 W.L.R. 521;
 [2021] 7 WLUK 190. 16-003
Tuke v Hood [2020] EWHC 2843 (Comm); [2020] 10 WLUK 302 . . . . . . 13-013, 13-041, 15-046,
 49-036A
Tuke v Hood [2021] EWHC 74 (Comm); [2021] 1 WLUK 146 . . . . 49-036A
Unite the Union v Freitas [2022] EWHC 666 (QB); [2022] 3 WLUK 315; [2022] I.C.R.
 D7 46-037
Van Zuylen v Whiston-Dew [2021] EWHC 2219 (Ch); [2021] 8 WLUK 21 19-068
Various Claimants v Giambrone and Law (A Firm); sub nom. Main v Giambrone & Law
 (A Firm) [2017] EWCA Civ 1193; [2017] 7 WLUK 765; [2018] P.N.L.R. 2 8-050
Vento v Chief Constable of West Yorkshire; sub nom. Chief Constable of West Yorkshire v
 Vento (No.2) [2002] EWCA Civ 1871; [2002] 12 WLUK 676; [2003] I.C.R. 318;
 [2003] I.R.L.R. 102; [2003] Po. L.R. 171; (2003) 100(10) L.S.G. 28; (2003) 147
 S.J.L.B. 181. . . . . 43-007, 43-020, 48-008C
Villeneuve v Gaillard [2011] UKPC 1; [2011] 2 WLUK 302 . . . . 1-021B
Ward v Newalls Insulation Co Ltd; Ward v Cape Contracts Ltd [1998] 1 W.L.R. 1722;
 [1998] 2 All E.R. 690; [1998] 2 WLUK 407; [1998] P.I.Q.R. Q41; (1998) 95(15) L.S.G.
 32; (1998) 142 S.J.L.B. 103 CA (Civ Div) 41-082A
Watson Norie v Shaw [1967] 1 Lloyd's Rep. 515; [1967] 2 WLUK 3; 117 N.L.J. 157;
 (1967) 111 S.J. 117 CA (Civ Div). 37-016
Watson v Kea Investments Ltd [2019] EWCA Civ 1759; [2019] 4 W.L.R. 145; [2019] 10
 WLUK 319; [2020] W.T.L.R. 351 19-068
Welsh Ambulance Services NHS Trust v Williams [2008] EWCA Civ 81; [2008] 2 WLUK
 387; (2008) 105(9) L.S.G. 30. . . . . 41-082A
White Lion Hotel (A Partnership) v James [2021] EWCA Civ 31; [2021] 2 W.L.R. 911;
 [2021] 1 WLUK 111; [2021] P.I.Q.R. P11 8-121
Willson v Ministry of Defence; sub nom. Wilson v Ministry of Defence [1991] 1 All E.R.
 638; [1990] 7 WLUK 78; [1991] I.C.R. 595 QBD 40-007A
Wood v Commercial First Business Ltd (Dissolved) [2021] EWHC 1403 (Ch); [2021] 6
 WLUK 646 19-068
Woodward v Grice [2017] EWHC 1292 (QB); [2017] 6 WLUK 82 46-071
WXY v Gewanter [2013] EWHC 589 (QB); [2013] 3 WLUK 341; [2013] Info. T.L.R. 281 . 43-019
XXXX (known as Hatchet) v Varma [2021] EWHC 1709 (QB); [2021] 6 WLUK 375 46-030
YJB Port Ltd v M&A Pharmachem Ltd [2021] EWHC 42 (Ch); [2021] 1 WLUK 56 10-001
Young v Chalkley (1867) 16 L.T. 286 . . . . 16-027B
Young v Downey [2020] EWHC 3457 (QB); [2020] 12 WLUK 254 13-008
Zeromska-Smith v United Lincolnshire Hospitals NHS Trust [2019] EWHC 980 (QB);
 [2019] 4 WLUK 293. 40-269

TABLE OF STATUTES

1858 Chancery Amendment Act (Lord Cairns'
    Act) 1858 (c.27) ... 3-012A, 29-005
1934 Law Reform (Miscellaneous Provisions)
    Act 1934 (c.41)
    s.1 40-007
1976 Congenital Disabilities (Civil Liability)
    Act 1976 (c.28) 40-289
    s.1(1) 40-289
        (2)(a) 40-289
        (b) 40-289
1976 Fatal Accidents Act 1976 (c.30)
    s.1A 41-019
        (1) 41-019
        (2) 41-019
        (2A) 41-019

1981 Senior Courts Act 1981 (c.54)
    s.35A 19-053
    s.50 .... 3-012A
1982 Administration of Justice Act 1982 (c.53)
    s.3(1) 41-019
1997 Protection from Harassment Act 1997
    (c.40)
    s.3(2) 39-022A
1998 Data Protection Act 1998 (c.29)
    12-008
    s.4(4) 14-037
    s.13 .... 14-037, 47-015
2004 Civil Partnership Act 2004 (c.33)
    s.83(7) 41-019

TABLE OF STATUTORY INSTRUMENTS

2020 Fatal Accidents Act 1976 (Remedial) Order 2020 (SI 2020/316)
    art.1(1) 41-019

art.2(3) 41-019

CHAPTER 1

THE MEANING OF DAMAGES AND COMPENSATION AT COMMON LAW AND IN EQUITY

TABLE OF CONTENTS

1. A DEFINITION OF DAMAGES 1-001
   (1) The requirement of a wrong 1-004
   (2) The omission of the reference to pecuniary compensation . 1-008
   (3) The omission of the reference to tort and breach of
       contract .... 1-011■
2. THE COVERAGE OF DAMAGES 1-022

1. A DEFINITION OF DAMAGES

(3) The omission of the reference to tort and breach of contract

(b) Damages and compensation in equity

(ii) Damages in equity's exclusive jurisdiction

After para.1-021, add new paragraphs:

Most recently in *Davies v Ford*[63a] one issue was the manner of calculation of **1-021A** equitable compensation for losses suffered by a company when two of its directors breached their fiduciary duties by diverting business to a new company in which they were the directors and shareholders. David Holland QC held that there was a claim for substitutive compensation for funds that had been diverted from the principal company but otherwise the claim against the directors did not involve any misapplication of pre-existing corporate assets and could not be brought as a claim for substitutive compensation.[63b] It was held that for the substitutive compensation claim it was not open to the trustee or fiduciary in breach to "argue the counterfactual, that is that the trust property would have been lost or paid away even if he or she had not been in breach".[63c] But for the claim for misappropriation of existing company property, the reparative compensation, or "the reparative basis", required the court to consider questions of causation of loss. Hence, the directors succeeded in part by establishing that some of the loss suffered by the principal company would have been suffered in any event.[63d]

[63a] [2021] EWHC 2550 (Ch).

[63b] [2021] EWHC 2550 (Ch) at [109]–[110].

[63c] [2021] EWHC 2550 (Ch) at [100], [103], [106].

[63d] [2021] EWHC 2550 (Ch) at [109]–[110], [272].

1-021B   Similarly, in a claim for reparative compensation for dishonest assistance in a breach of fiduciary duty, when Foxton J was confronted with the difficult question of whether losses for which equitable compensation was sought should be set off against profits made on other transactions, he applied the same common law approach of asking whether the profits were made as part of transactions for which any action would have been a separate cause of action.[63e] Indeed, Foxton J even described the award of equitable compensation for breach of fiduciary duty as "damages".[63f]

[63e] *Hotel Portfolio II UK Ltd v Ruhan* [2022] EWHC 383 (Comm) at [279]–[283], referring to *Brown v KMR Services Ltd* [1995] 2 Lloyd's Rep. 513; and *Charles Villeneuve Kyoto Securities Ltd v Joel Gaillard H Holdings Ltd* [2011] UKPC 1.

[63f] *Hotel Portfolio II UK Ltd v Ruhan* [2022] EWHC 383 (Comm) at [291].

PART 1A COMPENSATORY DAMAGES: OBJECT AND TERMINOLOGY

CHAPTER 2

THE OBJECT OF AN AWARD OF COMPENSATORY DAMAGES

TABLE OF CONTENTS
1. THE PRINCIPLE OF COMPENSATION 2-001
2. COMPENSATION LESS THAN LOSS 2-005
3. COMPENSATION GREATER THAN LOSS .... 2-006☐
4. COMPENSATION IS NOT DISCRETIONARY 2-011

3. COMPENSATION GREATER THAN LOSS

Replace the paragraph with:

2-008   There is a second group of cases, which have been described as "normal loss", that appear to permit compensation greater than loss if the concept of loss is viewed narrowly. In these cases the money award, subject to rules of mitigation, is measured by the cost to rectify the breach rather than to remedy the consequences to the plaintiff. In those cases, the award is a money substitute for performance which, in some instances, can be the value of a licence to have permitted as lawful that conduct which was committed unlawfully.[41] Whether these cases involve damages exceeding loss depends upon the breadth given to the concept of loss. A central illustration from the law of contract is the "broad ground" considered by the House of Lords in *Alfred McAlpine Construction Ltd v Panatown Ltd*.[42] That principle permits the recovery of the cost of rectifying defective performance even if the benefit, and hence the loss, of the contract work was ultimately for another party. Hence if A contracts with B for building work to be done on the land of C then, under this exception, A can recover the cost of the defects in the work even if the rectification work is only for the benefit of C. In *Alfred McAlpine Construction Ltd* that principle was accepted by Lords Goff and Millett, in the minority in the result, and was assumed to be correct by Lord Browne-Wilkinson.[43] Lord Sumption later explained that there was "much to be said" for this broad principle but that it was an exception to the basic principle of compensation which required the objectively manifested intent of the contracting party to benefit another.[44] It has subsequently been confined in this way to the construction context,[45] although it may have a broader operation elsewhere.[46] It has also been applied recently in the shipping context involving a long-term contract of affreightment.[46a]

[41] See paras 3-012 to 3-013 and Ch.14, below, in relation to licence fee damages.

[42] [2001] 1 A.C. 518. See below at para.31-004.

[43] [2001] 1 A.C. 518 at 577 (Lord Browne-Wilkinson).

[44] *Lowick Rose LLP v Swynson Ltd* [2017] UKSC 32; [2018] A.C. 313 at 324 [16]–[17]. See also at 350 [104] (Lord Neuberger).

[45] *BV Nederlandse Industrie van Eiprodukten v Rembrandt Enterprises Inc* [2019] EWCA Civ 596; [2020] Q.B. 551 at 579 [72]–[73].

[46] See Ch.3 at paras 3-011 to 3-012 discussing *Van der Garde v Force India Formula One Team Ltd* [2010] EWHC 2373 (QB).

[46a] *Palmali Shipping SA v Litasco SA* [2020] EWHC 2581 (Comm) at [49]–[50].

Replace the paragraph with:

2-010   The fourth variety where, at first glance, it appears that compensation is awarded beyond loss is where the claimant recovers an award commonly, but misleadingly, described as "transferred loss". In *Lowick Rose LLP v Swynson Ltd*,[58] Lord Sumption, delivering the decision with which three other members of the Supreme Court agreed, said that the principle applies where the:

> "… known object of a transaction is to benefit a third party or a class of persons to which a third party belongs, and the anticipated effect of a breach of duty will be to cause loss to that third party."

For instance, in cases of carriage of goods by sea, even if title and risk to the goods has passed to the consignee, the shipper can still sue the shipowner for negligence causing loss or damage to the cargo.[59] The rationale was given by Lord Diplock as being that, unless the terms provide otherwise, the shipper enters the contract with the shipowner for the benefit of all persons who may acquire an interest in the goods.[60] But expressed only in these terms, this principle of "transferred loss" is an anomaly because it is contrary to rules of privity of contract. As applied to owners of property it became known as the "narrow ground". However, the principle was extended to commercial contracts generally in *Linden Gardens Trust v Lenesta Sludge Disposals Ltd*,[61] where Lord Griffiths re-explained it on a "broad ground" and reconciled it with privity of contract by explaining that the loss was genuinely suffered by the claimant because of the claimant's interest in providing the third party the intended benefit. However, as Lord Sumption emphasised in *Lowick Rose LLP v Swynson Ltd*, the principle can only be applied where (i) there would be a "black hole" because the third party cannot recover themselves and (ii) the claimant enters the contract with the manifested object of benefitting the third party.[62] Provided that these conditions are satisfied there is no reason in principle why transferred loss on this narrow ground should be confined to claims for breach of contract. A tortious claim based upon an assumption of responsibility, which Lord Devlin described as "equivalent to contract",[62a] should not be treated any differently. The same must be true of a liability for equitable compensation for breach of equitable obligations that are also "equivalent to contract"[62b] where the equitable obligation is derived from a contract and imposed upon the equitable assignee of a contract right that is qualified by that obligation.[62c]

[58] [2017] UKSC 32; [2018] A.C. 313.

[59] *Dunlop v Lambert* (1839) 2 Cl. & F. 626.

[60] *The Albazero* [1977] A.C. 774 at 847.

[61] *Linden Gardens Trust v Lenesta Sludge Disposals Ltd* [1994] 1 A.C. 85. See also *Alfred McAlpine Construction Ltd v Panatown Ltd* [2001] 1 A.C. 518 at 547–548, per Lord Goff, 568, per Lord Jauncey, 577–578, per Lord Browne-Wilkinson, 582–583, per Lord Millett.

[62] [2017] UKSC 32; [2018] A.C. 313 at [15]–[16].

[62a] *Hedley Byrne & Co Ltd v Heller & Partners Ltd* [1964] A.C. 465 at 529.

[62b] *Nocton v Lord Ashburton* [1914] A.C. 932 at 972.

[62c] *Argos Pereira Espana SL v Athenian Marine Ltd* [2021] EWHC 554 (Comm); [2021] Bus. L.R. 866 at [24].

CHAPTER 3

THE TERMINOLOGY IN COMPENSATORY DAMAGES AND IN
CONSEQUENTIAL LOSS CLAUSES

TABLE OF CONTENTS
1.   GENERAL AND SPECIAL DAMAGE   3-001
2.   NORMAL AND CONSEQUENTIAL LOSSES   3-007
   (1)   Scope of what is normal loss   . . . .   3-011□
   (2)   Normal and consequential loss in contract clauses   . . . . .   3-013■
   (3)   Normal and consequential loss in indemnity clauses   . . . .   3-019□

2.   NORMAL AND CONSEQUENTIAL LOSSES

(1)   Scope of what is normal loss

After para.3-012, add a new paragraph:

Another example of normal losses is those awards made under what was the   **3-012A**
Chancery Amendment Act 1858, commonly called Lord Cairns' Act and now
contained in s.50 of the Senior Courts Act 1981, which gave statutory jurisdiction
for a court of equity to award damages in addition to or in substitution for grant-
ing either an injunction or specific performance.[49a] It has been said that this jurisdiction is a change only in method and not in substance from common law damages.[49b]
But it has also been said that these remarks must be treated with care since Lord
Cairns' Act damages are available on a different basis, in different circumstances,
and for different types of wrong.[49c] Nevertheless, Lord Cairns' Act damages neatly
divide into those which represent normal losses and those which are concerned with
consequential losses. As a "money substitute" for specific performance or for an
injunction the damages need to give "an equivalent for what is lost by the refusal
of the injunction [or specific performance]".[49d] That equivalent is provided by a
money amount to undo, repair, or licence the actual or anticipated wrongful act
(normal loss) as well as a payment for any further consequential loss suffered.
Where the wrong is no longer continuing, the normal loss can be measured at the
date of the wrongdoing but if the claimant was entitled to performance or inaction
at the date of judgment then the normal loss should be measured at that time. For
instance, in an excellent judgment on a strike out claim in *Rahman v Rahman*,[49e]
Master Clark held that Lord Cairns' Act damages for a claim for breach of an oral
agreement to allot shares were to be assessed at the date of judgment since that was
the date at which the claimant's "entitlement to the shares is treated as coming to
an end and being replaced by financial compensation".

[49a] See para.1-015 above.

[49b] See Lord Wilberforce in *Johnson v Agnew* [1980] A.C. 367 at 400C and G, saying that Lord Cairns' Act "does not provide for the assessment of damages on any new basis" and gives "no warrant for the court awarding damages differently from common law damages".

[49c] *One Step (Support) Ltd v Morris-Garner* [2018] UKSC 20; [2019] A.C. 649 at [47].

[49d] *One Step (Support) Ltd v Morris-Garner* [2018] UKSC 20; [2019] A.C. 649 at [44], quoting *Leeds Industrial Co-operative Society Ltd v Slack* [1924] A.C. 851; [1924] All E.R. Rep. 264 at 859.

[49e] [2020] EWHC 2392 (Ch).

(2)   Normal and consequential loss in contract clauses

After para.3-018, add new paragraph:

3-018A   Again, where a clause provided for something less than "total loss", such as a clause that excluded only "loss of profit, revenue, savings", it was, quite rightly, understood against the background of decades of legal principle that has treated a claim for wasted expenditure as an alternative claim.[86a] That background was a powerful factor in the interpretation of the contract as not extending to claims for wasted expenditure.[86b]

[86a] See below at paras 4-022 to 4-025.

[86b] *Soteria Insurance Ltd v IBM United Kingdom Ltd* [2022] EWCA Civ 440; (2022) 202 Con. L.R. 1.

After para.3-018A, add a new sub-section heading and paragraph:

(3)   Normal and consequential loss in indemnity clauses

3-019   A contract clause which provides for an indemnity for losses flowing from a particular event creates rights akin to debt, and not damages.[87] Rules such as mitigation or remoteness of damage would not apply at all. But it is necessary to mention here the recovery of such contractual losses because there can be a fine line between a contractual indemnity clause and a clause limiting or governing recovery for a breach of contract. In *Pullman Foods Ltd v Welsh Ministers*,[88] one issue was the meaning of a contractual clause requiring the promisor to "indemnify ... against all losses", among other things. Applying an earlier approach of Rix J, it was held by Marcus Smith J that the clause was a "true" indemnity clause rather than one concerned with the scope of damages for breach of contract. In the latter case, the same failure which triggered the indemnity would also constitute a breach of contract and in many cases there should be no "difference in overall responsibility".[89] The same principles described above should usually apply to indemnity clauses that are concerned with breach of contract. But since the clause in *Pullman Foods Ltd* was a true indemnity, applying irrespective of whether there was a breach of contract, the rules of mitigation and remoteness of damage did not apply.[90]

[87] See para.1-005, above.

[88] [2020] EWHC 2521 (TCC).

[89] *Pullman Foods Ltd v Welsh Ministers* [2020] EWHC 2521 (TCC) at [190], quoting from *Total Transport Corp v Arcadia Petroleum Ltd (The "Eurus")* [1996] 2 Lloyd's Rep. 408 at 432; [1996] C.L.C. 1084.

[90] [2020] EWHC 2521 (TCC) at [200].

PART 1B THE HEADS OF COMPENSATORY DAMAGES

CHAPTER 5

NON-PECUNIARY LOSSES

TABLE OF CONTENTS

I. **Tort** 5-002
    1. PAIN AND SUFFERING AND LOSS OF AMENITIES 5-004
    2. PHYSICAL INCONVENIENCE AND DISCOMFORT 5-010
    3. SOCIAL DISCREDIT 5-011
    4. MENTAL DISTRESS . . . . 5-012□

II. **Contract** 5-015
    1. PHYSICAL INCONVENIENCE AND DISCOMFORT 5-017
    2. PAIN AND SUFFERING AND LOSS OF AMENITIES 5-020
    3. MENTAL DISTRESS 5-023
    4. SOCIAL DISCREDIT 5-036

I. TORT

4. MENTAL DISTRESS

Replace the paragraph with:

On the other hand, once liability has been established, then compensation for **5-013** injury to feelings may be included in the damages, and indeed in torts infringing family relationships the injury to feelings represented the principal loss. These torts, however, have all been abolished by statute,[45] so that what were once the most important illustrations of this head of non-pecuniary loss have been removed from the scene, and there are left at common law only those torts in which injury to feelings generally forms a subsidiary element in the damages. Thus injury to feelings would seem to be allowable in torts which primarily protect reputation, certainly in libel and in slanders actionable per se[46] and most probably in malicious prosecution. The same is true of assault[47] and has been recognised as being true of deceit.[48] Invasion of privacy, stemming from breach of confidence in its personal as distinct from its commercial form, has from the beginning of the century begun to attract damages for injured feelings.[49] Increasingly in trespass to property or nuisance there has been an award for mental distress or anxiety[50]; on the other hand, it has been held that this head of non-pecuniary loss cannot be claimed in the tort of conspiracy[51] while the position with injurious falsehood is not yet settled.[52] Negligence resulting in economic loss[53] is unlikely to lead to damages for mental distress.[54] Statutory torts involving discrimination which formerly appeared in separate statutes[55] have now been brought under the umbrella of the Equality Act 2010 where it is provided, as it had been before, that an award of damages in respect of discrimination "may include compensation for injured feelings".[56] The statutory tort involving harassment[57] allows for damages "for any anxiety caused by the harassment".[58] Another example is the tort of intentional infliction of emotional harm. In *ABC v WH*,[59] damages for the tort of intentional infliction of emotional harm were awarded for "pain, suffering and loss of amenity" including a component for mental distress. It has been held, however, that injury to feelings is not recoverable, seemingly even if it is not too remote, for unlawful interference with chattels.[59a] There is no obvious reason why this should be the case, and the decisions seem to be based solely on the absence of any decided authority on the point (which is not authority for unavailability of such a head of loss). Indeed, it is well recognised that such damages can be aggravated by injury to feelings.[59b]

[45] Law Reform (Miscellaneous Provisions) Act 1970 ss.4 and 5.

[46] *Goslin v Corry* (1844) 7 M. & G. 342 at 346 (damages "for the mental suffering arising from the apprehension of the consequences of the publication"); *Ley v Hamilton* (1935) 153 L.T. 384 HL at 386 (damages for "the insult offered or the pain of a false accusation"); *McCarey v Associated Newspapers* [1965] 2 Q.B. 86 CA at 104 (damages "may also include the natural injury to the feelings"); *Fielding v Variety Inc* [1967] 2 Q.B. 841 CA at 855 ("entitled to be compensated ... for the anxiety and annoyance"); *John v MGN* [1997] Q.B. 586 CA at 607F (the sum awarded "must ... take account of the distress, hurt and humiliation which the defamatory publication has caused").

[47] See *Lane v Holloway* [1968] 1 Q.B. 379 CA.

[48] *Doyle v Olby (Ironmongers)* [1969] 2 Q.B. 158 CA at 170 (may be appropriate to consider "worry, strain, anxiety and unhappiness"); *Mafo v Adams* [1970] 1 Q.B. 548 CA at 558 (damages may be increased where there are "circumstances which aggravate the suffering and injury"); *Shelley v Paddock* [1978] Q.B. 120; *Saunders v Edwards* [1987] 1 W.L.R. 1116 CA; *East v Maurer* [1991] 1 W.L.R. 461 CA; *A v B* [2007] EWHC 1246 (QB); *Kinch v Rosling* [2009] EWHC 286 (QB).

[49] *Cornelius v de Taranto* [2001] E.M.L.R. 12 at 329 (damages not in issue in CA); *Campbell v MGN Ltd* [2002] E.M.L.R. 30, at 617 (damages not in issue in CA or HL); *Archer v Williams* [2003] E.M.L.R. 38 at 869; *Douglas v Hello! Ltd* [2004] E.M.L.R. 2 at 13 (these damages not in issue in CA); *McKennitt v Ash* [2006] E.M.L.R. 10 at 178 (damages not addressed in CA); *Mosley v News Group Newspapers Ltd* [2008] E.M.L.R. 20 at 679. These first instance cases are considered at paras 47-005 to 47-007, below.

[50] Owen and *Smith v Reo Motors* (1934) 151 L.T. 274 CA (explained on these lines by Lord Devlin in *Rookes v Barnard* [1964] A.C. 1129 at 1229); *Drane v Evangelou* [1978] 1 W.L.R. 455 CA; *Millington v Duffy* (1984) 17 H.L.R. 232 CA; and the other cases at para.39-073, below. Also *Scutt v Lomax* (2000) 79 P. & C.R. D31 CA; *Bryant v Macklin* [2005] EWCA Civ 762; *Anslow v Norton Aluminium Ltd* [2012] EWHC 2610 (QB) and compare *Barr v Biffa Waste Services Ltd* [2011] 4 All E.R. 1065: all at para.39-020, below.

[51] *Lonrho v Fayed (No.5)* [1993] 1 W.L.R. 1489 CA.

[52] Against: *Fielding v Variety Inc* [1967] 2 Q.B. 841 CA at 850 ("the claimants ... can only recover damages for their probable money loss, and not for their injured feelings"); in favour: *Joyce v Sengupta* [1993] 1 W.L.R. 337 CA at 348E ("instinctively recoil from the notion that in no circumstances can an injured claimant obtain recompense ... for understandable distress").

[53] The damages recoverable for non-economic loss by a car owner deprived of their car through negligence would seem to be for inconvenience rather than distress: see *Beechwood Birmingham Ltd v Hoyer Group UK Ltd* at para.37-062, below.

[54] *Verderame v Commercial Union Insurance Co Plc* [2000] Lloyd's Rep. P.N. 557 CA, a case of professional negligence, held that where the duty of care arises in respect of economic loss there will be no recovery of damages for mental distress any more than there would be if the professional negligence claim were brought, as is more common, in contract. For mental distress in contract where professional negligence can occasionally lead to an award see paras 5-023 and following, below.

[55] Notably the Sex Discrimination Act 1975, Race Relations Act 1976 and Disability Discrimination Act 1995. All three and the Regulations that go with them are repealed by the provisions, in force and prospective, of the Equality Act 2010.

[56] Section 119(4); adding, as before, "(whether or not it includes compensation on any other basis)". By contrast, in *R. v Secretary of State for Transport, Ex p. Factortame Ltd (No.7)* [2001] 1 W.L.R. 942 (TCC), one of the *Factortame* cases involving discrimination by the UK against the owners of foreign fishing vessels, it was held that Art.52 of the European Communities Treaty, which gives the right to

nationals of one Member State to establish themselves in another Member State, was concerned only with economic loss.

[57] Protection from Harassment Act 1997, which has survived the arrival of the Equality Act 2010.

[58] Section 3(2). Awards were made on this basis in *S&D Property Investments Ltd v Nisbet* [2009] EWHC 1726 (Ch) (where it was rightly said that anxiety need not amount to mental illness: [2009] EWHC 1726 (Ch) at [72] and following), in *Rayment v Ministry of Defence* [2010] EWHC 218 (QB) (£5,500 for bullying, humiliating and insulting an employee) and *Roberts v Bank of Scotland* [2013] EWCA Civ 882 CA (£7,500 for bombardment of phone calls to customer by bank).

[59] [2015] EWHC 2687 (QB).

[59a] *Cash & Brown v Chief Constable of Lancashire* [2008] EWHC 396 (Ch); [2008] Po. L.R. 182 at [57]; *R. (on the application of Linse) v Chief Constable of North Wales* [2020] EWHC 3403 (Admin) at [38].

[59b] Below at para.5-014.

PART 1C THE LIMITS OF COMPENSATORY DAMAGES

CHAPTER 6

THE GENERAL PROBLEM OF LIMITS

TABLE OF CONTENTS

1. INTERRELATION OF EXISTENCE OF LIABILITY AND EXTENT OF
   RESPONSIBILITY 6-002
   (1) Duty, scope of duty and remoteness .... 6-003□
   (2) Volenti non fit injuria, remoteness and contributory
       negligence 6-006
2. INTERRELATION OF VARIOUS FACETS OF THE EXTENT OF
   RESPONSIBILITY 6-010
   (A1) Causation, scope of duty and remoteness .... 6-010A□
   (1) Contributory negligence, remoteness and mitigation 6-011
   (2) Remoteness and certainty 6-021

1. INTERRELATION OF EXISTENCE OF LIABILITY AND EXTENT OF RESPONSIBILITY

(1) Duty, scope of duty and remoteness

Replace the paragraph with:

The Wagon Mound,[16] however, leaves us with one particularly important area of   **6-005**
difference between the existence and the extent of liability. It drew a distinction,
which later cases have built upon, between damage different in degree and damage different in type, so that, provided the type of damage inflicted was foreseeable and the duty of care thereby satisfied, tortfeasors may be liable in damages for
a more extensive degree of damage of that type than they could have anticipated.[17]
Finally, there is Lord Hoffmann's speech in *South Australia Asset Management
Corp v York Montague Ltd*,[17a] commonly called *SAAMCO*, in which an additional
limit, previously present but not always recognised, was acknowledged. That limit,
was reiterated by the Supreme Court in *BPE Solicitors v Hughes-Holland*[17b] and
then clarified and entrenched in the couplet of cases decided together by the
Supreme Court: *Manchester Building Society v Grant Thornton UK LLP*[17c] and
Khan v Meadows.[17d] The limit is that loss can only be recovered where the loss
concerns damage which is within the scope of the defendant's duty. In practice, this
issue has arisen most often in cases of negligence based upon an assumption of
responsibility where the central question is ascertaining the scope of the duty
assumed. In each of these cases the scope of duty enquiry was: "what is the risk
which the service [or action] which the defendant undertook was intended to
address?"[17e]

[16] [1961] A.C. 338; see paras 8-033 and 8-088, below.

[17] See paras 8-092 to 8-096, below.

[17a] [1997] A.C. 191; [1996] 3 W.L.R. 87.

[17b] [2017] UKSC 21; [2018] A.C. 599.

[17c] [2021] UKSC 20; [2021] 3 W.L.R. 81.

[17d] [2021] UKSC 21; [2021] 3 W.L.R. 147.

[17e] *Khan v Meadows* [2021] UKSC 21; [2021] 3 W.L.R. 147.

2. INTERRELATION OF VARIOUS FACETS OF THE EXTENT OF RESPONSIBILITY

After para.6-010, add a new sub-section:

(A1) Causation, scope of duty and remoteness

6-010A   Nomenclature can cause a lot of difficulty. One difficulty is sometimes caused by the conflation of remoteness and causation by describing remoteness as "legal causation". The description "legal causation" is really just shorthand for legal limits to liability for a cause "in fact" (or, more accurately, a metaphysical cause since causation does not happen as a fact in the world). Hence, "legal causation" is better described as "remoteness". Also essential to distinguish from both causation and remoteness of damage is the enquiry into whether loss falls within the scope of a defendant's duty. As the Privy Council and the Supreme Court have emphasised, the scope of duty criterion is a separate limitation from remoteness of damages.[31a] In the tort of negligence, the Supreme Court has divided the scope of duty criterion into two aspects. First there must be precision in the duty of care enquiry: "[w]hat are the risks of harm to the claimant against which the law imposes on the defendant a duty to take care?" Secondly, and described as a "duty nexus question" is whether there is a sufficient nexus between the subject matter of that duty of care and the harm for which the claimant seeks damages.[31b] In many instances, the application of the scope of the duty will be simple. A duty to take care to avoid physical injury or damage to property will include any physical injury or property damages and consequential loss in the scope of the duty. But, as we will see in Ch 8, the issues can become more difficult in cases of assumption of responsibility where pure economic loss is suffered.[31c]

[31a] *Attorney General of the Virgin Islands v Global Water Associates Ltd* [2020] UKPC 18; [2020] 3 W.L.R. 584 at [26], [29]; *Manchester Building Society v Grant Thornton UK LLP* [2021] UKSC 20; [2021] 3 W.L.R. 81 at [179]; *Khan v Meadows* [2021] UKSC 21; [2021] 3 W.L.R. 147 at [56]–[58], [68], [79].

[31b] *Khan v Meadows* [2021] UKSC 21; [2021] 3 W.L.R. 147 at [28].

[31c] See above paras 8-047 to 8-055.

CHAPTER 7

REDUCTION OF DAMAGES FOR CONTRIBUTORY NEGLIGENCE

TABLE OF CONTENTS
1. LIABILITY IN TORT 7-003
    (1) Scope 7-003
    (2) Apportionment .... 7-006■
2. LIABILITY IN CONTRACT 7-015
    (1) Scope 7-015
    (2) Apportionment 7-020
3. LIABILITY UNDER THE MISREPRESENTATION ACT 7-023

1. LIABILITY IN TORT

(2) Apportionment

Replace paragraph with:

That the decision on apportionment is so much a matter of impression is dramati- **7-007**
cally illustrated by *Jackson v Murray*,[20] a case from Scotland of a child running into
the path of an oncoming vehicle, a not unfamiliar story in the annals of contributory negligence. Not only was the trial judge's reduction of the 13-year-old girl's
damages by 90 per cent changed down by the Scots appeal court to 70 per cent and
further changed down by the Supreme Court to 50 per cent but the reduction by the
Supreme Court was only by a bare majority, the minority agreeing with the Scots
appeal court's 70 per cent. Reference was made to the potentially dangerous nature
of driving a car, which could do much more damage to a person than a person was
likely to do to a car. And it was agreed that an appeal court could only interfere with
an apportionment made if it could be said that it lay outside the generous ambit
within which reasonable disagreement was possible. Clearly, however, different
views were taken as to whether here this generous ambit had or had not been
crossed. The majority speech and the minority one are both worth perusal. That each
case will depend on its particular facts is illustrated by *Gul v McDonagh*,[20a] in which
a 13-year-old boy wearing headphones was crossing the road when he was struck
by a car travelling at about 40mph on a street where the maximum speed was
20mph. The trial judge, in a decision upheld by the Court of Appeal, reduced damages by 10 per cent for contributory negligence by the claimant, whose actions were
assessed against the standard of a reasonable 13-year-old.

[20] [2015] UKSC 5; [2015] 2 All E.R. 805.

[20a] [2021] EWCA Civ 1503; [2022] R.T.R. 9.

Replace paragraph with:

7-011   An assessment of a claimant's relative blameworthiness will be based upon all the circumstances but a key factor will be the extent to which the claimant could have foreseen their loss. This foreseeability will, in turn, be affected by the extent to which the claimant has been "reasonably induced to believe that he may proceed with safety",[28] and particularly where they have been so induced by the defendant. As the focus on the claimant's age in cases such as *Jackson v Murray* and *Gul v McDonagh* illustrate, the foreseeability by the claimant is generally assessed by reference to the claimant's circumstances. But the focus is not entirely subjective. A claimant cannot rely on the fact that they were drunk to reduce or prevent the extent of contributory negligence in the act of accepting a lift from a driver who would reasonably have been known also to be drunk. As the Court of Appeal held in the leading judgment in *Campbell v Advantage Insurance Co Ltd*,[28a] the assessment is made by reference to a reasonable person in the claimant's position without regard to intoxication. In other words, the claimant's position is their usual characteristics, not the characteristics of the particular moment.

[28] *AssetCo Plc v Grant Thornton UK LLP* [2019] EWHC 150 (Comm) at [1098]–[1099].

[28a] [2022] Q.B. 354. See especially at 367 [42], citing *Booth v White* [2003] EWCA Civ 1708; (2003) 147 S.J.L.B. 1367.

Replace the paragraph with:

7-012   One particular issue concerning the operation of apportionment troubled the courts in the wake of the landmark decision in *South Australia Asset Management Corp v York Montague Ltd*,[29] commonly called *SAAMCO*, that a claimant lender suing for professional negligence cannot claim for their real loss, however foreseeable, but is restricted to the loss, when less, which is attributable to the breach of duty for which the defendant alone is liable.[30] If, as in so many of these cases, the claimant's negligent lending practices have contributed to its loss,[31] is the apportionment to be made on the real loss or on the lesser attributable loss? The House of Lords decided for the first of these alternatives, and thereby in the claimant's favour, in *Platform Homes Loans Ltd v Oyston Shipways Ltd*,[32] reversing the Court of Appeal and resolving a conflict between many earlier first instance decisions. The issue did not arise in the later decision of *Manchester Building Society v Grant Thornton UK LLP*,[32a] where accountants were negligent in advising about the accounting treatment of hedge transactions which led to a loss by the Society of £26.7 million, but where the Society was 50% contributorily negligent in failing to take care in relation to the accounting treatment and also in entering swaps which substantially exceeded the duration of the mortgages that they were supposed to hedge. The reason that the issue did not arise was because the Supreme Court held that all of the Society's loss (after credit for the value of the benefits from the transaction) was recoverable so the 50% reduction for contributory negligence was calculated on the whole of the actual loss and the recoverable loss.

[29] [1997] A.C. 191.

[30] See para.34-077, below.

[31] See the cases at para.7-022, below.

[32] [2000] 2 A.C. 190. On the particular facts and figures in the case, applying the 20 per cent contributory negligence to the real loss of some £600,000 brought the figure to £480,000 and therefore within the £500,000 overvaluations by the defendants for which alone they were liable and therefore that amount was fully recoverable. Had application of the 20 per cent reduction not taken the claimant's loss within the overvaluation, then the overvaluation figure would have applied to fix the amount recoverable. In either situation no reduction of the overvaluation figure comes into play.

[32a] [2021] UKSC 20; [2021] 3 W.L.R. 81 at [173]–[174]. At [39], Lord Hodge and Lord Sales (Lord Reed, Lady Black and Lord Kitchin agreeing) agreed with Lord Leggatt.

CHAPTER 8

CAUSATION OF DAMAGE, SCOPE OF DUTY, AND REMOTENESS OF DAMAGE

TABLE OF CONTENTS

I. **Torts** 8-003
  1.   CAUSATION 8-003
    (1)   The "but for" test of necessary contribution .... 8-003■
    (2)   Applying the "but for" test when a later event causes the
         same or further harm .... 8-007□
    (3)   The exceptions to the "but for" test of necessary
         contribution .... 8-014□
  2.   DAMAGE OUTSIDE THE SCOPE OF THE CLAIMANT'S LEGAL DUTY . 8-032□
    (1)   The need to identify the interests protected .... 8-034■
    (2)   Where the tort is based on an assumption of
         responsibility .... 8-047■
    (3)   Where the damage caused is coincidental 8-056
  3.   REMOTENESS OF DAMAGE 8-057
    (1)   Nomenclature .... 8-057■
    (2)   The Wagon Mound test 8-060
    (3)   Foreseeable damage of that type 8-063
    (4)   Type of damage not affected by existing abnormalities of
         claimants or property .... 8-072■
    (5)   Consequences following upon a new intervening force . 8-095□

II. **Contract** 8-140
  1.   CAUSATION .... 8-141□
  2.   DAMAGE OUTSIDE THE SCOPE OF THE CLAIMANT'S LEGAL DUTY .. 8-145
    (1)   The scope of duty constraint: assumption of responsibility
         for that type of damage 8-145
    (2)   The scope of duty constraint has a long history 8-147
    (3)   The decision in The Achilleas in 2008 8-153
    (4)   The decisions concerning scope of duty since 2008 8-160
  3.   REMOTENESS OF DAMAGE 8-166
    (1)   A need for further restriction upon responsibility for
         consequences 8-166
    (2)   The rule in Hadley v Baxendale 8-168
    (3)   Hadley v Baxendale as a ceiling on recovery beyond
         ordinary losses 8-170
    (4)   The rule restated in Victoria Laundry v Newman in 1949 . 8-171
    (5)   The restated rule as qualified in The Heron II in 1967 ... 8-173

(6)   The degree of likelihood required 8-176
(7)   The type of loss and the manner or degree of loss 8-181
(8)   The degree of knowledge required 8-188
(9)   Consequences following upon a new intervening force   . 8-199

I.   TORTS

1.   CAUSATION

(1)   The "but for" test of necessary contribution

Replace paragraph with:

8-005   The "but for" test thus requires the court to consider whether the wrongdoer's act or omission was necessary for the loss that was suffered. The basic question is whether the loss would still have been suffered if the wrongful act had not occurred. One qualification to this basic question, designed to ensure that a victim is not made worse off by further wrongdoing, is that the court often asks whether the loss would have been *lawfully* suffered. When asking this question no other facts should be changed or assumed other than to remove the wrongful act. The only question is whether the loss could and would lawfully have occurred within the existing legal regime if the wrongful act had not occurred. For instance, in *R. (Hemmati) v Secretary of State for the Home Department*,[11] the Secretary of State unlawfully detained the claimants pending deportation. The Supreme Court held that it was not relevant to causation of loss that if the Secretary of State had known of the illegality a new regulation would have been enacted to permit lawful detention:

> "It can be no answer to a claim for damages for unlawful imprisonment that the detention would have been lawful had the law been different."[12]

It should be noted, however, that the broader the characterisation of the wrongful act that is to be removed in the assessment of what would have happened, the less likely that causation of loss will be established. For instance, in *Parker v Chief Constable of Essex Police*[12a] the Court of Appeal held that only nominal damages were available for the false imprisonment of the claimant following his unlawful arrest because the arrest would still have been made if the officer had appreciated, as she could have done, what the law required. That characterisation has been doubted in the High Court of Australia, adopting the approach of the UK Supreme Court, on the basis that the correct enquiry should be whether things had been done "as they should have been" (i.e. without the wrong) rather than whether things had been done as they could have been.[12b] A better understanding of the reasoning in *Parker* was given by Philip Mott QC, sitting as a Deputy High Court judge in *Fittschen v Chief Constable of Dorset Police*,[12c] who treated the wrongdoing in Parker as an arrest without a proper briefing for the arresting officer about procedures.

[11] [2019] UKSC 56; [2019] 3 W.L.R. 1156. See para.17-018 below.

[12] *R. (Hemmati) v Secretary of State for the Home Department* [2019] UKSC 56; [2019] 3 W.L.R. 1156 at 1193 [112].

[12a] [2018] EWCA Civ 2788; [2019] 1 W.L.R. 2238.

[12b] *Lewis v Australian Capital Territory* (2020) 271 CLR 192 at 262–263 [182], citing *R. (Hemmati) v Secretary of State for the Home Department* [2019] UKSC 56; [2019] 3 W.L.R. 1156 at 1193 [112]; [2020] 1 All E.R. 669 at 702; and *Kuchenmeister v Home Office* [1958] 1 Q.B. 496 at 512; [1958] 2 W.L.R. 453 QBD.

[12c] [2022] EWHC 399 (QB) at [9].

After para.8-005, add new paragraph:

8-005A Since the rationale of a counterfactual enquiry into what would *lawfully* have occurred without the defendant's wrong is to ensure that the claimant is not made worse off by some other hypothetical wrong for which the claimant cannot recover, the rationale does not apply where the loss would have occurred in any event due to another wrong that would have been committed by the claimant themselves. In *Brearley v Higgs*,[12d] in relation to a claim for causation in relation to a loss of a chance, Falk J correctly held that causation had not been satisfied in circumstances in which, but for the defendant solicitors' breaches of duty in providing negligent advice, the claimant would nevertheless have dishonestly failed to follow that advice.[12e] Falk J said[12f]:

> "[W]hilst a court would fairly start with a presumption of honest behaviour, it cannot be right that honesty must continue to be presumed in favour of a claimant whom the court is satisfied after the rigours of a full trial would, in fact, have behaved dishonestly."

[12d] [2021] EWHC 2635 (Ch).

[12e] [2021] EWHC 2635 (Ch) at [393]–[395], [412].

[12f] [2021] EWHC 2635 (Ch) at [362].

(2) Applying the "but for" test when a later event causes the same or further harm

Replace the paragraph with:

8-007 As explained above, the "but for" test is usually applied by asking whether but for the wrongdoing the loss would have been *lawfully* suffered, a point recognised by Bryan J in *Lakatamia Shipping Co Ltd v Su*.[13a] This qualification ensures that a victim is not made worse off by further wrongdoing. This also means that one wrongdoer will be responsible for losses even if those losses would otherwise have occurred by another's later wrongdoing.

[13a] [2021] EWHC 1907 (Comm) at [938]. And see para.8-005 above.

(3) The exceptions to the "but for" test of necessary contribution

After para.8-013, add a new paragraph immediately after the sub-section heading "(3) The exceptions to the 'but for' test of necessary contribution":

8-013A In *Financial Conduct Authority v Arch Insurance (UK) Ltd*,[32a] Lords Hamblen and Leggatt (with whom Lord Reed agreed) said that for most purposes the "but for" test is a minimum threshold test for causation. But they acknowledged that there were some situations in which causation could be established even if the but for test is not satisfied. The situations to which they referred, which are discussed below, were exceptional cases of material contribution such as one of 20 individuals who push a car off a cliff when any 13 individuals would have been sufficient or one director who was part of a unanimous vote of directors when a majority would have been sufficient.[32b]

[32a] [2021] UKSC 1; [2021] 2 W.L.R. 123 at [181].

[32b] [2021] UKSC 1; [2021] 2 W.L.R. 123 at [183]–[185]. See below at paras 8-019 to 8-020.

(a) "Material contribution" by a wrongdoer to the claimant's loss

Replace the paragraph with:

8-018 The two decisions in *Williams* and *Heneghan* were confronted by Picken J in *John v Central Manchester and Manchester Children's University Hospitals NHS Foundation Trust*.[47] That case involved the defendant hospital's negligence in delaying a CT scan of Dr John's brain after an accident. Dr John suffered a brain injury from his accident which was exacerbated by a post-operative infection. However, a further factor was the hospital's delay. If Dr John's CT scan had not been delayed by an hour, he would have been operated upon an hour earlier and he would have avoided a period of raised intra-cranial pressure for an hour. The primary judge considered the three categories from *Heneghan*, as he was required to do, and held that since Dr John's case was not an industrial disease case, it was not concerned with contribution to risk (category (3)). He treated Dr John's case as concerned with material contribution to injury or damage (category (2)). He concluded that since the material contribution test applied to multi-factor cases as well as single-factor cases, full damages should be recovered, without apportionment for the extent to which any other cause contributed to the injury. In other words, Dr John recovered not merely for the amount by which the hospital's delay increased his injury. He recovered for the whole of the injury. The negligence was a "but for" cause of the increase in the injury but not for the whole of the injury. Yet, the primary judge held[48] that if the "material contribution" test is satisfied, then causation is made out and the entirety of the loss can be recovered if it is not possible to attribute particular damage to a specific cause. A more orthodox approach was taken by the trial judge in *Davies v Frimley Health NHS Foundation Trust*[48a] where the issue was whether the unreasonable failure of the hospital to start IV antibiotics in a timely way caused the death of Mrs Davies from the indivisible disease of bacterial meningitis. After an exhaustive discussion of the authorities, the trial judge held that causation had been established but only because the "but for" test had been established, rejecting the sufficiency of any test for material contribution.[48b]

[47] [2016] EWHC 407 (QB); [2016] 4 W.L.R. 54.

[48] [2016] EWHC 407 (QB); [2016] 4 W.L.R. 54 at [98].

[48a] [2021] EWHC 169 (QB); [2021] P.I.Q.R. P14.

[48b] [2021] EWHC 169 (QB); [2021] P.I.Q.R. P14 at [209].

2. DAMAGE OUTSIDE THE SCOPE OF THE CLAIMANT'S LEGAL DUTY

Replace the paragraph with:

8-033 The question of the scope of the duty was concisely stated by Denning LJ in *Roe v Minister of Health*[109]: "Is the consequence within the risk?" This problem was for long little explored so that the strands of authority were few. It was propelled into the limelight by the decisions of the House of Lords and Supreme Court in *South Australia Asset Management Corp v York Montague Ltd*[110] and *Hughes-Holland v BPE Solicitors*[111] respectively.[112] And then a couplet of decisions of the Supreme Court heard together firmly established scope of duty as a restrictive criterion for the tort of negligence. Those decisions, *Manchester Building Society v Grant Thornton UK LLP*[112a] and *Khan v Meadows*,[112b] are considered in detail below in the context of the scope of liability for an assumed duty. Simple illustrations can be given of instances where the initial damage was beyond the scope of the duty owed. These are *Saddington v Colleys Professional Services*[113] and *Moore v Zerfah*.[114]

Loans on mortgage were made to wives and their husbands, and the money lent was lost by the husband or by the husband's company. Actions were brought by the wives against valuers and brokers respectively on the basis that the wives would not have agreed to the loans but for negligence on the part of the defendant professionals. Both claims failed.[115] As Lord Sumption expressed the point in *Hughes-Holland v BPE Solicitors*[116]:

> "... the law distinguishes between a mere precondition or occasion for a loss and an act which gives rise to a liability to make it good by way of damages."

The scope of duty limitation is not a "rigid rule of law" but it is an important tool that, like remoteness of damage, constrains the extent of liability.[117]

[109] [1954] 2 Q.B. 66 CA at 85.

[110] [1997] A.C. 191.

[111] [2017] UKSC 21; [2018] A.C. 599.

[112] For this aspect see paras 8-047 and following, below.

[112a] [2021] UKSC 20; [2021] 3 W.L.R. 81.

[112b] [2021] UKSC 21; [2021] 3 W.L.R. 147.

[113] [1999] 1 Lloyd's Rep. P.N. 140 CA.

[114] [1999] 1 Lloyd's Rep. P.N. 144 CA.

[115] *Galoo v Bright Grahame Murray* [1994] 1 W.L.R. 1360 CA, an equivalent case in contract (at para.8-055, below), was followed and applied. It was further said that the same result would be achieved by holding that loss of the money was not damage of a kind that was foreseeable—this in *Saddington*—or in respect of which the defendants owed a duty to protect the claimants—this in *Moore*.

[116] [2017] UKSC 21; [2018] A.C. 599 at 616 [20].

[117] *AssetCo Plc v Grant Thornton LLP* [2020] EWCA Civ 1151 at [102].

(1)   The need to identify the interests protected

(c)   Where some, but not all, damage falls within a protected interest

Replace paragraph with:

Damages for injury to reputation have also been claimed in torts to goods. Thus   **8-043**
in *Thurston v Charles*,[181] the defendant, a member of a town corporation, wrongfully communicated to the other members a letter written to the claimant by a third party which contained statements defamatory of the claimant. The claimant brought suit both for defamation and for trespass or conversion. The count on defamation failed because the communication was held privileged, but the other succeeded with damages being given in effect for the injury to the claimant's reputation. This case is probably now bad law. A recent contrast is with *BDW Trading Ltd v URS Corporation Ltd*[181a] where it was held, on a strike out application, that a structural engineering designer, who was assumed to have been negligent in the structural design of a high-rise building, was not liable for losses flowing only from the damage to the reputation of a developer, such as loss of potential future projects. On the other hand, in *Dixon v Calcraft*,[182] an action not in tort but upon a statute, the damage alleged was that, by seizing the claimant's ship on a suspicion of her being unsafe, an imputation was cast on the claimant's character as a shipowner. Lord Esher MR said:

> "No such claim for damages was ever yet sustained in an action for seizing a chattel. If compensation were given for such an injury, it would be a kind of compensation unknown

to the English law. It seems to me clear that this damage could not be recovered in an action for such a detention of a chattel, if wrongful. It could not be given by way of aggravation of damages in respect of wounded feelings. Such a thing was never heard of. Nor could it be given for injury to character, because that would really be giving damages as for libel or slander, though the matter complained of is not anything written or spoken."[183]

[181] (1905) 21 T.L.R. 659.

[181a] [2021] EWHC 2796 (TCC); 200 Con. L.R. 192.

[182] [1892] 1 Q.B. 458 CA.

[183] [1892] 1 Q.B. 458 CA at 464; see, too, at 466, per Lopes LJ.

Replace the paragraph with:

8-044   In *Lonrho v Fayed (No.5)*,[184] a case of conspiracy far removed from the field of torts to goods, the Court of Appeal held that *Thurston v Charles*[185] is unsound and cannot stand; the view stated in *Dixon v Calcraft*[186] is to be preferred. Yet it may be questioned how far this essentially obiter pronouncement affects torts to goods generally. *Thurston v Charles* was said to be inconsistent with a cache of cases in 1993 which declined to allow claims to be made for injury to the reputation other than in defamation; for such damages suit could not be brought in injurious falsehood,[187] in negligence[188] or in conspiracy.[189] However, it should be noted that in all these cases, including *Thurston v Charles*, the claimants' complaints centred upon the making of statements for which, for one reason or another, they could not, or did not wish to, sue in defamation and the courts' concern has been that defendants are not denied the familiar defences of justification, privilege and fair comment by allowing claimants to proceed by a different cause of action. Where, however, a statement is not involved and these defences are of no relevance, then the rationale for overturning *Thurston v Charles* itself has nothing upon which to operate. Even if a statement is involved, a less blunt approach might be to consider whether allowing recovery of losses flowing from the non-protected interest would be too remote, particularly in light of the rules concerning the protection of that interest. For that reason, until the decision in *Sicri v Associated Newspapers*[189a] it had been thought that there was no obstacle in principle to the recovery of non-pecuniary loss consequent upon loss of reputation merely because the action was brought for a misuse of private information rather than for defamation.[189b] The denial of this proposition in *Sicri* was primarily due to a concern that non-pecuniary losses flowing from damage to reputation could be recovered in the hypothetical case of the publication of information about the arrest of a person later convicted of terrorism. Yet, the later conviction surely rendered very minimal the extent of any contribution to loss of reputation by the misuse of private information. Any non-pecuniary loss from lost reputation would be too remote to recover.

[184] [1993] 1 W.L.R. 1489 CA.

[185] (1905) 21 T.L.R. 659.

[186] [1892] 1 Q.B. 458 CA.

[187] *Joyce v Sengupta* [1993] 1 W.L.R. 337 CA.

[188] *Spring v Guardian Assurance* [1993] I.C.R. 412 CA. But Spring was later reversed: [1995] 2 A.C. 296; the Lords were unimpressed by the argument that a claim in negligence should not be allowed to overtake an action in defamation.

[189] *Lonrho v Fayed (No.5)* [1993] 1 W.L.R. 1489 CA, itself.

[189a] [2020] EWHC 3541 (QB); [2021] 4 W.L.R. 9 at [163]. Applied in *Hayden v Duckworth* [2020] EWHC 1033 (QB) at [28]. See below at para.47-010A.

[189b] *Khuja v Times Newspapers Ltd* [2017] UKSC 49; [2017] 3 W.L.R. 351 at [21], [34], [381].

(2) Where the tort is based on an assumption of responsibility

Replace the paragraph with:

When the tort in issue is negligence, the Supreme Court has said that the scope of duty enquiry is essentially twofold. The first involves precision in the duty of care enquiry: "[w]hat are the risks of harm to the claimant against which the law imposes on the defendant a duty to take care?" The second is whether there is a sufficient nexus between the subject matter of that duty of care and the harm for which the claimant seeks damages.[200a] In many instances, this application will be routine. A duty to take care to avoid physical injury will, at the second stage, include any physical injury and consequential loss in the nexus of harm. A duty to take care to avoid damage to property will, at the second stage, include any damage to the property and consequential loss in the nexus of harm. Perhaps the most important application of the scope of duty restriction in negligence lies in cases of negligence where the tort is based upon an assumption of responsibility, and where the definition of the duty and ascertaining the nexus of harm with the duty has sometimes proved difficult. The requirement for damage to fall within the scope of an assumption of responsibility has always been embedded in the law but it was given a great boost, in the context of a claim for negligence based on an assumption of responsibility, by Lord Hoffmann's speech in *South Australia Asset Management Corp v York Montague Ltd*,[201] commonly called *SAAMCO*, the gist of which was reiterated by the Supreme Court in *BPE Solicitors v Hughes-Holland*.[202] This requirement has been clarified and entrenched in the couplet of cases decided together by the Supreme Court: *Manchester Building Society v Grant Thornton UK LLP*[202a] and *Khan v Meadows*.[202b] In each case of assumption of responsibility the central question for scope of duty is the same: "what is the risk which the service [or action] which the defendant undertook was intended to address?"[202c]

8-047

[200a] *Khan v Meadows* [2021] UKSC 21; [2021] 3 W.L.R. 147 at [28].

[201] [1997] A.C. 191.

[202] [2017] UKSC 21; [2018] A.C. 599. Followed by the Court of Appeal in *AssetCo Plc v Grant Thornton LLP* [2020] EWCA Civ 1151, rejecting an appeal by the auditors—see [76] and [78].

[202a] [2021] UKSC 20; [2021] 3 W.L.R. 81.

[202b] [2021] UKSC 21; [2021] 3 W.L.R. 147.

[202c] *Khan v Meadows* [2021] UKSC 21; [2021] 3 W.L.R. 147.

Replace the paragraph with:

Whether a person has assumed the responsibility for damage arising from a transaction will depend upon the express or implied terms of the person's undertaking. Where implied terms are concerned, the nature of the transaction can be important. As Lord Sumption explained in *Hughes-Holland*, the extent to which an assumption of responsibility will concern the risks of a transaction might depend upon whether the transaction is one of "advice", involving the underlying concept of an adviser who guides the "whole decision making process" including entry into the transaction and is responsible for the consequences of entry,[210] or whether the transaction is one for provision of "information" involving the concept of a general information provider who does not take responsibility for the decision to enter the transaction.[211] However, ultimately it is the underlying concept of whether the loss flows from the wrongful feature of the transaction that is important rather than the descriptively inadequate[212] labels of "advice" or "information". As five members of the Supreme Court held in *Manchester Building Society v Grant Thornton UK*

8-049

LLP[212a] "the distinction between 'advice' cases and 'information' cases ... should not be treated as a rigid straitjacket". Thus, in *Large v Hart*,[212b] the Court of Appeal correctly held that concepts of "advice" or "information", both of which could partly describe the transaction, were not useful in assessing whether a negligent surveyor was liable for the consequences of latent defects in a property, the purchase of which would not have occurred if the surveyor's report had not been negligent.[212c]

[210] [2017] UKSC 21; [2018] A.C. 599 at 623 [40]. See *AssetCo Plc v Grant Thornton LLP* [2020] EWCA Civ 1151 at [76] and *LIV Bridging Finance Ltd v EAD Solicitors LLP (In Administration)* [2020] EWHC 1590 at [35].

[211] [2017] UKSC 21; [2018] A.C. 599 at 623 [41].

[212] [2017] UKSC 21; [2018] A.C. 599 at 623 [39].

[212a] [2021] UKSC 20; [2021] 3 W.L.R. 81 at [4] (Lord Hodge and Lord Sales; Lord Reed, Lady Black and Lord Kitchin agreeing).

[212b] [2021] EWCA Civ 24; [2021] B.L.R. 189.

[212c] [2021] EWCA Civ 24; [2021] B.L.R. 189 at [67]–[68].

Replace the paragraph with:

8-050   In *Manchester Building Society v Grant Thornton UK LLP*,[213] the respondent accountants were negligent in their advice about accounting treatment of long-term interest rate swaps entered by the Society. The accountants had not been asked to, and had not, advised the Society about the commercial issues concerning entry into the swaps. Nevertheless, the Society would not have entered the swaps but for the accountants' advice about the accounting treatment of them which was thought to free the Society from regulatory capital requirements. When, after the intervention of the regulator, the Society realised the error, the swaps were closed, with £32.5 million in break costs. The Supreme Court unanimously concluded that the loss suffered by closing out the swaps, at market value, on discovery of the error was within the scope of the duty assumed by the accountants, although damages were reduced by 50% for the contributory negligence of the Society. In reaching the conclusion that losses from closing out the swap agreements were within the scope of the accountants' duties, and not external commercial losses, the Supreme Court departed from the conclusions of both the trial judge and the Court of Appeal, which had been forcefully expressed. The Supreme Court decision is ultimately compelling, especially in circumstances in which the accountants knew that the advice they were giving was to be used for the business model adopted by the Society and the break costs of the swaps were the costs of abandoning that business model. But the result was not obvious. In contrast, other cases will be simpler. For instance, in *Main v Giambrone*,[214] the defendant law firm advised English and Irish claimants that they would be protected by bank loan guarantees when buying Italian property off the plan. The firm received and then paid out the claimant's deposits without guarantees being in place. The firm, with its Italian lawyers, were found to have guided the "whole decision making process" and therefore to have assumed responsibility for the whole transaction which turned out to be a money laundering scam.[215] It was therefore liable for the deposits lost by the claimants.

[213] [2021] UKSC 20; [2021] 3 W.L.R. 81.

[214] [2017] EWCA Civ 1193; [2018] P.N.L.R. 2.

[215] [2017] EWCA Civ 1193; [2018] P.N.L.R. 2 at [82].

After para.8-050, add a new paragraph:

8-050A   The *Manchester Building Society* case was decided at the same time, and by the same panel, as *Khan v Meadows*.[216] The decision in *Khan v Meadows* also involved the scope of an assumed duty but in the different context of medical negligence. The decision of the House of Lords in *McFarlane v Tayside Health Board*[217] had rejected the view of nearly two decades that the scope of the duty of a doctor carrying out a failed sterilisation extended to liability for the costs of the upbringing of the child. Subsequently, however, the Court of Appeal concluded that the scope of the doctor's duty did extend to the extra costs of providing for the special needs and care of a child with disabilities.[217a] The issue in *Khan* was whether the scope of the duty of a doctor extended only to costs related to the disabilities about which negligent advice was given or whether it extended to all disabilities. The facts of *Khan* involved negligent advice from a doctor that led the claimant patient to believe that she was not a carrier of the haemophilia gene. But for the advice, the claimant would not have had a baby. The Supreme Court unanimously held that although the doctor was liable for the extra costs incurred by the claimant of bringing up the child with haemophilia, the doctor was not liable for the extra costs of the unrelated autism condition of the child. The scope of the doctor's duty extended only to advising about haemophilia.

[216] [2021] UKSC 21; [2021] 3 W.L.R. 147.

[217] [2000] 2 A.C. 59; [1999] 3 W.L.R. 1301.

[217a] *Parkinson v St James and Seacroft University Hospital NHS Trust* [2001] EWCA Civ 530; [2002] Q.B. 266; *Groom v Selby* [2001] EWCA Civ 1522; [2002] Lloyd's Rep. Med 1.

Replace the paragraph with:

In other cases it is much more difficult to determine whether the loss flows from **8-052** the feature that makes the conduct wrongful. These cases can be difficult to resolve as is shown by the opposing views often taken of a case, *Aneco Reinsurance Underwriting v Johnson & Higgins*,[223] by the House of Lords, the Court of Appeal and the court of first instance. Whereas in *SAAMCO* the valuers were held liable only for the loss resulting from the over-valuation and not for the much greater loss from the property market collapse, in *Aneco* where brokers had failed to effect valid insurance, they were held liable not just for the loss resulting from their failure properly to insure but for the much greater loss resulting from their client having no reinsurance at all. Ultimately, although defending the result in *Aneco*, Lord Sumption giving the reasons of the Supreme Court in *Hughes-Holland v BPE Solicitors*[224] emphasised that the decision "is not authority for any general proposition of law beyond the particular factual context of that case". Easier to reconcile with cases that refuse liability is *Large v Hart*[224a] where the Court of Appeal held that a negligent surveyor was liable for the consequences of latent defects that, on one view, he could never have spotted. The reason for liability was that the surveyor should have seen enough of the defects for him to give different advice which would have avoided the purchase of the property and the subsequent expense of knocking down the building and reconstructing it.[224b] On the other hand, it was rightly not suggested that the surveyor was liable for any funding costs, or increase in funding costs, or for any fall in property values.[224c]

[223] [2002] 1 Lloyd's Rep. 157 HL.

[224] [2017] UKSC 21; [2018] A.C. 599 at 625 [44].

[224a] [2021] EWCA Civ 24; [2021] B.L.R. 189.

[224b] [2021] EWCA Civ 24; [2021] B.L.R. 189 at [52]–[53].

[224c] [2021] EWCA Civ 24; [2021] B.L.R. 189 at [56].

After para.8-052, add new paragraphs:

8-052A   Another reasonably straightforward application of *SAAMCO* was in *Charles B Lawrence & Associates v Intercommercial Bank Ltd.*[224a] A valuer negligently valued land at $15 million. On the basis of that valuation the lender made a loan of $3 million with a mortgage over the land provided by a guarantor as security for the loan. It was later discovered that the guarantor did not have title to the land being provided as security, so the mortgage was worthless to the lender. The Privy Council held that the lender's loss was not within the scope of duty owed by the valuer. As Lord Burrows and Lady Rose explained, the purpose of the duty, assessed objectively, was to obtain a valuation of the land. It was not, as the valuer had disclaimed, a duty to investigate title. The loss at the date the loan was made (being the relevant date assumed by the parties) that was attributable to the valuation was therefore $625,000, being the difference between the loan sum, $3 million, and the residential value of the land, $2,375,000. A settlement reached by the lender with its conveyancing attorneys, for their negligent failure to reveal the lack of title, was therefore irrelevant because it concerned only the aspect of the scope of duty that had been excluded.

[224a] [2021] UKPC 30; [2022] P.N.L.R. 7.

8-052B   Another example is *Radia v Marks*,[224b] where a claim was brought against a medical expert on the basis that the alleged negligence of the expert led to the claimant being found to be a dishonest witness. Lambert J held that it had been no part of the expert's retainer to advise or assist on issues concerning the credibility of the claimant and, indeed, he was not qualified to do so. Indeed, to extend the scope of a duty on the part of the expert to protect against adverse credibility findings could conflict with the expert's duty to a court or tribunal.[224c]

[224b] [2022] EWHC 145 (QB); [2022] P.N.L.R. 12.

[224c] [2022] EWHC 145 (QB); [2022] P.N.L.R. 12 at [61].

8-053   *Delete para.8-053.*

Replace the paragraph with:

8-055   In light of the modern understanding of this limit on responsibility for damage that is caused by a wrongful act, some older cases that refuse liability on the basis of causation might be better understood now as cases where the damage was beyond the scope of assumed liability for torts based upon an assumption of responsibility. Though primarily brought in contract, *Galoo v Bright Grahame Murray*[230] was a case also for an assumption of responsibility in the law of torts, as is generally so with the professional negligence claims which today take up much of the time of the courts.[231] The negligent failure of auditors to discover and report upon inaccuracies in the audited accounts of the claimant companies, which would have shown the companies to be insolvent, led the companies to continue to trade and so incur further losses. The auditors were held not liable for these further losses on the ground that they had not caused them but had only provided the opportunity for them to be incurred.[232] But the case is better now understood as turning not upon causation, which was satisfied, but upon scope of duty. Certainly in *Equitable Life Assurance Society v Ernst & Young*,[233] a not dissimilar case, Langley J confessed to finding it easier to analyse *Galoo* in terms of scope of duty than causation,[234] and Lord Hoffmann has himself effectively said so extra-judicially.[235] In *Manchester Building Society v Grant Thornton UK LLP*,[235a] Lord Leggatt also analysed *Galoo* in this way although, as explained above, the Supreme Court concluded that the *losses* were within the scope of the duty assumed by the defendant accountants. The Supreme Court also gave very short shrift to the submission that the negligence of the accountants was too remote in that it had merely provided the opportunity for the losses to be made.[235b]

[230] [1994] 1 W.L.R. 1360 CA.

[231] Exceptionally, the obligation of care will arise only in contract as with the solicitor's negligence in *Haugesund Kommune v Depfa ACS Bank* [2011] 3 All E.R. 655 CA, where Norwegian law applied: facts at para.34-011, below.

[232] See the case at para.8-208, below.

[233] [2003] Lloyd's Rep. P.N. 88.

[234] [2003] Lloyd's Rep. P.N. 88 at [85]. The decision itself was reversed in part: [2004] P.N.L.R. 16 CA at 269.

[235] In a paper, *Common Sense and Causing Loss*, to the Chancery Bar Association, 15 June 1999. There are, however, cases in which cause necessarily predominates over scope of duty, as appears to have been the case on one of the issues in *Green v Alexander Johnson* [2005] EWCA Civ 775 CA, an appeal on the computation of damages arising out of a barrister's negligence: see the discussion at [2005] EWCA Civ 775 CA at [23] and following.

[235a] [2021] UKSC 20; [2021] 3 W.L.R. 81 at [116].

[235b] [2021] UKSC 20; [2021] 3 W.L.R. 81 at [39], [173]–[174], [211].

3. REMOTENESS OF DAMAGE

(1) Nomenclature

Replace footnote 241 with:

[241] [2017] UKSC 80; [2018] 1 W.L.R 192. The application of this reasoning, but not its correctness, was also rejected in *FS Cairo (Nile Plaza) LLC v Lady Brownlie* [2021] UKSC 45; [2021] 3 W.L.R. 1011 at [48]–[51].

8-057

(4) Type of damage not affected by existing abnormalities of claimants or property

(a) Physical abnormalities of claimants or their property

Replace footnote 341 with:

[341] Though a necessary condition, reasonable foreseeability is not a sufficient condition in secondary victim cases. In *Alcock v Chief Constable of the South Yorkshire Police* [1992] 1 A.C. 310, from Lord Oliver's speech in which the classification of primary and secondary victims apparently derives, the House of Lords required that there be not only reasonable foreseeability but also proximity to the event in time and space and proximity of relationship between primary and secondary victims. The *Alcock* limitations were extended to rescuers and employees, who are put into the position of secondary victims, by the further House of Lords decision in *White v Chief Constable of the South Yorkshire Police* [1999] 2 A.C. 455, reversing *Frost v Chief Constable of the South Yorkshire Police* [1998] Q.B. 254 CA (see the case further at para.8-112, below). The *Alcock* limitations are regarded as control mechanisms, intended to keep cases of this nature within acceptable bounds and in formulating them in *Alcock*, in the words of Lord Hoffmann in *White* (otherwise *Frost*), at [1999] 2 A.C. 455 at 511B, the search for principle had been called off. The latest decision is that of the Court of Appeal in *Taylor v A. Novo (UK) Ltd* [2014] Q.B. 150 CA where a daughter was denied recovery for a psychiatric illness induced by witnessing her mother's collapse and death from an injury at work three weeks earlier caused by her employers' negligence. The Master of the Rolls in the only reasoned judgment meticulously examined a whole series of cases in the field, leading and other, to conclude that to allow recovery where the death was witnessed but the accident itself was not would be taking a step too far: [2014] Q.B. 150 CA at [29] and following. But the horrific event witnessed must be proximate in time to the event of negligence: *Paul v Royal Wolverhampton NHS Trust* [2022] EWCA Civ 12; [2022] 2 W.L.R. 917.

8-077

(b) Pecuniary abnormalities of claimants or their property

(ii) Abnormal weakness

After para.8-093, add new paragraph:

8-093A   The only abnormal financial weaknesses which are relevant, however, are those that concern the claimant's general financial position, not weaknesses that arise from particular contracts. Hence, in *Armstead v Royal and Sun Alliance Insurance Co Ltd*,[429a] although Mrs Armstead could have recovered damages for any loss of use of her hired car that was damaged by the negligence for which the defendant insurer was responsible, she was unable to recover, as too remote, particular contractual "loss of use" expenses owed by her to her hire company (which were set at a credit hire rate) during the period in which the car was being repaired. Those losses were too remote.

[429a] [2022] EWCA Civ 497; [2022] R.T.R. 23. See further the discussion at para.37-028A.

(5)   Consequences following upon a new intervening force

Replace footnote 435 with:

8-097   [435] *Clay v TUI UK Ltd* [2018] EWCA Civ 1177; [2018] 4 All E.R. 672 distinguished in *James v White Lion Hotel* [2020] P.I.Q.R. P10 at [99], [100]–[105]. An appeal to the Court of Appeal in *James* was dismissed: [2021] EWCA Civ 31.

(a)   Intervening acts where the claimant or third party has insufficient autonomy

(ii)   Insufficient autonomy due to the defence of the person's own rights

Replace footnote 468 with:

8-105   [468] [2018] EWCA Civ 1177; [2018] 4 All E.R. 672. Compare *James v White Lion Hotel* [2020] P.I.Q.R. P10 at [103]–[105] where a smoker's act of sitting on a window sill was a "clear misjudgement" but was not so unreasonable to "break the chain of causation". An appeal to the Court of Appeal in *James* was dismissed including with a rejection of a defence of *volenti non fit iniuria*: [2021] EWCA Civ 31.

Replace the paragraph with:

8-109   The complementary situation is of course where the master of the claimant's ship acts in such a way as to class him as a free agent: here the defendant is relieved of liability for any further damage following on from the intervening act. These cases, collected above,[497] should be compared and contrasted with those just dealt with. *SS Singleton Abbey v SS Paludina*[498] is the leading case on damage to a ship which was held to be too remote owing to an intervening act, though an act of a third party in that case; *The Metagama*,[499] is the leading case on damage to a ship which was held to be not too remote despite an intervening act; and the difference between such cases, as Lord Wright pointed out in *The Oropesa*,[500] is basically a question of fact. It should also be borne in mind that a third and intermediate solution has been put forward by Brandon J in *The Calliope*,[501] where he held that further damage to a ship was not too remote despite an intervening act, but that the damages must be reduced because of the contributory negligence inherent in the intervening act.[502] The test in that case, adopted half a century later in *The Owners of the Vessel Sakizaya v The Owners of the Vessel Panamax Alexander*,[502a] was whether the defendant's fault in relation to a first collision was "continuing" in the sense that it did not merely provide the opportunity for the later collision. In that case, the defendant shipowners of the Panamax Alexander were liable for a further collision by another ship that was still "in the grip of the first collision" and was not a "free agent"[502b] meaning that the controllers of the other ship had limited options to avoid further damage and the further collision was the consequence of their attempt to protect the ship.

[497] See para.8-106, above.

[498] [1927] A.C. 16: facts at para.8-130, below.

[499] (1927) 29 Ll. L. Rep. 253 HL.

[500] As reported at [1943] 1 All E.R. 211 CA at 213: "I am confirmed in my view that the problem here is a question of fact by the curious difference of opinion which seems to have occurred in the two leading cases."

[501] [1970] P. 172.

[502] See para.6-015, above, for a detailed consideration of this decision. *The Metagama* at para.8-109, above and the other shipping cases at para.8-106, above were referred to the court in *Morris v Richards* [2004] P.I.Q.R. Q3 CA at 30 in the context of holding that a physically injured claimant taking new employment and then losing it was not thereby disqualified from recovering damages for loss of earnings in respect of the period following the loss of her new position.

[502a] [2020] EWHC 2604 (Admlty) at [297]–[299].

[502b] [2020] EWHC 2604 (Admlty) at [298].

(iv)   Insufficient autonomy due to impairment from the tort

Replace the paragraph with:

Other examples of an adult's act for which the adult was not fully responsible due to impairment of autonomy as a result of the tort are *Pigney v Pointers Transport Services*[536] and *Reeves v Commissioner of Police of the Metropolis*.[537] In *Pigney*, the defendant injured a man who, as a result of neurosis induced by the injury took his own life. It was held that his widow could recover[538] in respect of his death: the damage she suffered was not too remote.[539] In *Reeves*, a man who was a known suicide risk killed himself while in police custody, the police were held liable to his estate for their failure to take care to prevent him from committing suicide. His act of self-destruction was the precise outcome against which the police were under a duty to guard. The House of Lords in *Corr v IBC Vehicles Ltd*,[540] then went even further in allowing recovery, for the defendant was not custodian but employer, so that it could not be said that the suicide was a consequence from which there was a duty to protect the employee. A horrific accident at work resulting in terrible head injuries led not only to appalling physical consequences but to a deep depressive illness which drove the victim after several years to kill himself. It was held that his suicide had been a direct result of the depressive illness at a time when his capacity to make reasoned judgments about his future was impaired and that therefore the chain of causal consequences for which the defendant was liable had not been broken by the suicide as a novus actus interveniens.[541] Subsequently, in *Gray v Thames Trains Ltd*,[542] where the claimant, after being injured in a train crash which affected him psychologically, had killed a stranger leading to hospitalisation for manslaughter, the Court of Appeal, relying on the reasoning of the House of Lords in *Corr*,[543] considered that it was strongly arguable that the claimant should not be disentitled from recovering for loss of earnings during his hospitalisation, as killing another should no more than killing oneself be regarded in the particular circumstances as a novus actus breaking the chain of causation.[544] However, when the case reached the House of Lords it was held that recovery was barred by the ex turpi causa rule, thus removing the need to consider remoteness.[545]

8-117

[536] [1957] 1 W.L.R. 1121.

537 [2000] 1 A.C. 360.

538 Strictly in this case, and the cases that follow in the text, the claimant was not the intervening actor but these cases bear a closer analogy to claimant's than to third party's intervening act.

539 But see *Pigney* further in the footnote at the end of this paragraph.

540 [2008] 1 A.C. 884.

541 On novus actus see in particular the speech of Lord Bingham at [2008] 1 A.C. 884 at [14]–[16].

542 [2009] A.C. 1339 CA.

543 [2009] 1 A.C. 1339 CA at [36]–[44].

544 [2009] A.C. 1339 CA at [45].

545 [2009] A.C. 1339. Also followed in *Henderson v Dorset Healthcare University NHS Foundation Trust* [2020] UKSC 43; [2020] 3 W.L.R. 1124. The Court of Appeal in *Corr v IBC Vehicles Ltd* [2007] Q.B. 46 CA held *Pigney* (in text above) to have been correctly decided—there is no reference to *Pigney* in the House of Lords in *Gray v Thames Trains*—but on a ground which is no longer acceptable (see [2007] Q.B. 46 CA at [101], per Wilson LJ). For another ground, now otiose, of the decision in *Pigney* see para.41-011, below.

(b)   Intervening acts where the claimant or third party has sufficient autonomy

Replace footnote 559 with:

8-121   559 [1982] A.C. 225. See also *James v White Lion Hotel* [2021] EWCA Civ 31 at [58] where the Court of Appeal upheld a finding of liability, notwithstanding a high, but not very high, degree of unreasonableness by the deceased, with a 60% reduction for contributory negligence.

II.   CONTRACT

1.   CAUSATION

After para.8-142, add new paragraphs:

8-142A   As with torts,653a the "but for" question is whether the loss could and would lawfully have occurred within the existing legal regime if the wrongful act had not occurred. The counterfactual does not vary any fact other than those involving the breach of contract. An example is *British Gas Trading Ltd v Shell UK Ltd*.653b In that case, the Court of Appeal held that sellers of gas under long term agreements had breached terms of those agreements that obliged the sellers to maintain a capacity to deliver natural gas at a specified rate. Although the sellers had met their delivery obligations to the buyers, the buyers argued that in order to avoid being in breach of their capacity obligation the sellers would have served variation notices reducing the capacity which they were required to maintain, which would in turn have reduced the price to the buyers by £61 million. Males LJ, in the leading judgment, held that the relevant counterfactual was what the sellers were required to do, which was to maintain the relevant capacity, even though this was impossible for them to do. The counterfactual was not concerned with what the sellers might have done if they had known that they were in breach, but did not do, namely to issue variation notices.653c Hence, only nominal damages could be awarded. Both Andrews LJ and Peter Jackson LJ recognised the curiosity of this conclusion,653d which arises because performance was impossible and if the sellers had known that they were in breach then their likely action may have been to issue the variation notice. But the normal measure of damages entitles a buyer to the value of performance promised even if it is impossible. And the counterfactual for the recovery of consequential losses depends upon a finding of what would have happened if the seller had not been in breach. It does not ask what would have happened if the seller had known that it would be in breach.

653a See above at para.8-005.

653b [2020] EWCA Civ 2349.

653c [2020] EWCA Civ 2349 at [79].

653d [2020] EWCA Civ 2349 at [97], [105].

Another example is *Medstead Associates Ltd v Canaccord Genuity Wealth* **8-142B**
*(International) Ltd.*653e In that case, the defendant breached its contract with the claimant by performing trading for clients introduced by the claimant without paying commission to the defendant on those trades. The defendant argued that if it had not chosen to breach the contract it would also have been open with the clients and required payment of extra commission which, in turn, would have led to less trading and therefore less commission. Nicholas Vineall QC, sitting as a Deputy High Court judge, rightly held that the defendant was not entitled to vary any of the facts on the counterfactual other than its breach of contract in failing to pay the claimant. The only facts that are changed on the counterfactual are the facts that constituted the breach of contract.653f

653e [2020] EWHC 2952 (Comm).

653f See, especially, [2020] EWHC 2952 (Comm) at [42].

Chapter 9

MITIGATION OF DAMAGE

Table of Contents

I. **Various Meanings of the Term "Mitigation"** 9-001
    1.   Principal Meaning: The Three Rules as to the Avoiding of the Consequences of a Wrong 9-002
    2.   The Two Subsidiary or Residual Meanings 9-008

II. **The First Rule: No Recovery for Avoidable Loss Which the Claimant Ought Reasonably to have Avoided** 9-014
    1.   Various Aspects of the Rule 9-015
       (1)   Application to contract and tort 9-015
       (2)   A question of fact not a question of law 9-016
       (3)   The question of duty 9-018
       (4)   The question of causation 9-019
       (5)   The question of onus 9-020
       (6)   Whether need to mitigate before contractual breach 9-021
       (7)   Whether need to mitigate by discontinuing contractual performance 9-024
       (8)   Application of mitigation to the actual loss or the recoverable loss 9-037
    2.   The Rule and its Relationship to the Normal Measure of Damages 9-039
    3.   Illustrations of Circumstances Raising the Issue of Whether Loss Should have been Avoided 9-047
       (1)   Contract 9-048
       (2)   Torts .... 9-064■
    4.   Standard of Conduct Claimants Must Attain 9-079
       (1)   The criterion of reasonableness and the standard of reasonableness .... 9-079□
       (2)   Illustrative decisions .... 9-083■

III. **The Corollary (Second Rule): Recovery for Loss Incurred in Attempts to Mitigate Damage** 9-102

IV. **The Third Rule: No Recovery Generally for Loss Which has been Avoided by Reasonably Necessary Means** 9-109
    1.   The Three Subdivisions of the Rule 9-109
    2.   Various Aspects of the Rule 9-113
       (1)   Application to contract and tort 9-114
       (2)   The question of onus 9-115

	(3)	The preliminary issue of mitigation of loss or no loss ...	9-116
3.	ACTIONS TAKEN AFTER THE WRONG BY THE CLAIMANT		9-117
	(1)	Situations where the benefit is generally taken into account	9-121
	(2)	Situations where the benefit is generally ignored	9-133■
	(3)	Situations where the position is unclear	9-153
4.	ACTIONS TAKEN AFTER THE WRONG BY THIRD PARTIES		9-154
	(1)	The particular case of gratuitous assistance afforded	9-157
	(2)	The particular case of converted or distrained goods applied to pay debts	9-159
	(3)	Miscellaneous situations	9-162
5.	ACTIONS TAKEN BEFORE THE WRONG BY THE CLAIMANT		9-166
	(1)	Insurance taken out before injury against the eventuality of injury	9-167
	(2)	Sub-contracts already made before breach	9-171

II.   THE FIRST RULE: NO RECOVERY FOR AVOIDABLE LOSS WHICH THE CLAIMANT OUGHT REASONABLY TO HAVE AVOIDED

3.   ILLUSTRATIONS OF CIRCUMSTANCES RAISING THE ISSUE OF WHETHER LOSS SHOULD HAVE BEEN AVOIDED

(2)   Torts

(a)   In general: where the door to mitigation is not opened by the party in default

(ii)   Goods: damage and destruction

Replace paragraph with:

9-068   Where goods have been damaged and their owner seeks to recover their expenditure in repairing them, the cost of repair is generally categorised as an expense incurred in order to mitigate loss. Whether the cost is recoverable turns therefore upon the reasonableness or otherwise of effecting the repairs. This is well illustrated by two contrasting cases concerning the repair of cars, *Darbishire v Warran*[269] and *O'Grady v Westminster Scaffolding*,[270] in both of which the claimant had had his damaged car repaired at a cost in excess of its market value instead of trying to replace it. These are fully considered when dealing specifically with damage to goods.[271] A simple example where it is not reasonable to repair is where the claimant intends to sell the damaged item and the reduction in market value from the damage is less than the cost of repair.[272] A similar test of reasonableness for the purposes of mitigation is applied where the claimant's claim is for the cost of hiring a substitute while the damaged article is being repaired. Again the cases involve cars. A series of cases from *Watson Norie v Shaw*[273] to *Hussain v EUI Ltd*[274] consider the question of whether hiring a prestige car, or hiring a car for a prolonged period, indicates a failure to mitigate. These cases too are fully considered when dealing specifically with damage to, and destruction of, goods.[275] The principle for which recovery is permitted subject to mitigation, as explained by the High Court of Australia in *Arsalan v Rixon*,[275a] is that the claimant will usually have suffered both physical inconvenience and a loss of the amenity value of using the damaged prestige car so it will not generally be unreasonable conduct, disqualifying the claimant from recovery of the loss, if the claimant hires an alternative car which is a substitute in terms of quality.

269 [1963] 1 W.L.R. 1067 CA.

270 [1962] 2 Lloyd's Rep. 238.

271 See para.37-005, below.

272 *Endurance Corporate Capital Ltd v Sartex Quilts and Textiles Ltd* [2020] EWCA Civ 308 at [36]–[38].

273 [1967] 1 Lloyd's Rep. 515 CA.

274 [2019] EWHC 2647 (QB).

275 See paras 37-015, 37-016 and 37-069, below.

275a [2021] HCA 40.

4. STANDARD OF CONDUCT CLAIMANTS MUST ATTAIN

(1) The criterion of reasonableness and the standard of reasonableness

Replace the paragraph with:

Reasonableness is assessed objectively by reference to all the circumstances in which the claimant finds themself.[313a] In mitigating their loss, claimants are only required to act reasonably and the standard of reasonableness is not high in view of the fact that the defendant is an admitted wrongdoer.[314] Lord Macmillan put this point well for contract in *Banco de Portugal v Waterlow*[315]; his remarks apply equally to tort. He said:

9-079

> "Where the sufferer from a breach of contract finds himself in consequence of that breach placed in a position of embarrassment the measures which he may be driven to adopt in order to extricate himself ought not to be weighed in nice scales at the instance of the party whose breach of contract has occasioned the difficulty. It is often easy after an emergency has passed to criticise the steps which have been taken to meet it, but such criticism does not come well from those who have themselves created the emergency. The law is satisfied if the party placed in a difficult situation by reason of the breach of a duty owed to him has acted reasonably in the adoption of remedial measures and he will not be held disentitled to recover the cost of such measures merely because the party in breach can suggest that other measures less burdensome to him might have been taken."[316]

Whether the claimant has acted reasonably is in every case a question of fact, not of law.[317]

313a *Deutsche Bank AG v Total Global Steel Ltd* [2012] EWHC 1201 (Comm); [2012] Env. L.R. D7 at [159]; *McMahon v Grant Thornton UK LLP* [2020] CSOH 50; [2020] S.T.C. 1732 at [125].

314 See also *Rabilizirov v A2 Dominion London Ltd* [2019] EWHC 186 (QB) at [76] and *Natixis SA v Marex Financial* [2019] EWHC 2549 (Comm) at [543].

315 [1932] A.C. 452 at 506.

316 Words adopted and applied in *Bacon v Cooper (Metals)* [1982] 1 All E.R. 397 (facts at para.25-083, below) and in *Al Rawas v Pegasus Energy Ltd* [2007] EWHC 2427 (QB) (claimant subject to search and freezing orders had not been shown to have acted unreasonably in taking out a loan so as to be able to pay a very large sum into court). See the similar remarks of Roskill J in *Harlow and Jones v Panex (International)* [1967] 2 Lloyd's Rep. 509 at 530, rejecting the argument that the claimants, suing for non-acceptance of goods sold, acted unreasonably, in the light of their liability for storage charges, in not accepting any offer they could get for the goods. See also *Hayes v James & Charles Dodd* [1990] 2 All E.R. 815 CA at 820e, where the claimants might have surrendered the lease of premises at a much earlier date so as to avoid continuing accrual of rent (facts at para.34-016, below), per Staughton LJ:

"but they were placed in a difficult situation through the fault of the defendants, and I would not criticise them for failing to adopt that course".

[317] See para.9-016, above. For a whole series of ways in which the defendant argued unsuccessfully that the claimant should have acted to mitigate his loss see, at great length, *BSkyB Ltd v HP Enterprise Services UK Ltd* [2010] EWHC 86 (TCC) at [1712]–[1800].

(2) Illustrative decisions

(b) Illustrations of what is not required of the claimant in mitigation

(ii) A claimant need not risk their person too far in the hands of surgeons

After para.9-088, add new paragraph:

9-088A   The same principles apply in relation to a claimant's choice to take a medicine whose side-effects, or experimental nature, could expose the claimant to risks of greater harm to person or lifestyle. In *Mathieu v Hinds*,[355a] the defendant failed to establish that the claimant had acted unreasonably in refusing to take medicine for regular, debilitating headaches. Two side effects of the medicine were drowsiness and cognitive decline in the form of dementia. As the claimant was an artist, the trial judge, Hill J, accepted that it was "hard to imagine two side-effects he would be less willing to tolerate" and that his position was "understandable".[355b]

[355a] [2022] EWHC 924 (QB); [2022] P.I.Q.R. Q4.

[355b] [2022] EWHC 924 (QB); [2022] P.I.Q.R. Q4 at [116].

IV. THE THIRD RULE: NO RECOVERY GENERALLY FOR LOSS WHICH HAS BEEN AVOIDED BY REASONABLY NECESSARY MEANS

3. ACTIONS TAKEN AFTER THE WRONG BY THE CLAIMANT

(2) Situations where the benefit is generally ignored

(b) Other situations

(i) Other contracts

After para.9-142, add new paragraph:

9-142A   Contrary in result to these decisions stands the decision of Sir Nigel Teare in *Space Shipping Ltd v ST Shipping and Transport Pte Ltd*.[578a] In that case, Space Shipping, bareboat charterers, fixed a vessel on time charter to ST Shipping. The vessel was seized and detained for more than three years due to a cargo being unauthorised for export. Later the vessel was towed to Port of Spain where, as a consequence of the long detention, she was declared by Space Shipping to be a constructive total loss. The arbitrator held ST Shipping liable for more than $US 24 million in costs of hire and damages for breach of a contractual term not to expose the vessel to capture or seizure. But the arbitrator deducted $US 1.4 million for the costs of drydocking that Space Shipping had saved because drydocking and repair was impossible while the vessel was detained and impractical once the vessel was a constructive total loss. In upholding this award, in effect Sir Nigel Teare distinguished the decisions above on the basis that the drydocking costs were part and parcel of the value of the lost hire and were not an independent commercial decision by Space Shipping.[578b]

[578a] [2021] EWHC 2288 (Comm).

578b [2021] EWHC 2288 (Comm), especially at [60]–[62].

CHAPTER 10

CERTAINTY OF DAMAGE, PRESUMPTIONS OF DAMAGE, AND LOSS
OF CHANCE

TABLE OF CONTENTS

I.   The Problem of Certainty   .... 10-001■

II. Circumstances in Which Damages May be Awarded Although
     the Nature of the Damage Prevents Absolute Certainty of
     Proof   10-010
     1.   WHERE DAMAGE IS PRESUMED   .... 10-010□
     2.   WHERE THE LOSS IS NON-PECUNIARY   10-013
     3.   WHERE IT IS UNCERTAIN HOW A PECUNIARY LOSS IS TO BE
          MEASURED   .... 10-014■
     4.   UNCERTAINTY AS TO AMOUNT OF LOSS ATTRIBUTABLE TO THE
          BREACH   10-016
     5.   UNCERTAINTY AS TO EXISTENCE OR POSSIBILITY OF PECUNIARY LOSS   . 10-029
          (1)   Prospective expenses   .... 10-030□
          (2)   Prospective earnings   10-034
          (3)   Loss of general business and professional profits   10-035
          (4)   Loss of a chance   .... 10-041■
          (5)   Where certainty of loss is dependent upon the defendant's
                actions   .... 10-111■
          (6)   Where certainty as to the loss suffered is dependent on
                future events   10-119

I.   THE PROBLEM OF CERTAINTY

To the end of the paragraph, add:
   The loss must, however, be an immediate adverse consequence and not merely   **10-001**
a risk of some adverse consequence.[4a]

[4a] *YJP Port Ltd v MAandA Pharmachem Ltd* [2021] EWHC 42 (Ch) at [68]. See also *Marathon Asset
Management LLP v Seddon* [2017] EWHC 300 (Comm); [2017] 2 C.L.C. 182 at [162].

Replace paragraph with:
   Further cases presenting this difficulty of showing the amount of profitable sales   **10-006**
that would have been made by the claimant had there been no tort or breach of
contract by the defendant have indicated that the claimant is assisted by the principle
in the very old case of *Armory v Delamirie*,[22] which has today received a new lease
of life, the principle being that the court is required to resolve uncertainties by making assumptions generous to the claimant where it is the defendant's wrongdoing
which has created those uncertainties. That principle was endorsed by the Supreme

[47]

Court in *Morris-Garner v One Step (Support) Ltd*[23] but there remains doubt about the extent of its application. The doubt concerns whether the principle is one of general application or whether it applies only to assist the judge in resolving evidential disputes. The remarks of Lord Reed JSC in *Morris-Garner* suggest the latter. So too, do the remarks of Longmore LJ (with whom Arden and Aikens LJJ agreed) in *Keefe v The Isle of Man Steam Packet Co Ltd*,[24] adopted in *Fluor v Shanghai Zhenhua Heavy Industry Co Ltd*,[25] that when the defendant's breach of duty makes it difficult or impossible for a claimant to adduce relevant evidence the defendant "must run the risk of adverse factual findings". To similar effect are the remarks of Sir Michael Burton in *MAD Atelier International BV v Manes*,[25a] that where a defendant's wrongdoing has created uncertainties, "in the case of a loss whose existence has been proved, the court will err on the side of generosity in the calculation of it if its exact calculation is difficult if not impossible to arrive at".

[22] (1722) 1 Str. 505.

[23] [2018] UKSC 20; [2019] A.C. 649 at [38].

[24] [2010] EWCA Civ 683 at [19].

[25] [2018] EWHC 1 (TCC) at [53].

[25a] [2021] EWHC 3335 (Comm) at [30].

II. CIRCUMSTANCES IN WHICH DAMAGES MAY BE AWARDED ALTHOUGH THE NATURE OF THE DAMAGE PREVENTS ABSOLUTE CERTAINTY OF PROOF

1. WHERE DAMAGE IS PRESUMED

Replace the paragraph with:

10-012   Contract, on the other hand, having less concern with matters involving interference with the claimant's relationships with other people generally, provides few situations in which the court is ready to presume damage. The one clear case is that damages may be given for the general pecuniary loss by injury to credit and reputation caused by the defendant's failure to pay the claimant's cheques or honour their drafts,[33] a pecuniary loss which it is difficult to estimate at all accurately. Established as long ago as *Rolin v Steward*,[34] confirmed in *Kpohraror v Woolwich Building Society*,[35] and still applied as in *Nicholson v Knox Ukiwa & Co*,[36] the clearest explanation of the rule appears in Lord Birkenhead's speech in *Wilson v United Counties Bank*,[37] where he said that:

> "... the ratio decidendi in such cases is that the refusal to meet the cheque, under such circumstances, is so obviously injurious to the credit of a trader[38] that the latter can recover, without allegation of special damage, reasonable compensation for the injury done to his credit."

Nevertheless, there must still be some evidence of damage to credit before the presumed general damage will attract a significant award, albeit that the evidence can be at a high level of generality and the assessment will remain a broad brush approach.[38a] Further, where the claimant's credit rating is already substantially impaired, then general damages will be much lower than the £8,000 awarded to the claimant with a reasonably healthy credit rating in *Durkin v DSG Retail Ltd and HFS Bank Plc*.[38b]

[33] For details see paras 34-091 to 34-093, below.

[34] (1854) 14 C.B. 595.

[35] [1996] 4 All E.R. 119 CA.

[36] [2008] P.N.L.R. 33 at 782.

[37] [1920] A.C. 102 at 112.

[38] No longer limited to a trader: see *Kpohraror v Woolwich Building Society* [1996] 4 All E.R. 119 CA at para.34-091, below.

[38a] *Kerrigan v Elevate Credit International Ltd (t/a Sunny) (in admin)* [2020] EWHC 2169 (Comm); [2020] C.T.L.C. 161 at [153].

[38b] [2008] GCCG 3651 discussed in *Kerrigan v Elevate Credit International Ltd (t/a Sunny) (in admin)* [2020] EWHC 2169 (Comm); [2020] C.T.L.C. 161 at [150], [153].

3. Where it is Uncertain how a Pecuniary Loss is to be Measured

Replace paragraph with:

A different case of uncertainty of loss appeared in *Gerber Garment Technology* **10-015** *Inc v Lectra Systems Ltd*,[45] where the claimant holding company was unable to prove that the loss of profits of its wholly-owned subsidiaries was a loss to itself. By contrast, the claimant, again a holding company, was held to have overcome this hurdle in *George Fischer (Great Britain) Ltd v Multi Construction Ltd*,[46] and recovered pound for pound the loss of its subsidiary.[47] Again in *MAD Atelier International BV v Manes*,[47a] the claimant was able to prove the substantial dividends that would have been paid to it by the subsidiaries, despite numerous imponderables concerning the profit that would have been achieved from restaurants that would have been run by the subsidiaries. Also in the context of nuisance it was recognised in *Jan de Nul (UK) v NV Royale Belge*,[48] where silt had been deposited in an estuary, that damages could be awarded although it was impossible to assess the effects of the nuisance with any degree of monetary precision.

[45] [1997] R.P.C. 443 CA.

[46] [1995] 1 B.C.L.C. 260 CA.

[47] There is also in this area the uncertainty over shareholders' losses where the direct loss is to the company; such losses being termed reflective losses. While the general rule is that the shareholder cannot sue where the company has an action, the no reflective loss principle is not to be over-indulged and does not always stand in the way of the shareholder claiming damages, as *Shaker v Al-Bedrawi* [2003] Ch. 350 CA; *Giles v Rhind* [2003] Ch. 618 CA (the damages assessment follows at [2004] 1 B.C.L.C. 385) and *Pearce v European Reinsurance Consultants and Run-Off Ltd* [2006] P.N.L.R. 8 at 142 show. *Webster v Sandersons Solicitors* [2009] P.N.L.R. 37 at 773 CA is another case involving, inter alia, shareholders' reflective losses. The application of the reflective loss principle in relation to damages is further discussed in the factual context of *Malhotra v Malhotra* [2014] EWHC 113 (Comm) at [53]–[63], *Energenics Holdings Pte Ltd v Ronendra Nath Hazarika* [2014] EWHC 1845 (Ch) at [60]–[70], and *Barnett v Creggy* [2014] EWHC 3080 (Ch) at [92]–[99].

[47a] [2021] EWHC 3335 (Comm).

[48] [2000] 2 Lloyd's Rep. 700.

5. Uncertainty as to Existence or Possibility of Pecuniary Loss

(1) Prospective expenses

Replace the paragraph with:

If a particular expense has already been incurred but not yet paid by the claim- **10-031** ant, the amount thereof may be included in the damages where the claimant is under a legal liability to pay the third party. Thus in *Mason v Barker*,[107] where a penalty had been paid in order to bring about the release of the claimant from a false imprisonment, it was held that the claimant could recover as damages the amount so paid whether it had been paid by himself or by some third party whom he was liable to reimburse. In *Randall v Raper*,[108] where the claimant buyer had been sued by his sub-buyer for damages, he recovered this amount from his seller although he had not paid the sub-buyer.[109] A further and modern illustration of a sale and sub-sale of goods, here of a cargo of gasoline in defective condition, is provided by *Total Liban SA v Vitol Energy SA*.[110] Should, however, it be clear and certain that the liability will never be discharged, and the expense never paid by the claimant, recovery will be denied them so as to avoid their reaping a windfall; it was so held in *Biffa Waste Services Ltd v Maschinenfabrik Ernst Hese GmbH*.[111] Thus, as Foxton J said in *Palmali Shipping SA v Litasco SA*,[111a] a liability which would have been waived or forgiven in any event will not count towards the calculation of loss.

[107] (1843) 1 C. & K. 200.

[108] (1858) E.B. & E. 84.

[109] A similar result was reached about the same time in *Smith v Howell* (1851) 6 Exch. 730 where, however, the action was not for damages but was an action on an indemnity. The claimant lessee assigned his lease to the defendant, taking an indemnity against all "costs, damages, and expenses which he might incur" from breaches by the assignee of the covenants in the lease. The assignee did commit breaches, for which the claimant was sued by his lessor and judgment recovered against him by default. It was held that he might recover the amount of the damages and the costs of the judgment by default, in an action on the indemnity, though he had not yet paid them himself.

[110] [1999] 2 Lloyd's Rep. 700.

[111] [2009] P.N.L.R. 1 at 1.

[111a] [2020] EWHC 2581 (Comm) at [37].

(4)   Loss of a chance

(b)   The range of the loss of a chance doctrine: general principles

Replace paragraph with:

10-044   Before turning to the authorities which in modern times have cascaded over the law reports, it is important to address the question which has much troubled the courts, of how wide ranging is the loss of a chance doctrine. In short, when does a claimant have to prove on a balance of probabilities that a particular result would have come about and when need he prove only that a chance, which may be less than a probability, of achieving that particular result has been lost. The distinction is of immense importance, separating as it does the cases where the claimant will be awarded all or nothing and the cases where a percentage of loss will come their way. A broad summary of the overall position is made, with crystal clarity, by Andrew Burrows QC sitting as a High Court judge prior to his appointment to the Supreme Court of the United Kingdom in *Palliser Ltd v Fate Ltd*.[176] He said:

> "The correct picture of the law on proof in relation to damages is therefore that where the uncertainty is as to past fact, the 'all or nothing balance of probabilities' test applies. Where the uncertainty is as to the future, proportionate damages are appropriate. Where the uncertainty is as to hypothetical events, the correct test to be applied depends on the nature of the uncertainty: if it is uncertainty as to what the claimant would have done, the all or nothing balance of probabilities test applies; if it is as to what a third party would have done, damages are assessed proportionately according to the chances."

To this can be added two points. First, once a claimant elects to claim damages on the basis of a loss of a chance, it is not open to the claimant to seek to recover full damages by proving what a third party would have done on the balance of probabilities.[176a] Secondly, as set out below, the all-or-nothing approach where the uncertainty concerns something that the claimant would have done applies also to things that a defendant would have done and things that a third party would have done where the third party's actions are attributable to the claimant or the defendant.[176b]

[176] [2019] EWHC 43 (QB) at [27].

[176a] *Phoenicks Ltd v Bellrock Property & Facilities Management Ltd* [2021] EWHC 2639 (Comm) at [103], citing *Assetco v Grant Thornton LLP* [2019] EWHC 150 (Comm); [2019] Bus. L.R. 2291 (which was not doubted on appeal in *AssetCo v Grant Thornton LLP* [2020] EWCA Civ 1151; [2021] Bus. L.R. 142).

[176b] See below at paras 10-058 to 10-071.

(ii)   The distinction between causation of loss and quantification of loss

In the ninth sentence, after "This then makes for three stages in the enquiry", add new footnote 188a:

10-048

[188a] These three stages were approved, and the content of this paragraph was cited with approval, in *F P McCann Ltd v Department for Regional Development* [2020] NIQB 51 at [93].

(iii)   A loss of chance requires a real and substantial chance

Replace paragraph with:

10-052

There are two simple and basic points to bear in mind when considering proof of loss of chance. The first is the pragmatic view we have seen above that loss of chance is a broad brush assessment. The second point is that a loss of chance claim requires a real chance. A chance of bringing a claim which has no underlying substance, such as a "nuisance claim" or a dishonest claim, is not a real chance.[221] Further, a chance which is negligible will not permit recovery. The difficult question then is what is a negligible chance? In *Harding Homes (East Street) Ltd v Bircham Dyson Bell (a firm)*,[222] the defendant solicitors were negligent by including an all moneys clause in a guarantee given by the claimant builders to a bank in relation to a property development. The guarantee should have been limited to interest shortfall and cost overruns. The claimants alleged that they lost the opportunity for a more profitable result arising from negotiations about the development with the bank. The trial judge, Proudman J, considered whether the loss of opportunity was of something of value, that is, something that had a real and substantial rather than a merely negligible prospect of success. In concluding that the prospects of success were negligible, the trial judge[223] followed *Thomas v Albutt*,[224] where Morgan J said that if "the prospects were 10 per cent or less, then I should regard them as negligible". It is difficult to justify such mathematical precision in relation to a broadly expressed approach to "negligible" prospects of success. But even if this point were to be expressed in mathematical terms, the better approach is that a "negligible" prospect should be assessed in light of the circumstances. For instance, a 10 per cent prospect of succeeding in relation to a transaction worth billions of pounds might not be negligible for the same company compared with one which is worth thousands. A clear example is *Ocean Outdoor UK Ltd v Hammersmith & Fulham LBC*[225] where the claimants sought damages on the basis of a lost chance of success based on allegations that the defendant council breached procurement rules in a tender process. In the leading judgment in the Court of Appeal, Coulson J held that even if the rules had been breached, the claimant had been outbid on a scale of 3:1 so that "there can be no uncertainty as to the hypothetical outcome of a lawful competition". Another example is *Recorded Picture Co Ltd v Alfama Films Production*[225a] where producers claimed for the breach of an agreement by a London production company which granted the producers an option to make a film, after the London production company gave an option to another company which ultimately made the film. Judge Hacon held that a combination of factors including financing problems meant that the producers never had anything above a speculative chance of making the film.

²²¹ *Perry v Raleys Solicitors* [2019] UKSC 5; [2020] A.C. 352 at 643–644 [26].

²²² [2015] EWHC 3329 (Ch).

²²³ [2015] EWHC 3329 (Ch) at [167].

²²⁴ [2015] EWHC 2817 (Ch) at [461].

²²⁵ [2019] EWCA Civ 1642; [2020] 2 All E.R. 966 at [92].

^{225a} [2020] EWHC 3481 (Ch) at [141].

After para.10-052, add a new paragraph:

10-052A   However, in *PCP Capital Partners LLP v Barclays Bank Plc*,[225b] Waksman J considered the authorities and discussion above and held that 10% should be a cut-off point since there must be some threshold and the percentage threshold should be the same no matter what the circumstances of the case. There are three basic problems with this approach of mathematical precision. The first is that it is arbitrary. In many cases, the assignment of a percentage, 8%, 11% or 16%, will have no rational economic basis. The exercise that a trial judge will be likely to have performed is to assess whether the chance was substantial and then to assign an arbitrary percentage to reflect the assessment of whether the chance was substantial. Secondly, as already mentioned, whether a chance is substantial or not might depend upon the circumstances. Consider, for example, a venture capitalist considering whether to provide £100 million in funding for two large ventures. Both have a 10% chance of success. If the first succeeds the profit will be £500 million. If the second succeeds, the profit will be £1 million. The venture capitalist might consider the 10% chance in the first case to be substantial but not in the second case. Thirdly, sometimes there will not be a single percentage chance. In other words, the outcome might not be binary. For instance, in the first hypothetical case there might be a 5% chance of a £500 million recovery, a 50% chance of a £50 million recovery (i.e. 50% loss) and a 40% chance of complete failure. The expected recovery across all these chances in such a case is £50 million for £100 million in funding. Should a 10% threshold chance be assessed for recovery of at least £100 million even though this is not the expected recovery? Or some lesser amount?

^{225b} [2021] EWHC 307 (Comm) at [559]–[561].

(iv)   The distinctions as they apply to personal injury cases

After para.10-057, add a new paragraph:

10-057A   For the moment, nevertheless, apart from cases of mesothelioma and related diseases, the assessment of chances in relation to personal injury or death will only be relevant to a balance of probabilities conclusion. Hence, in *Schembri v Marshall*[248a] the Court of Appeal, applying *Gregg*, upheld the conclusion of the trial judge that the respondent's wife's death from pulmonary embolism would probably have been avoided if the deceased had been sent straight to hospital when presenting with symptoms to her general practitioner. Although various chances were considered in the process of reaching that conclusion, as well as statistical evidence concerning the prospects of survival if the deceased fell within the statistical groups, the ultimate question is a single question to be assessed as whether but for the negligence the deceased would have survived.

(v) The distinction between acts of the claimant and acts of third parties

Replace paragraph with:

10-065 While at first glance it may seem somewhat strange to have different tests applicable to hypothetical acts of the claimant and hypothetical acts of third parties, it can be seen to make sense, with nothing at all arbitrary about it and with no need to bring in public policy to justify it. Claimants can hardly claim for the loss of the chance that they *might* have acted in a particular way; they must show that they *would* have; it cannot surely be enough for claimants to say that there was a *chance* that they would have so acted. The onus is on claimants to prove their case and they therefore must be able to show how they would *in fact* have behaved. There is no such onus on third parties.[267] The claimant's position in this is well illustrated by *McWilliams v Arrol*,[268] a House of Lords case from Scotland, where a widow, suing for the death of her husband because of his employers' failure to provide him with a safety belt, failed in her action because she could not show that he would have used the safety belt had it been provided; it was not enough to show that he *might* have used it. Would not Miss Chaplin have had to show on the balance of probabilities that, if she had been given adequate notice of the interviews by Seymour Hicks, she would have attended?[269] As a matter of principle, the same reasoning must also apply to the hypothetical behaviour of defendants.[269a] This is especially because the defendant is exposed to the "full rigours of the litigation regime" and is likely to have led evidence on the counterfactual.[269b]

[267] The proposition in this sentence was quoted and endorsed by Andrew Burrows QC, sitting as a High Court judge in *Palliser Ltd v Fate Ltd* [2019] EWHC 43 (QB) at [27].

[268] [1962] 1 W.L.R. 295 HL.

[269] Facts of *Chaplin v Hicks* at para.10-041, above. In *Floyd v John Fairhurst & Co* [2004] P.N.L.R. 41 CA at 795 (facts at para.10-082, below) it was accepted on all sides that the claimant had to establish on the balance of probabilities what his own actions would have been.

[269a] Assumed in *AerCap Partners 1 Ltd v Avia Asset Management AB* [2010] EWHC 2431 (Comm); [2010] 2 C.L.C. 578 at [76(iii)]. See also *Phoenicks Ltd v Bellrock Property & Facilities Management Ltd* [2021] EWHC 2639 (Comm) at [105].

[269b] *PCP Capital Partners LLP v Barclays Bank Plc* [2021] EWHC 307 (Comm) at [551]–[553]. And see also *Hirtenstein v Hill Dickinson* [2014] EWHC 2711 at [85].

Replace paragraph with:

10-068 There will, however, be difficult cases where the rationale for the rule might make it difficult to draw such a sharp distinction between claimants and defendants, on the one hand, and third parties on the other. For instance, is a director to be treated in the same way as the claimant or as a third party where the claimant is a company seeking recovery from a defendant for breach of duty by the company? The answer should probably depend upon whether the actions of the director are attributable to the company, in which case the director's conduct is the conduct of a party.[275a] Another difficulty with this sharp distinction is how a court should deal with a contingency that depends upon the actions of *both* a claimant/defendant and a third party.[275b] One solution would divide the contingency according to the action involved, with an overall assessment of loss of chance requiring a standard of proof on the balance of probabilities for actions by the claimant and defendant, and an assessment of chance for the actions of the third party.[275c] This approach could become extraordinarily unwieldy and complicated, especially where third party action is interrelated with actions by a party. A more pragmatic and simpler approach would be to ask whether the action of a party or a third party is dominant or controlling of the hypothetical outcome.

[275a] *Barrowfen Properties Ltd v Patel* [2021] EWHC 2055 (Ch) at [327]–[328]. See also *AerCap Partners 1 Ltd v Avia Asset Management AB* [2010] EWHC 2431 (Comm); [2010] 2 C.L.C. 578 at [76(iii)].

[275b] A question raised but not answered in *PCP Capital Partners LLP v Barclays Bank Plc* [2021] EWHC 307 (Comm) at [565].

[275c] *Brooke Homes (Bicester) Ltd v Portfolio Property Partners Ltd* [2021] EWHC 3015 (Ch) at [220].

After para.10-068, add new paragraph:

10-068A   Another difficult issue arises where the third parties are joined to the action or give full evidence so that they are in much the same position, from the claimant's perspective, as a defendant. Again, coherent principle would treat them in the same way as a claimant or defendant. Judge Hodge QC in *Stone Heritage Developments Ltd v Davis Blank Furniss*[276] applied the balance of probabilities test to third-party actions in such a case,[277] and since he held that the balance of probabilities test was not satisfied,[278] the claimants in that case could not succeed. There was in fact no need for Judge Hodge QC so to decide as he had already held against the claimants on other grounds, and the Court of Appeal was able to bypass the issue by dismissing the appeal on the ground that the defendant had not been negligent, ending its single judgment by simply saying that:

> "... the proper test by which to assess the likelihood or otherwise of a third party ... acting in any particular manner should be considered in a wider context than that which this appeal affords".[279]

[276] *Stone Heritage Developments Ltd v Davis Blank Furniss* unreported 1 June 2006 Ch D.

[277] See *Stone Heritage Developments Ltd v Davis Blank Furniss* unreported 1 June 2006 at [330]–[334] of the extremely long judgment.

[278] See *Stone Heritage Developments Ltd v Davis Blank Furniss* unreported 1 June 2006 at [335].

[279] [2007] EWCA Civ 765 at [47]; [2007] 31 E.G. 80 (C.S.).

(d)   Assessment of the value of the lost chance

Replace the paragraph with:

10-098   And in *Nautica Marine Ltd v Trafigura Trading LLC,*[432a] Foxton J held that if a contract had been concluded and if it had required only approval for loading of a vessel then the chance of approval of a vessel for loading was so high that no discount would have needed to be made for the possibility that approval might not have been forthcoming. Sometimes the court has an easy ride and can satisfy itself without difficulty that no chance has been lost, or that the chance lost was at most wholly speculative. Thus in *Halifax Building Society v Urquart-Dykes and Lord,*[433] that the negligent advice of a trade mark agent had prevented his principal from reaching a better deal with a competitor than was achieved was considered purely speculative so that there was no loss of a valuable chance[434]; in *Casey v Hugh James Jones & Jenkins,*[435] there was held to have been no real or substantial, but only a speculative, chance that the claimant's personal injury claim would have succeeded; in *Gosfield School Ltd v Birkett Long,*[436] the chance lost was held to be too speculative to have a money value put on it.[437] Conversely, the court may find itself satisfied that realisation of the chance was a virtual certainty so that it becomes appropriate to award what would have been awarded against the original defendant. Thus in the Irish *McGrath v Kiely and Powell,*[438] the claimant was awarded against her solicitor and her doctor the whole of the extra damages she would have obtained in her successful personal injury claim had the full extent of her injuries been revealed to the court. Full recovery was also allowed by the Court of Appeal in *White v Jones*,[439] and in *Nicholson v Knox Ukiwa & Co*,[440] there was held to be no chance that the claimant's action against his bank would have failed.[441] So too in *Nicholas Prestige Homes v Neal*,[442] there was no chance that the estate agents would not have succeeded in selling the defendant's property[443] so that, as Ward LJ said, no discount had to be made for imponderables.[444]

[432a] [2020] EWHC 1986 (Comm); [2021] 1 All E.R. (Comm) 1157 at [119].

[433] [1997] R.P.C. 55.

[434] [1997] R.P.C. 55 at 87, line 18.

[435] [1999] Lloyd's Rep. P.N. 115.

[436] [2006] P.N.L.R. 19 at 342.

[437] [2006] P.N.L.R. 19 at [125]–[131]; the claim, against solicitor and barrister, would have failed on earlier issues of breach of duty and causation. For other cases of chances too speculative to permit any recovery see the wrongful death cases at para.10-095, above, *Cancer Research Campaign v Ernest Brown & Co* [1998] P.N.L.R. 592; *Veitch v Avery* (2007) 115 Con. L.R. 70; and *Checkprice (UK) Ltd v Revenue and Customs Commissioners* [2010] EWHC 682 (Admin) at para.38-009, below.

[438] [1965] I.R. 497.

[439] [1995] 2 A.C. 207 CA.

[440] [2008] P.N.L.R. 33 at 782; facts at para.34-092, below.

[441] [2008] P.N.L.R. 33 at 98 and following.

[442] [2010] EWCA Civ 1552 CA.

[443] Facts at para.10-098, above.

[444] [2010] EWCA Civ 1552 CA at [33].

(5) Where certainty of loss is dependent upon the defendant's actions

(b) Where there is a discretion as to the manner of contractual performance

After para.10-117, add a new paragraphs:

There is, however, an important distinction between a discretion which concerns **10-117A** how the contract would be performed if there had been no breach and a discretion which the contract breaker could have exercised, but did not exercise, to prevent the breach, if the contract breaker had known that it was in breach. In *British Gas Trading Ltd v Shell UK Ltd*,[520a] the correct approach taken by the Court of Appeal, overturning the primary judge on this point, was to examine the position of the innocent party absent the breach of contract, but not to examine the position of the innocent party absent the breach of contract and with additional knowledge of the law by the contract breaker.

[520a] [2020] EWCA Civ 2349. Facts at para.8-142A above.

The decisions in *Durham Tees Valley Airport Ltd* and *British Gas Trading Ltd* **10-117B** were applied in *Mallino Development Ltd v Essex Demolition Contractors Ltd*[520b] where the judge, Mr Martin Bowdery QC, held that the principle that damages are based on the least onerous contractual obligation did not apply in cases where the discretion was how to perform a contractual obligation. Those cases were instead governed by a question that asks how the obligation would have been performed, had there been no breach, on the balance of probabilities.[520c]

[520b] [2022] EWHC 1418 (TCC).
[520c] [2022] EWHC 1418 (TCC) at [32]–[34].

PART 2 NON-COMPENSATORY DAMAGES

CHAPTER 12

NOMINAL DAMAGES

Table of Contents

1. Circumstances Giving Rise to an Award of Nominal
    Damages 12-001
    (1) Where there is iniuria sine damno 12-001
    (2) Where loss is shown but its amount is not sufficiently
         proved 12-004
2. Amount Awarded; Nominal and Small Damages
    Distinguished .... 12-008□
3. Practical Functions of Nominal Damages 12-010

2. Amount Awarded; Nominal and Small Damages Distinguished

Replace the paragraph with:
   "Nominal damages", said Maule J in *Beaumont v Greathead*,[21] "means a sum of   **12-008**
money that may be spoken of, but that has no existence in point of quantity". Thus
in *Joule v Taylor*,[22] where the claimant sued for a debt of £50 and this amount
represented the extent of the court's jurisdiction, it was held that the nominal damages which he claimed for the purpose of obtaining costs did not place the debt
beyond the court's jurisdiction. Nevertheless a token sum is awarded, which, after
an early period in which the amount could be miniscule,[23] eventually crystallised
at the figure of £2, a figure that lasted for a hundred years.[24] For some time at the
end of the last century £5 had become common if not the norm,[25] but the new
century has seen a reversion to £2[26] which amount has even been said to be "the
traditional sum".[27] Although, the House of Lords in *Grobbelaar v News Group
Newspapers Ltd*,[28] unaccustomed to having to set a figure for a nominal damages
award, reverted to £1, a figure which has since appeared in a number of cases.[29]
With issues of proportionality in litigation it could hardly matter whether a figure
awarded is £1 or £2. Yet a point will come when the allegedly nominal amount is
too great to be nominal so that the quantum awarded will be erroneous. Such a case
might be the award in the course of the voluminous *Douglas v Hello!* litigation in
which the allegedly nominal sum awarded to each of two claimants for breach of
the Data Protection Act 1998 was £50.[30] Similarly, in the older case of *Constantine
v Imperial Hotels*,[30a] the award was of 5 guineas which had a value of not far from
£50. Until the 21st edition of this work, that amount was described as "curious".
In *Beattie Passive Norse v Canham Consulting Ltd*,[30b] Fraser J went further and
described the amount as "simply wrong". Clearly, today a substantial damages
award would be made to the claimant cricketer for the humiliation and distress suffered when the innkeeper refused him accommodation in breach of the innkeeper's

duty of common calling. But the size of the award was much more than a token amount to affirm a breach with no real loss. Again in *Checkprice (UK) Ltd v Revenue and Customs Commissioners*,[31] the surprising amount of £500 was awarded.[32] This must be wrong; while £500 may mean little or nothing to the Revenue and Customs Commissioners sued in *Checkprice*, it is for most people even today a considerable amount of money and far from being a nominal sum.

[21] (1846) 2 C.B. 494 at 499.

[22] (1851) 7 Ex. 58.

[23] *Feize v Thompson* (1808) 1 Taunt. 121 (sixpence, now 2.5p); *Mostyn v Coles* (1862) 7 H. & N. 872 (farthing, now 0.1p); *Sapwell v Bass* [1910] 2 K.B. 486 (shilling, now 5p).

[24] Starting with *Child v Stenning* (1879) 11 Ch. D. 82 CA and running as far as *The Kismet* [1976] 2 Lloyd's Rep. 585; a good number of intermediate cases, all of contract, are listed in earlier editions. Occasionally £1 has been awarded in the latter part of this period, as in *James v Hutton* [1950] 1 K.B. 9 CA; further such cases are listed in earlier editions. In the curious case of *Constantine v Imperial Hotels* [1944] K.B. 693, the award was of 5 guineas (now £5.25): see at 708.

[25] *Brandeis Goldschmidt & Co v Western Transport* [1981] Q.B. 864 CA (see at 874); *Dean v Ainley* [1987] 1 W.L.R. 1729 (but substantial damages awarded by the Court of Appeal: see at 1729); *Surrey CCl v Bredero Homes* [1993] 1 W.L.R. 1361 CA; *Berkowitz v MW (St John's Wood)* (1993) 48 E.G. 133. £5 as the award reappears in *The Queen on the application of Mohammed) v The Secretary of State for the Home Department* [2014] EWHC 1898 (Admin).

[26] See, e.g. *The Football League Ltd v Edge Ellison* [2007] P.N.L.R. 2 at 38 (£2 for each of two contract breaches); *Multi Veste 226 BV v NI Summer Row Unitholder BV* [2011] EWHC 2026 (Ch).

[27] In *Village Investigations Ltd v Gardner* [2005] EWHC 3300 at [77].

[28] [2002] 1 W.L.R. 3024 HL.

[29] In the two false imprisonment cases of *R. (on the application of OM) v Secretary of State for the Home Department* [2011] EWCA Civ 909 CA at [57] and *R. (on the application of Moussaoui) v Secretary of State for the Home Department* [2012] EWHC 126 (Admin) at [194], and in *Halliday v Creation Consumer Finance Ltd* [2013] EWCA Civ 333 CA, a claim in respect of damage under s.13(1) of the Data Protection Act 1998 (at [6]). In *Hodge Jones & Allen v McLaughlin* [2011] EWHC 2402 (QB) the nominal damages were provisionally assessed at £10 (at [323]).

[30] See *Douglas v Hello! Ltd* [2003] EWHC 786 (Ch); [2003] 3 All E.R. 996 at [239] and *Douglas v Hello! Ltd* [2003] EWHC 2629 (Ch); [2004] E.M.L.R. 2 at 13, [12].

[30a] [1944] K.B. 693 at 708; [1944] 2 All E.R. 171.

[30b] [2021] EWHC 1116 (TCC); [2021] P.N.L.R. 22 at [138].

[31] [2010] EWHC 682 (Admin); [2010] S.T.C. 153.

[32] [2010] EWHC 682 (Admin); [2010] S.T.C. 153 at [63].

CHAPTER 13

EXEMPLARY DAMAGES

Table of Contents

I.   **The Exceptional Nature of Exemplary Damages**   . . . . 13-001□

II. **Cases in which Exemplary Damages may be Awarded**   13-009
     1.   Types of Claim in which Exemplary Damages are Possible   . 13-011■
     2.   The Three Categories in which Exemplary Awards are
          Possible   13-017
          (1)   First common law category: oppressive, arbitrary or
                unconstitutional conduct by government servants   13-017
          (2)   Second common law category: conduct calculated to
                result in profit   . . . . 13-021■
          (3)   Authorisation by statute   13-028

III. **Computation of the Exemplary Award**   13-031
     1.   Various Criteria Applied by the Courts   13-031
          (1)   The claimant to be the victim of the behaviour requiring
                deterrence   13-033
          (2)   Moderation in awards   13-034
          (3)   The means of the parties   13-038
          (4)   The conduct of the parties   13-039
          (5)   The relevance of the amount awarded as compensation   . 13-040□
          (6)   The relevance of any criminal penalty   13-044
          (7)   The position with joint wrongdoers   13-045
          (8)   The position with multiple claimants   13-046
     2.   The Question of Vicarious Liability   13-047
     3.   The True Rationale of the Second Common Law Category   . 13-050

I.   The Exceptional Nature of Exemplary Damages

Replace the paragraph with:

Thus the debate continues and it is not likely to be long before the courts return   **13-008**
to this controversial question. Indeed there was a chance that the issue would have
been resurrected in *Kuddus* itself. For the House of Lords having decided, disagree-
ing with the courts below, that the claimant's action should not be struck out, the
defendants could have gone ahead and responded to the virtual invitation to chal-
lenge the existence of exemplary damages in their entirety. But the case settled.
From the opposite perspective, there will also be challenges in the future to the
arbitrary confinement of exemplary damages to the three categories described by
Lord Devlin in *Rookes*. For instance, in *Young v Downey*,[39a] the claimant's 19-year-

old father was murdered in a terrorist attack for which the defendant was a joint tortfeasor. But criminal proceedings against the defendant collapsed. The claimant argued that only a small extension was required from the first category to recognise exemplary damages in a case where punishment and deterrence was needed but the criminal justice system had failed to fulfil that purpose. Spencer J held that such an extension was for Parliament or higher courts, probably the Supreme Court.[39b] When the issue reaches the Supreme Court it is to be hoped that the law will not be left in a state where it is recognised that deterrence is required in three arbitrary categories which do not include circumstances of a terrorist attack, in which a 19-year-old father was murdered.

[39a] [2020] EWHC 3457 (QB).

[39b] [2020] EWHC 3457 (QB) at [38].

II. CASES IN WHICH EXEMPLARY DAMAGES MAY BE AWARDED

1. TYPES OF CLAIM IN WHICH EXEMPLARY DAMAGES ARE POSSIBLE

Replace footnote 48 with:

13-011 [48] Including torts based upon breach of statutory duty, as in *Design Progression Ltd v Thurloe Properties Ltd* [2005] 1 W.L.R. 1; facts at para.13-025, below. Yet in *Mosley v News Group Newspapers Ltd* [2008] E.M.L.R 20 at 679, Eady J ruled that exemplary damages are not admissible in a claim for invasion of privacy: [2008] E.M.L.R 20 at [197]. However, this was in part due to his doubt as to whether it was proper to classify invasion of privacy as a tort since claims founded on privacy have evolved from claims in equity for breach of confidence: see the discussion in his judgment at [2008] E.M.L.R 20 at [181]–[185]. His further argument that exemplary damages need not be available in all torts (at [187] to [192]) is, after *Kuddus*, not at all convincing. Lindsay J in the earlier *Douglas v Hello! Ltd* [1996] 3 All E.R. 996 had been content to assume, without deciding, that exemplary damages were available in this type of case: [1996] 3 All E.R. 996 at [273]. In any event, both Eady J and Lindsay J considered exemplary damages to be inappropriate on the particular facts. In *Salt Ship Design AS v Prysmian Powerlink Srl* [2021] EWHC 2633 (Comm); [2022] F.S.R. 16 at [452] the approach of Eady J was described as "controversial" by Jacobs J in the course of recognising that exemplary damages were available for unlawful means conspiracy which existed concurrently with a breach of confidence and invasion of privacy.

Replace the paragraph with:

13-013 Deceit had curiously produced no exemplary damages awards before *Rookes*. Nor have there been any decisions in either direction since *Rookes* but views have been expressed both in favour and against. On the one hand, Widgery LJ in *Mafo v Adams*[52] was quite confident that exemplary damages could be awarded and Peter Pain J in *Archer v Brown*[53] thought likewise. On the other hand, Sachs LJ in *Mafo v Adams*[54] said he still had to be persuaded and *Metallund Rohstoff AG v Acli Metals (London)*[55] proceeded on the basis that exemplary damages could not,[56] or arguably could not,[57] be awarded. Today the dicta and views in favour must prevail. Indeed Lord Scott in *Kuddus* said specifically that, if exemplary damages were to be retained,[58] deceit should in a suitable case attract them.[59] And they were, rightly, recognised by Jacobs J to be available in *Global Display Solutions Ltd v NCR Financial Solutions Group Ltd*.[59a] The best approach is to recognise that deceit can give rise to exemplary damages but that not every case of deceit will do so. The garden variety case of deceit involves a fraudulent misrepresentation causing loss to another but an order for compensation for that loss will commonly be sufficient. As Jacobs J and Bryan J have said in *Tuke v Hood*,[59b] and *Lakatamia Shipping Co Ltd v Su*,[59c] in nearly all cases of fraud in the Commercial Court the conduct might be described as "outrageous". Exemplary damages should, however, be available in circumstances such as where the loss is fortuitously small or the fraud was committed cynically, taking into account the likelihood of compensation, but with a view to profit.

⁵² [1970] 1 Q.B. 548 CA at 558.

⁵³ [1985] Q.B. 401 at 423F.

⁵⁴ [1970] 1 Q.B. 548 CA at 555.

⁵⁵ [1984] 1 Lloyd's Rep. 598 CA.

⁵⁶ [1984] 1 Lloyd's Rep. 598 CA at 612, col.1.

⁵⁷ [1984] 1 Lloyd's Rep. 598 CA at 603, col.2.

⁵⁸ Which he regretted: see para.13-007, above.

⁵⁹ [2002] 2 A.C. 122 at [122].

⁵⁹ᵃ [2021] EWHC 1119 (Comm) at [536].

⁵⁹ᵇ [2020] EWHC 2843 (Comm) at [193].

⁵⁹ᶜ [2021] EWHC 1907 (Comm) at [964].

2.   THE THREE CATEGORIES IN WHICH EXEMPLARY AWARDS ARE POSSIBLE

(2)   Second common law category: conduct calculated to result in profit

After para.13-025, add new paragraph:

In every case discussed immediately above, exemplary damages depended upon   **13-025A**
an admission or evidence from which an inference could be drawn as to the contumelious motives of gain by the landlord. The inference will often be easily drawn where the landlord has acted in a contumelious way and profited from their conduct. But in some exceptional cases, such as *Gabb v Farokhzad*,¹⁵⁵ᵃ the landlord may simply be being difficult for the sake of it. Whilst the *Rookes v Barnard* categories continue to govern, contumelious conduct without a motive for profit will not suffice.¹⁵⁵ᵇ

¹⁵⁵ᵃ [2022] EWHC 212 (Ch); [2022] 1 W.L.R. 2842 at [121].

¹⁵⁵ᵇ See paras 13-006 to 13-008 above.

III.   COMPUTATION OF THE EXEMPLARY AWARD

1.   VARIOUS CRITERIA APPLIED BY THE COURTS

(5)   The relevance of the amount awarded as compensation

Replace the paragraph with:

The principle was fully endorsed by all seven of their Lordships in *Broome v Cas-*   **13-041**
sell & Co,²⁴⁰ and its operation is well illustrated by *Drane v Evangelou*,²⁴¹ where a landlord resorted to trespass by forcible entry in order to evict his protected tenant and the Court of Appeal upheld the County Court judge's decision that such monstrous behaviour called for exemplary damages of £1,000. While Lord Denning MR was content to view the award simply as one of exemplary damages and endorse it as such, Lawton and Goff LJJ thought that it could be justified as an amalgamation of aggravated damages and exemplary damages. Both indeed considered that the award was not excessive as one for aggravated damages only, but said that, even assuming in the landlord's favour that it was excessive as such, they had, in Goff LJ's words, "not the slightest doubt that the aggregate included an element of punishment which was not in the circumstances excessive".²⁴² And

in *Guppy (Bridport) v Brookling and James*,[243] where a similar action by tenants against their landlord succeeded in nuisance rather than trespass, an award of £1,000 which combined exemplary and compensatory elements was again upheld by the Court of Appeal.[244] In *John v MGN*,[245] Lord Devlin's "if, but only if" test, as it was there called, was explicitly applied; the result of its application was still to require an exemplary award.[246] On the other hand, in *Tuke v Hood*,[246a] Jacobs J held that a standard case of fraud was not sufficient for an exemplary damages award in circumstances in which a large award of compensation left no need for further deterrence.

[240] [1972] A.C. 1027. It is stated very clearly by Lord Reid: at 1089B–F.

[241] [1978] 1 W.L.R. 455 CA.

[242] [1978] 1 W.L.R. 455 CA at 463D. See similarly Lawton LJ at 461H.

[243] (1983) 14 H.L.R. 1 CA.

[244] See especially (1983) 14 H.L.R. 1 CA at 26.

[245] [1997] Q.B. 586 CA.

[246] See [1997] Q.B. 586 CA at 626A to B.

[246a] [2020] EWHC 2843 (Comm) at [193].

Replace the paragraph with:

13-043   One of the central factors for a court to consider when assessing whether compensatory damages are sufficient to fulfil the functions of punishment, including the central concern of deterrence, is the size of the compensatory award. But the size of a compensatory award is not conclusive. In *Ramzan v Brookwide Ltd*,[250] where the total compensatory damages arrived at were in excess of £500,000, the trial judge nevertheless considered it appropriate to make an award of exemplary damages of £60,000. This award she thought was called for because she foresaw the financially powerful defendant company repeating its expropriatory actions elsewhere should it find an opportunity to do so.[251] The award of exemplary damages was upheld by the Court of Appeal although reduced by two-thirds.[252] And, in *AXA Insurance UK Plc v Financial Claims Solutions Plc*,[253] where the profit sought to be made from fraudulent insurance claims would have been entirely eradicated by the award of £85,000 compensation, the court nevertheless made an additional award of £20,000 in exemplary damages. And in *Global Display Solutions Ltd v NCR Financial Solutions Group Ltd*,[253a] Jacobs J was left in the difficult position of assessing exemplary damages in circumstances in which the parties had defined the issues for trial as including an assessment of exemplary damages but had deferred consideration of compensatory damages. Nevertheless, Jacobs J considered that it was still possible to assess whether compensatory damages were inadequate and awarded £125,000 in exemplary damages in circumstances in which this was only a small fraction of the economic benefit obtained by deceit and in which there was a subjective calculation made, which was objectively accurate, that the defendant's conduct would lead to substantial economic advantage outweighing any penalty.

[250] [2011] 2 All E.R. 38 Ch.

[251] See [2011] 2 All E.R. 38 Ch at [73].

[252] [2012] 1 All E.R. 903 CA. This reduction is thought somewhat difficult to justify, as is suggested at para.13-032, above.

[253] [2018] EWCA Civ 1330.

[253a] [2021] EWHC 1119 (Comm).

CHAPTER 14

LICENCE FEE (NEGOTIATING AND USER) DAMAGES

TABLE OF CONTENTS
1. NOMENCLATURE AND JURISDICTION 14-001
2. LICENCE FEE DAMAGES AS A MEASURE OF COMPENSATION 14-004
3. LICENCE FEE DAMAGES AS A MEASURE OF BENEFIT BEFORE 2019 . 14-010■
4. THE DECISION IN MORRIS-GARNER: ONLY ONE MEASURE
      SURVIVES 14-015
   (1) Licence fee damages for a breach of contract as a measure
         of compensation 14-015
   (2) A purely restitutionary analysis is not undertaken 14-017
5. FOR WHICH CATEGORIES ARE LICENCE FEE DAMAGES AVAILABLE? . 14-019
   (1) Breach of a contractual right which protects a non-
         economic interest 14-019
   (2) Tortious interference with land or goods . . . . 14-027■
   (3) Intellectual property wrongs, breach of confidence and
         infringement of privacy 14-031
   (4) No availability for torts that require proof of loss or which
         cannot be licensed 14-033
6. AVAILABILITY CONSIDERED IN CASES AFTER MORRIS-GARNER . . . 14-036■
7. VALUATION OF LICENCE FEE DAMAGES 14-039
   (1) The method of the hypothetical negotiation 14-039
   (2) Relevant factors to consider in the hypothetical
         negotiation . . . . 14-043□
   (3) Other methods of calculation 14-057
8. ALTERNATIVES TO LICENCE FEE DAMAGES AND ELECTION
      REQUIREMENTS 14-059
   (1) Injunctions 14-059
   (2) Other types of damages 14-063

3. LICENCE FEE DAMAGES AS A MEASURE OF BENEFIT BEFORE 2019

Replace paragraph with:

The restitutionary measure was rejected, or at least sidelined, in England and **14-014**
Wales in *One Step (Support) Ltd v Morris-Garner*.[60] Nevertheless, even after that
decision, the force of preceding authority and principle for ensuring that a
wrongdoer should not obtain a benefit at the expense of the claimant has seen at
least one judge, Judge Paul Matthews sitting as a Judge of the High Court, assert
that claims for licence fee damages (or mesne profits) are generally "measured by

[65]

reference to the *benefit* obtained by the [wrongdoer] rather than by reference to the actual *loss* suffered by the claimant" (emphasis in original).[60a]

[60] [2018] UKSC 20; [2019] A.C. 649.

[60a] *Axnoller Events Ltd v Brake* [2022] EWHC 1162 (Ch) at [58].

5. FOR WHICH CATEGORIES ARE LICENCE FEE DAMAGES AVAILABLE?

(2) Tortious interference with land or goods

(a) Wrongful user and occupation of land or goods

Replace paragraph with:

14-028   It has also long been accepted that if a defendant tortiously makes use of the claimant's goods then the claimant is entitled to damages for the use even if the claimant would not have used them itself. A classic statement of the Earl of Halsbury in *The Mediana*[96] envisaged the tortfeasor taking away another's chair for a year and asked rhetorically whether anybody could say that the tortfeasor had a right to diminish the damages by showing that the owner who had plenty of other chairs in the room did not usually sit in the chair taken.[97] One leading case in this area is *Strand Electric Co v Brisford Entertainments*.[98] There the claimant recovered as damages in detinue the market rate of hire of electrical equipment for the whole period of its tortious detention by the defendant although it was highly unlikely that the claimant, in the absence of its detention, could have hired out all of the equipment for all of the time. Although Denning LJ said in his forthright and far-sighted way that this was a restitutionary remedy,[99] a conclusion that is not presently open in English law, Somervell and Romer LJJ were content to reserve their opinions on whether the remedy was compensatory or restitutionary.[100] As we have seen above, in the post-*One Step (Support)* era, where an exclusively restitutionary analysis of these damages is denied, the best approach is to treat benefit to a defendant as a factor relevant to the measure of the price of rectifying the wrongful act.[100a] Thus, although it was inaccurate for Judge Paul Matthews in *Axnoller Events Ltd v Brake*[100b] to treat mesne profits as measured exclusively by reference to the benefit to a defendant, the benefit to the defendant remains relevant to assess the price of rectifying the wrongful act by which a valuable opportunity was conferred.

[96] [1900] A.C. 113.

[97] [1900] A.C. 113 at 117.

[98] [1952] 2 Q.B. 246 CA.

[99] At para.14-018, above.

[100] Details of the case are at para.38-067, below.

[100a] Above at paras 14-017 to 14-018.

[100b] [2022] EWHC (Ch) 1162 at [58], [67].

6. AVAILABILITY CONSIDERED IN CASES AFTER MORRIS-GARNER

Replace paragraph with:

14-037   A case on the other side of the line, albeit where the point did not need to be decided because no claim was brought for negotiating damages, is *Lloyd v Google LLC*.[132] That case involved an application for permission to serve a claim form on Google LLC, a foreign corporation. Mr Lloyd sought to bring a representative claim against Google alleging a breach by Google of s.4(4) of the Data Protection Act 1998 by secretly tracking, collating, using, and selling data concerning the internet activity of Apple iPhone users. The decision of the Supreme Court, in reasons given by Lord Leggatt, was that the claim could not be served out of the jurisdiction because no cause of action arose under s.13 of the Data Protection Act in the absence of proof that Google made some unlawful use of the data of a claimant and that damage was suffered as a result. Perhaps due to the need to establish a representative claim, no claim was brought by Mr Lloyd for misuse of private information. The claim was solely based upon s.13 of the Data Protection Act. But that claim could not succeed because it was held that a claim for damages under s.13 required material damage or distress. Since the mere "loss of control" of data is not material damage, the Supreme Court, overruling the Court of Appeal, held that the application to serve out of the jurisdiction was properly refused because no allegation of financial loss or distress had been made. If, however, an action had been brought by Mr Lloyd for misuse of private information, Lord Leggatt accepted that the claim "would naturally lend itself to an award of user damages".[133] As his Lordship observed, there is no inconsistency between a person insisting upon their privacy and claiming compensation on the basis that their information is a commercial asset. Just because the person did not wish to exploit the information commercially does not deny that the wrongdoer should rectify the wrongful act, because something was taken for nothing.[134] The information, here generated from an internet browser, remains a commercial asset whether exploited or not. Indeed, in one decision at first instance it was not even in dispute that licence fee damages should be awarded where the breach of a contractual obligation consisted of misuse of the other party's data concerning pets implanted with microchips.[135]

[132] [2021] UKSC 50; [2021] 3 W.L.R. 1268.

[133] [2021] UKSC 50; [2021] 3 W.L.R. 1268 at [141].

[134] [2021] UKSC 50; [2021] 3 W.L.R. 1268 at [142].

[135] *The Kennel Club Ltd v Micro-ID Ltd* [2019] EWHC 1639 (IPEC) at [85].

7. VALUATION OF LICENCE FEE DAMAGES

(2) Relevant factors to consider in the hypothetical negotiation

(a) The terms of the hypothetical licence

Replace the paragraph with:

14-044 We saw above that an important factor in identifying the nature and circumstances of the wrongful activity that is the subject of a hypothetical licence will be the way in which the claimant runs its case. Hence, in the case discussed, *Marathon Asset Management*, the trial judge observed that the claimant's case concerning breach of confidence did not rely upon any wrongful use of the information. Indeed, the use occurred only in relation to a few of the many files that were copied. Nor did the claimant identify the value of those files that were used.[155] Although the wrongful conduct might have gone further, the licence was therefore confined to the copying and return of the information. In contrast, in *32Red Plc v WHG (International) Ltd*,[156] the claimant submitted that the licence should not merely extend to the actual infringing mark that was used (32Vegas) for the limited period of its use but should be for the exclusive use of the trade mark itself (32 Red) and for an indefinite period. The trial judge, Newey J, rightly rejected that submission, confining the terms of the licence to the wrongful conduct (the actual trade mark used and the actual period of infringement).[157] However, the terms of the licence were for exclusive use where the circumstances of the infringement involved near-exclusivity.[158] In *FBT Productions LLC v Let Them Eat Vinyl Distribution Ltd*,[158a] the Deputy High Court judge assessed the notional licence as a licence to make the 2,891 copies that were infringing. It may be that, as in *32Red Plc*, a more realistic notional licence would be for 3,000 copies but the conservative approach usually adopted by the parties is to confine the extent of the licence to the precise circumstances of the infringement.

[155] [2017] EWHC 300 (Comm) at [281]–[282].

[156] [2013] EWHC 815 (Ch) at [38].

[157] [2013] EWHC 815 (Ch) at [50]–[52].

[158] [2013] EWHC 815 (Ch) at [55].

[158a] [2021] EWHC 932 (IPEC) at [68].

CHAPTER 15

ACCOUNT AND DISGORGEMENT OF PROFITS

TABLE OF CONTENTS

I.   Concept and Meaning of Disgorgement and Damages   15-001

II. Rationale of Disgorgement Damages   15-005

III. Circumstances Giving Rise to Disgorgement Damages   15-008
     1.   LIABILITY FOR EQUITABLE WRONGDOING   15-008
     2.   LIABILITY FOR BREACH OF CONTRACT   15-009
          (1)   Attorney General v Blake   15-009
          (2)   Where there is a legitimate interest in preventing profit   . 15-012
          (3)   Where there is no legitimate interest in preventing profit   . 15-023
     3.   LIABILITY FOR TORTS   15-029
          (1)   The principle   15-029
          (2)   Awards using the language of account of profits   15-031
          (3)   Awards using the language of "damages"   15-033
          (4)   Profit-stripping awards described as "money had and
                received"   15-036
          (5)   Awards concealed within exemplary damages   15-037
          (6)   Retrograde authority in relation to deceit   15-039
          (7)   Retrograde authority involving breach of statutory duty   . 15-045

IV. Measure of Profits, Causation and Remoteness of Profits   15-046
     1.   MEASURE OF PROFITS   . . . . 15-046■
     2.   SCOPE OF DUTY, CAUSATION AND REMOTENESS   . . . . 15-050■
     3.   DISGORGEMENT FROM MULTIPLE WRONGDOERS   15-056
     4.   CONCURRENT CLAIMS FOR COMPENSATION AND DISGORGEMENT   . . 15-057■

IV.   MEASURE OF PROFITS, CAUSATION AND REMOTENESS OF PROFITS

1.   MEASURE OF PROFITS

Replace the paragraph with:

The starting point in an accounting for profits is that it is only profits made by   **15-046**
the defendant that the defendant can be ordered to disgorge. Even if a defendant is
one of several wrongdoers, the defendant will not be liable to disgorge profits made
by another wrongdoer.[156a] A preliminary question in taking an account of profits is
which profits will count. Although the process of equitable accounting and how
profits are determined are generally questions for accounting expertise, there are
two matters of principle that should be addressed. The first is that the account of

profits can include sufficiently certain anticipated profits as well as profits already made. In *Ancient Order of Foresters in Victoria Friendly Society Ltd v Lifeplan Australia Friendly Society Ltd*,[157] a majority of the High Court of Australia held that profits that can be disgorged include both profits made as well as anticipated profits to which the defendant has a right conditional upon performance.

> "To confine the account in this way would sever the process of accounting for, and disgorgement of, profit from its rationale in the principle of ensuring that the wrongdoer should not be permitted to gain from the wrongdoing."[158]

[156a] *FM Capital Partners Ltd v Marino* [2020] EWCA Civ 245; [2021] Q.B. 1 at [52]–[53]. See also *Tuke v Hood* [2020] EWHC 2843 (Comm) at [172]; *Lifestyle Equities CV v Ahmed* [2021] EWCA Civ 675; [2021] Bus. L.R. 1020 at [10], [16].

[157] [2018] HCA 43; (2018) 265 C.L.R. 1.

[158] *Ancient Order of Foresters in Victoria Friendly Society Ltd v Lifeplan Australia Friendly Society Ltd* [2018] HCA 43; (2018) 265 C.L.R. 1 at 18 [24]; see also *Potton Ltd v Yorkclose Ltd* [1990] F.S.R. 11 at 15.

After para.15-049, add new paragraphs:

15-049A   The process of accounting for profits, consistently with the rationale of deterrence, is concerned with the net gain to the defendant. Hence, the measure of profit is net profit after tax.[165a] And all expenses can be deducted including salary paid to the wrongdoer upon the same principle which entitles a wrongdoer to an allowance in all cases other than where further punishment is required.[165b] But if the salary is not truly an allowance for work and effort and also represents a distribution of profit then to that extent it should be disgorged as profit. Thus, in *Lifestyle Equities CV v Ahmed*,[165c] the wrongdoers were required to account for and disgorge 10% of their salaries which represented profits from the trade mark infringements. The expenses incurred might not have been taken as salary but are still a non-monetary expense if they involved time and effort of the wrongdoer in earning the profit. It can sometimes be a very difficult exercise to determine when the time and effort was expended in the course of earning the profit, but a helpful approach, relied upon by Cockerill J in *Recovery Partners GP Ltd v Rukhadze*,[165d] is that of Professor Conaglen, who suggests that courts should consider whether: (i) the work done by the wrongdoer would otherwise have had to be done by another; and (ii) whether the work was beneficial to earning the profits.[165e]

[165a] *Blizzard Entertainment SAS v Bossland GmbH* [2019] EWHC 1665 (Ch) at [75]; *Lifestyle Equities CV v Ahmed* [2021] EWCA Civ 675; [2021] Bus. L.R. 1020 at [93]–[95].

[165b] *Broome v Cassell & Co Ltd* [1972] A.C. 1027 at 1129–1130; [1972] 2 W.L.R. 645.

[165c] [2021] EWCA Civ 675; [2021] Bus. L.R. 1020 at [84].

[165d] [2022] EWHC 690 (Comm) at [366]–[372].

[165e] M. Conaglen, "Identifying the profits for which a fiduciary must account" (2020) 79 *Cambridge Law Journal* 38, 63.

15-049B   In some circumstances, courts will deny a wrongdoer an allowance for expenses earned in the course of making profits, including the skill and effort expended to make the profits. The effect of this denial is that the wrongdoer will disgorge more than the true net profit. The cases have not spoken clearly on when this should occur. It has been said that the allowance could possibly be granted even for a knowing and deceitful wrongdoer.[165f] But it has also been said that an allowance should be granted sparingly.[165g] These remarks can be reconciled on the basis that, like an award of exemplary damages,[165h] the disgorgement of more than the net profit should depend upon whether the breach requires additional deterrence or punishment: "[t]he excess is punishment".[165i] Thus, one circumstance where the allowance will be denied is where, as Foxton J has put it, the wrongdoer's conduct was "conscious, calculated and sustained" and dishonest.[165j]

[165f] *Attorney General v Guardian Newspapers (No.2)* [1990] 1 A.C. 109 at 266; [1988] 3 W.L.R. 776 HL.

[165g] *Imageview Management Ltd v Jack* [2009] EWCA Civ 63; [2009] Bus. L.R. 1034 at [60]; *Hotel Portfolio II UK Ltd v Ruhan* [2022] EWHC 383 (Comm) at [259].

[165h] See above para.13-051.

[165i] *Broome v Cassell & Co* [1972] A.C. 1027 at 1129; [1972] 2 W.L.R. 645 HL.

[165j] *Hotel Portfolio II UK Ltd v Ruhan* [2022] EWHC 383 (Comm) at [260].

2. Scope of Duty, Causation and Remoteness

Replace paragraph with:

15-051 English courts have gone further when considering the disgorgement of profits for breach of fiduciary duty. In *Parr v Keystone Healthcare*,[167] it was held that "but for" causation was not required for any case of breach of fiduciary duty. The requirement is only for the requirements of scope of duty, considered below, of "some reasonable connection" or a "reasonable relationship" between the breach of duty and the profit.[168] In other words, courts will never refuse an order for disgorgement of profits for breach of fiduciary duty if those profits would have been made without the breach of fiduciary duty.[169] As the Court of Appeal said in *Gray v Global Energy Horizons Corp*,[169a] the "link or nexus" between the profit and the breach "does not need to be of a causal character" and it will usually be sufficient if it falls within the fiduciary's scope of duty, which need not require the use of the fiduciary's position to have generated the profit. As a general principle this state of the law is difficult to defend. If an account and disgorgement of profits is not to be punitive then it is hard to see why—other than in exceptional cases, such as deceit, where policy expands liability beyond strict causation —a wrongdoer should be required to disgorge profits that were not the result of a misuse of the fiduciary's position and would have been made even if there had been no breach of duty. Unsurprisingly, the nature of the "reasonable connection" that is said to suffice has been extremely elusive. It has been said to be "obviously a fact sensitive inquiry",[169b] but in the application of that approach, considering whether the profits were made "essentially because of [the] breach" sounds very much like a test for causation.[169c]

[167] [2019] EWCA Civ 1246; [2019] 4 W.L.R. 99 at [18] per Lewison LJ, with whom McCombe and Bean LJJ agreed.

[168] *Murad v Al-Saraj* [2005] EWCA Civ 959 at [112]; *CMS Dolphin Ltd v Simonet* [2001] EWHC 415 (Ch) at [97]; *Ultraframe (UK) Ltd v Fielding* [2005] EWHC 1638 (Ch), [2007] W.T.L.R. 835 at [1588].

[169] *Gwembe Valley Development Co Ltd v Koshy* [2004] B.C.L.C. 131; *Murad v Al-Saraj* [2005] EWCA Civ 959 at [76].

[169a] [2020] EWCA Civ 1668; [2021] 1 W.L.R. 2264 at [128].

[169b] *Recovery Partners GP Ltd v Rukhadze* [2022] EWHC 690 (Comm) at [285].

[169c] *Recovery Partners GP Ltd v Rukhadze* [2022] EWHC 690 (Comm) at [376].

Replace paragraph with:

15-055 The use of the remoteness principles can be seen in cases which insist that the profits to be disgorged have "some reasonable connection" with the breach of duty.[177] A good illustration is the United States case of *Frank Music Corp v Metro-Goldwyn Mayer Inc*.[178] The defendant hotel, in breach of copyright, had included a segment from the defendant's musical in its revue. The Court of Appeals for the 9th Circuit awarded the plaintiff 12 per cent of the profits from the revue (being a total of 9 per cent after an allowance to the hotel). The claimants argued that they were also entitled to: (i) a share of the profits from the hotel because the revue enticed people to the hotel and increased those profits; and (ii) a share of additional "downstream corporate benefits" received by the hotel's parent corporation. The Court held that the first set of indirect profits could be recovered but that the second were too remote. This decision was cited with approval by the High Court of Australia in *Ancient Order of Foresters in Victoria Friendly Society Ltd v Lifeplan Australia Friendly Society Ltd*[179] where it was also held that the onus is upon the party that is liable to account for profits to establish that they are too remote. In that case, the appellant company was a knowing participant in a breach of fiduciary duty by former employees of the respondent company who joined the appellant company and enticed employees of their old employer to it by means that included breaches of fiduciary duties. The new company was required to account for all of the profits made. This case contrasts with the decision of the High Court of Australia in *Warman International Ltd v Dwyer*.[180] A manager left his position at Warman and, in breach of fiduciary duty, set up new companies which entered a joint venture agreement with Warman's distributor. Warman claimed an account and disgorgement of all the profits of the new company. In a joint judgment, the High Court of Australia held that Warman was entitled to an account and disgorgement of the net profits before tax of the new companies only for the first two years of their operation. The concern of the court was that the "stringent rule requiring a fiduciary to account for profits can be carried to extremes".[181] So too, in *Davies v Ford*[181a] the disgorgement of any profits for which the defendant company could be ordered to account would, if relevant profits had been made, have been limited to a period that ended with financial contributions that had been lawfully made by third parties when the company had become insolvent.

[177] *CMS Dolphin Ltd v Simonet* [2001] EWHC 415 (Ch) at [97].

[178] 886 F. 2.d. 1545 (1989) 9th Cir CA.

[179] [2018] HCA 43; (2018) 265 C.L.R. 1 at 15 [15].

[180] (1995) 182 C.L.R. 544.

[181] (1995) 182 C.L.R. 544 at 561.

[181a] [2021] EWHC 2550 (Ch) at [148].

4. Concurrent Claims for Compensation and Disgorgement

After para.15-057, add new paragraph:

15-058   The same approach is taken to multiple wrongdoers. In *Davies v Ford*[186] the claimant was entitled to recover: (i) equitable compensation for losses suffered from two directors who had breached their fiduciary duties; and (ii) an account and disgorgement of profits for knowing receipt of property in breach of fiduciary duty, from a related company that was alleged to have received profits from the directors' breach. If only equitable compensation had been awarded against the directors then the company would have retained the profits from its separate wrongdoing. Ultimately, however, the company was found not to have received any relevant property.

[186] [2021] EWHC 2550 (Ch).

CHAPTER 16

LIQUIDATED DAMAGES AND PENALTIES

TABLE OF CONTENTS
1.   HISTORICAL DEVELOPMENT OF LIQUIDATED DAMAGES AND
     PENALTIES 16-004
  (1)   Penal bonds 16-004
  (2)   Sums agreed to be paid as damages for breach of contract . 16-006
  (3)   The intention of the parties and descriptions they use . . . 16-008
  (4)   The modern law 16-009
2.   NATURE AND EFFECT OF LIQUIDATED DAMAGES AND PENALTIES . . 16-010
  (1)   Nature of liquidated damages and penalties . . . . 16-010□
  (2)   Effect of holding a stipulated sum to be liquidated dam-
        ages or a penalty . . . . 16-024■
3.   RULES FOR DISTINGUISHING LIQUIDATED DAMAGES FROM
     PENALTIES 16-030
  (1)   The wording used by the parties is of marginal
        importance 16-031
  (2)   The circumstances must be viewed as at the time when the
        contract was made . . . . 16-032□
  (3)   The question of onus 16-034
  (4)   The test for a penalty 16-035
4.   APPLICATION OF THE EXTREME DISPROPORTION WITH A "LEGITIMATE
     INTEREST" TEST 16-043
  (1)   Where there is only a single obligation upon the breach of
        which the sum becomes payable or the property
        transferrable 16-044
  (2)   Where there are several obligations upon the breach of
        which the sum becomes payable or property
        transferrable . . . . 16-051■
5.   MAIN TYPES OF CONTRACT IN WHICH THE OLDER RULES WERE
     APPLIED 16-065
  (1)   Types of contract where the stipulated sum or property to
        be transferred is generally a penalty . . . . 16-066■
  (2)   Types of contract where the stipulated sum is generally
        liquidated damages . . . . 16-084■
6.   RELATED SITUATIONS 16-103
  (1)   Limitations of liability by way of liquidated damages . . . 16-103■
  (2)   Money paid or payable before breach: deposits and
        forfeiture clauses 16-108

Replace paragraph with:

16-002   Whether the agreed sum is recoverable from the party in breach depends primarily upon whether it constitutes liquidated damages, when it is recoverable, or a penalty, when it is not. The law as to liquidated damages and penalties has a long involved history, and a brief account of the development over the centuries is necessary for a full understanding of the modern law. But the underlying rationale of the doctrine can be stated briefly. "Parties to a contract cannot agree upon a remedy which is of a nature which the law would never have permitted".[a1] A separate doctrine, recognised in Australia and also described as a penalties doctrine, has not been accepted in the UK. The rationale of that separate doctrine is that a term in the nature of a security for performance cannot be "in terrorem" of the satisfaction of the secured right.[a2]

[a1]   See M. Arden and J. Edelman, "Mutual borrowing and judicial dialogue between the Apex courts of Australia and the United Kingdom" (2022) 138 L.Q.R. 217, 220.

[a2]   *Andrews v Australia and New Zealand Banking Group Ltd* (2012) 247 CLR 205 at 216 [10]. See Arden and Edelman, "Mutual borrowing and judicial dialogue between the Apex courts of Australia and the United Kingdom" (2022) 138 L.Q.R. 217, 220.

Replace the paragraph with:

16-003   There is, however, always an anterior question to ask before considering whether a clause is for liquidated damages or for a penalty. The question is whether the clause applies to the circumstances. This is particularly important where the breach of contract consists of a failure to complete, but the clause is concerned with liquidated damages for delay. An example is the decision in *Triple Point Technology Inc v PTT Public Co Ltd*.[1] Triple Point was a service provider which failed to perform any milestones for payment other than the first two. This led to termination of the contract. It failed in its claim to recover payment for the subsequent milestones that it did not complete. A counterclaim was brought by PTT for damages for breach of contract and "delay". PTT recovered for delay in relation to the first two milestones. But a major issue was whether the clause applied to failures to complete the later milestones. The liquidated damages clause for delay provided for damages calculated at a rate per day from the due date until the date that the work was "accepted" (which must have meant "accepted from Triple Point"). The Court of Appeal, Sir Rupert Jackson (Floyd and Lewison LJJ agreeing), relied upon a decision of the House of Lords, from Scotland, which held that a similar provision did not entitle a contractor to liquidated damages for delay where the contractor never completed the work.[2] As Sir Rupert Jackson observed, it can be:

> "... artificial and inconsistent with the parties' agreement to categorise the employer's losses as £x per week up to a specified date and then general damages thereafter."

Perhaps more fundamentally, the premise of the clause was that the work by Triple Point would ultimately be accepted by PTT. The whole purpose of the clause was to liquidate damages for delay in completion. It was not to liquidate damages for failure to complete. Although, as Sir Rupert Jackson rightly said, every contractual term must be interpreted in its own context,[3] the decision of the Court of Appeal must cast serious doubt upon earlier authorities that had allowed liquidated damages clauses to operate for delays until the point of termination.[4] The Supreme Court reversed the decision of the Court of Appeal confining the Scottish decision to its own facts. Although again recognising that the question is ultimately one of interpretation, Lady Arden (with whom Lord Leggatt and Lord Burrows agreed, and

Lord Sales and Lord Hodge agreed on this issue) held that the approach of the Court of Appeal was inconsistent with the commercial reality and the function of liquidated damages, which is to provide certainty of remedy until the contract is terminated.[4a] Unless a clause clearly provided otherwise, the ordinary position is that liquidated damages apply for any delay in completing the work, including failure to complete, until termination, at which point the contractor has no control over the delay and the objective intention of the parties is unlikely to be that the liquidated damages will continue.[4b] As Lord Leggatt added, the contrary approach would introduce considerable uncertainty at the time of contracting about the amount of damages recoverable in the event of a delay and would give contractors who overrun an incentive not to complete.[4c] In light of that commercial reality the words "up to the date PTT accepts such work" meant "up to the date (if any) PTT accepts such work".[4d] Lady Arden acknowledged that this had the effect that under that contract the employer had complete control over whether the damages were liquidated or general damages since the contract gave the employer the power to terminate. But that was the bargain that the parties had struck.[4e]

[1] [2019] EWCA Civ 230; [2019] 1 W.L.R. 3549.

[2] *British Glanzstoff Manufacturing Co Ltd v General Accident, Fire and Life Assurance Co Ltd* 1912 S.C. 591 (Court of Session) and 1913 S.C. (HL) 1.

[3] [2019] EWCA Civ 230; [2019] 1 W.L.R. 3549 at [110]. In *PBS Energo AS v Bester Generacion UK Ltd* [2020] EWHC 223 (TCC) at [438] to [442], Cockerill J questioned the result of *Triple Point* stating that deciding which of three outcomes is correct in any given case will turn on the wording of the clause in each case. An appeal to the Supreme Court in *Triple Point* is outstanding.

[4] *Greenore Port Ltd v Technical & General Guarantee Company Ltd* [2006] EWHC 3119 (TCC); *Shaw v MFP Foundations and Pilings Ltd* [2010] EWHC 1839 (TCC); *Hall v Van Der Heiden (No.2)* [2010] EWHC 586 (TCC); *Bluewater Energy Services BV v Mercon Steel Structures BV* [2014] EWHC 2132 (TCC); *GPP Big Field LLP v Solar EPC Solutions SL* [2018] EWHC 2866 (Comm).

[4a] *Triple Point Technology Inc v PTT Public Company Ltd* [2021] UKSC 29; [2021] 3 W.L.R. 521 at [35].

[4b] *Triple Point Technology Inc v PTT Public Company Ltd* [2021] UKSC 29; [2021] 3 W.L.R. 521 at [85]–[86].

[4c] *Triple Point Technology Inc v PTT Public Company Ltd* [2021] UKSC 29; [2021] 3 W.L.R. 521 at [80]–[81].

[4d] *Triple Point Technology Inc v PTT Public Company Ltd* [2021] UKSC 29; [2021] 3 W.L.R. 521 at [38].

[4e] *Triple Point Technology Inc v PTT Public Company Ltd* [2021] UKSC 29; [2021] 3 W.L.R. 521 at [49].

2. NATURE AND EFFECT OF LIQUIDATED DAMAGES AND PENALTIES

(1) Nature of liquidated damages and penalties

(a) The modern test for a penalty as stated in 2016

After para.16-018, add a new paragraph:

Many subsequent cases have involved a simple application of these principles, **16-018A** which are considered in more detail below particularly by reference to the older cases. For instance, in *Permavent Ltd v Makin*[47a] the issue was whether a price adjustment clause in a settlement agreement was an unenforceable penalty. The price adjustment clause was extremely harsh, including requiring repayment of everything received under the settlement agreement, and would result in a loss of the entitlement to a stream of future payments. But it was not out of all proportion to the claimant's legitimate interest and therefore it was not a penalty. The purpose of the price adjustment clause was to restrict the counterparty from interfering with or disputing title to intellectual property rights. The intellectual property rights were fundamental to the claimant's business, it was impossible to put a precise figure upon likely damage to those rights, and "an attack on them has the potential to damage the claimants' business in a similar way to an attack on the goodwill of the company in [*Makdessi*]."[47b]

[47a] [2021] EWHC 467 (Ch).

[47b] [2021] EWHC 467 (Ch) at [51].

(2) Effect of holding a stipulated sum to be liquidated damages or a penalty

(a) Effect of holding a sum to be liquidated damages

Replace paragraphs with:

16-027   The claimant will, however, be entitled to sue for unliquidated damages in the ordinary way, in addition to suing for the liquidated damages, if other breaches have occurred outside those which fall within the ambit of the liquidated damages provision or, it seems, if only part of the loss arising from a single breach is regarded as falling within the provision's ambit. This issue has most commonly arisen in the context of liquidated damages clauses concerning demurrage. Demurrage is a term that is generally used to mean the agreed compensation for the detention of a ship beyond an agreed or reasonable time for loading and unloading. This will usually include losses arising from the inability of the vessel to earn freight,[77] as well as the costs of keeping the vessel in port, including the running expenses, consumption of bunkers, and dock dues.[78] But difficult questions are raised concerning the scope of a demurrage clause to extend to other types of loss. For a long time, the leading decision on this issue was the difficult reasoning of the Court of Appeal in *Aktieselskabet Reidar v Arcos Ltd*.[79] Charterers, in breach of their obligation to load a full and complete cargo by a certain date, took so long to load that the time passed when the ship could carry a summer cargo and she was only able to carry a much smaller winter cargo. The charterparty contained the usual provision for demurrage as liquidated damages for the charterers' detention of the ship in loading, but the owners successfully claimed, in addition to the demurrage, unliquidated damages in the ordinary way for loss of freight caused by the charterers' failure to load a full and complete cargo. "The provisions as to demurrage", said Atkin LJ, "quantify the damages, not for the complete breach, but only such damages as arise from the detention of the vessel."[80]

[77] *Total Transport Corp v Amoco Trading Co (The Altus)* [1985] 1 Lloyd's Rep. 423 QBD (Comm Ct); *Suisse Atlantique Societe d'Armement Maritime SA v NV Rotterdamsche Kolen Centrale* [1965] 1 Lloyd's Rep. 533 CA at 540.

[78] See also R. Gay, "Damages in addition to demurrage" [2004] L.M.C.L.Q. 72, 89.

[79] [1927] 1 K.B. 352; (1926) 25 Ll. L. Rep. 513 CA.

[80] [1927] 1 K.B. 352 at 363; (1926) 25 Ll. L. Rep. 513 CA.

16-027A   Unfortunately, as Males LJ later observed giving the judgment of the Court of Appeal in *K Line PTE Ltd v Priminds Shipping (HK) Co Ltd (The Eternal Bliss)*,[81] the ratio decidendi of *Aktieselskabet Reidar v Arcos* is obscure. Bankes LJ had thought that there had been only one breach by the charterers but that the dead freight was "special damages" that was distinct from the claim for detention of the vessel. Sargant LJ thought that there had been two different breaches by the charterers and that the demurrage clause did not extend to the separate breach of failing to load a full and complete cargo. But passages in the judgment of Atkin LJ support each of the "one breach" and "two breach" positions.[82] After decades in which no approach had achieved conclusive and widespread acceptance,[83] the issue arose again in *K Line PTE Ltd v Priminds Shipping (HK) Co Ltd (The Eternal Bliss)*,[84] in which the question of recovery of unliquidated damages despite a demurrage clause was raised for consideration by the High Court in the course of an arbitration. In that case, the charterer's only breach was in delay in unloading a cargo of soybeans. The delays caused the cargo to deteriorate. The question was whether the liquidated damages for demurrage included the deterioration of the cargo. At first instance, Andrew Baker J held that even for a single breach it was possible to recover separately from the demurrage clause an amount of unliquidated damages for harm that was "separate from and different in kind than the detention of the ship".[85] The Court of Appeal disagreed. In a judgment with which the other members of the court agreed, Males LJ said, surely correctly, that the issue of whether there is one obligation or two is one of interpretation of the charterparty. In the absence of any contrary indication, however, Males LJ explained that demurrage, which generally intends to provide certainty, liquidates all damages arising from a breach of a charterparty, not merely some of the damages.[86]

[81] [2021] EWCA Civ 1712; [2022] Bus. L.R. 67 at [30].

[82] [2021] EWCA Civ 1712; [2022] Bus. L.R. 67 at [27]–[30].

[83] Although the leading, and still correct, decision was *The Bonde* [1991] 1 Lloyd's Rep. 136 QBD (Comm Ct). Compare *Chandris v Isbrandtsen Moller Co Inc* [1951] 1 K.B. 240; (1950) 84 Ll. L. Rep. 347 CA; *Suisse Atlantique Societe d'Armement Maritime SA v NV Rotterdamsche Kolen Centrale* [1965] 1 Lloyd's Rep. 533 CA at 540; *The Dias* [1978] 1 W.L.R. 261; [1978] 1 Lloyd's Rep. 325 HL; *Total Transport Corp of Panama v Amoco Transport Co (The Altus)* [1985] 1 Lloyd's Rep. 423 QBD (Comm); *The Adelfa* [1988] 2 Lloyd's Rep. 466 QBD (Comm); *The Luxmar* [2006] EWHC 1322 (Comm); [2006] 2 Lloyd's Rep. 543.

[84] [2021] EWCA Civ 1712; [2022] Bus. L.R. 67 at [30].

[85] [2020] EWHC 2373 (Comm); [2021] Bus. L.R. 213 at [48].

[86] [2021] EWCA Civ 1712; [2022] Bus. L.R. 67 at [52]–[59].

In some cases an injunction may prove a suitable remedy[87] but, although a claim- **16-027B** ant may elect[88] whether to ask for an injunction or for liquidated damages, it is generally held that the claimant cannot have both.[89] Thus in *Sainter v Ferguson*,[90] and again in *Carnes v Nesbitt*,[91] an injunction was refused because liquidated damages had already been awarded, and this view was adopted in *General Accident Assurance Co v Noel*,[92] where the claimant was put to his election. However, it would seem that the claimant should be entitled to have the two remedies where they relate to different breaches. The above three cases, in which an election was insisted upon by the court, concerned covenants in restraint of trade where a single stipulated sum was to become payable if the defendant started business in competition with the claimant, and it was reasonable to regard the two remedies as mutually exclusive. But the situation is different where there is a clause providing a graduated sum to be paid in line with the extent of the breach, as in covenants whereby one party has accepted restrictions on their right to sell their goods and has further agreed to pay the other a specific sum for every item sold in breach of covenant. Here it is reasonable to award liquidated damages for the past, i.e. on the number of items already sold in breach, and order an injunction as to the future. This result was reached, without exception being taken,[93] in *Imperial Tobacco Co v Parsley*.[94]

[87] Particularly in the case of covenants in restraint of trade.

[88] At first there was a tendency to refuse an injunction because of the very existence of a liquidated damages provision, as in *Young v Chalkley* (1867) 16 L.T. 286. But it soon became established that the claimant might elect for an injunction: this view was taken by the court in *Coles v Sims* (1854) 5 De G. M. & G. 1 (the view was not, as suggested by Wright J in *General Accident Assurance Co v Noel* [1902] 1 K.B. 377, that both an injunction and liquidated damages could be claimed) and an injunction was awarded in *Howard v Woodward* (1864) 34 L.J. Ch. 47 and *Jones v Heavens* (1877) 4 Ch. D. 636. The claimant can elect for an injunction even if the defendant has offered to pay the stipulated damages: *National Provincial Bank of England v Marshall* (1888) 40 Ch. D. 112 CA.

[89] Also the claimant can support their claim for an injunction by reliance on the liquidated damages being lower than their actual loss: *Bath and North East Somerset DC v Mowlem* (2005) 100 Con. L.R. 1 CA, at para.16-026 (first footnote), above.

[90] (1849) 7 C.B. 716.

[91] (1862) 7 H. & N. 778.

[92] [1902] 1 K.B. 377.

[93] The only issue before the Court of Appeal was whether the stipulated sum was penalty or liquidated damages.

[94] [1936] 2 All E.R. 515 CA.

(b) Effect of holding a sum to be a penalty

Replace paragraph with:

16-029   In most of the cases where the claimant has recovered for actual damage the stipulated penalty sum has been greater in amount. Just as the penalty cannot augment the damages, so too the claimant will not be restricted to the penalty in the rare cases where it is less than the actual damage. It might be thought impossible to have what has been categorised as "an extravagant and unconscionable sum" turning out to be less than the actual damage, but such a situation could occur where one sum is stipulated to be paid for a number of breaches of varying importance, as to one of which it is disproportionately large, and a serious breach occurs causing damage greater than the stipulated sum. This has found illustration in charterparties,[100] which early developed a clause stipulating for a single sum to be paid for any non-performance. It was early held in *Winter v Trimmer*,[101] and again in *Harrison v Wright*,[102] that the claimant could ignore this penal stipulation and recover for the greater loss. The same result was reached in the last century in *Wall v Rederiaktiebolaget Luggude*[103] where Bailhache J retraced the law in a very useful judgment which remains the clearest authority for the present rule. However the wording of the clause had become more complex[104] and the earlier cases provide more useful illustrations of circumstances in which a penalty is likely to turn out less than the actual damage. The decision itself was approved soon after as to its interpretation of the particular clause as a penalty by the House of Lords in *Watts v Mitsui*,[105] and, as Scrutton LJ pointed out in *Widnes Foundry v Cellulose Acetate Silk Co*,[106] Lord Sumner clearly took the view that:

> "... the clause did not prevent the shipowners or charterers from recovering the actual amount of damage, though it might be more than the estimated amount of freight."[107]

In view of this line of authority, the occasional dicta which state that the penalty marks the ceiling of recovery are unacceptable.[108] They are probably based upon the historical fact that the sum in a penal bond fixed the maximum amount recoverable.[109] But in light of the reasoning of the Supreme Court in *Makdessi*[109a] that penalty provisions cannot be partially enforced, it would also follow that they cannot have the limited effect of forming a cap on damages.[109b] Nevertheless, as O'Farrell J held in *Eco World - Ballymore Embassy Gardens Co Ltd v Dobler UK*

Ltd,[109c] a clause might also have a dual character as fixing the damages (whether that is a penalty or liquidated damages) *and* as a limitation of liability provision. In so far as it operates as a penalty it would be void. But it could be given its separate effect as a limitation of liability provision whether it is a penalty clause or a liquidated damages clause. In that case, a provision that "[l]iquidated damages will apply ... at the rate of £25,000 per week ... up to an aggregate maximum of 7% of the final Trade Contract Sum" was held to operate in two ways: (i) to fix damages at £25,000 per week for the relevant period; and (ii) independently of that fixing of damages, to operate as a limitation of all liability to the 7% of the contract price.

[100] Another illustration is *Maylam v Norris* (1845) 14 L.J.C.P. 95. On a sale of fixtures and fittings for £65, with a stipulation, held penal, that either party should pay £30 on any breach, the seller was held entitled to bring an action in respect of £61 which the buyer had failed to pay him.

[101] (1762) 1 Wm. Bl. 395.

[102] (1811) 13 East 343.

[103] [1915] 3 K.B. 66.

[104] It was held still to constitute a penalty mainly because of its history: see para.16-105, below, where the case is considered further.

[105] [1917] A.C. 227.

[106] [1931] 2 K.B. 393 CA.

[107] [1931] 2 K.B. 393 CA at 408.

[108] See *Wilbeam v Ashton* (1807) 1 Camp. 78, per Lord Ellenborough: "Beyond the penalty you shall not go; within it, you are to give the party any compensation which he can prove himself entitled to"; *Elphinstone v Monkland Iron & Coal Co* (1886) 11 App. Cas. 332 at 346, per Lord Fitzgerald: "The penalty is to cover all the damages actually sustained but it does not estimate them, and the amount of loss (not, however, exceeding the penalty) is to be ascertained in the ordinary way." In *Cellulose Acetate Silk Co v Widnes Foundry* [1933] A.C. 20 at 26 Lord Atkin wished "to leave open the question whether, where a penalty is plainly less in amount than the prospective damages, there is any legal objection to suing on it, or in a suitable case ignoring it and suing for damages". Diplock LJ in *Robophone Facilities v Blank* [1966] 1 W.L.R. 1428, referring to this express reservation of opinion, said that the matter was "by no means clear": at 1446. Lord Atkin's comments are not, however, quite on point as is shown by his reference to prospective damages; they are more allied to the issue of limitation of liability by way of liquidated damages, which is dealt with elsewhere: see paras 16-103 to 16-107, below.

[109] See para.16-004, above. And it did indeed remain true that if the claimant sued in debt for the penalty itself, until this, apparently, ceased to be possible (see para.16-005, above), they would impose a ceiling on their recovery and be entitled to no more than the penal sum. See *Wall v Rederiaktiebolaget Luggude* [1915] 3 K.B. 66 at 72, per Bailhache J: "The result of suing for the penalty is therefore that the claimant recovers proved damages, but never more than the penal sum fixed"; and similarly *Harrison v Wright* (1811) 13 East 343 at 348, per Lord Ellenborough.

[109a] [2015] UKSC 67; [2016] A.C. 1172. See above at para.16-016 point (7).

[109b] *Eco World - Ballymore Embassy Gardens Co Ltd v Dobler UK Ltd* [2021] EWHC 2207 (TCC); [2021] T.C.L.R. 7 at [110].

[109c] [2021] EWHC 2207 (TCC); [2021] T.C.L.R. 7 at [111].

After para.16-029, add a new paragraph:

Another consequence of a penalty clause being treated as truly void is that the **16-029A** penalty clause cannot be relied upon as an election by the claimant not to pursue common law damages. Even a clause as explicit as to provide that "the remedies described in this [clause] are exclusive of and in substitution for any and all other rights and remedies provided by law" will not exclude common law damages upon the clause being found to be void.[109d]

[109d] *De Havilland Aircraft of Canada Ltd v Spicejet Ltd* [2021] EWHC 362 (Comm) at [36]–[37].

3.   RULES FOR DISTINGUISHING LIQUIDATED DAMAGES FROM PENALTIES

(2)   The circumstances must be viewed as at the time when the contract was made

Replace the paragraph with:

16-033   The one circumstance, not really an exception at all, in which subsequent events can be used to determine whether a clause is a penalty is where those subsequent events demonstrate what could have been anticipated at the time of the contract. In other words, the subsequent events are no more than "valuable evidence as to what could reasonably be expected to be the loss at the time the contract was made."[129]

[129] *Philips Hong Kong v Attorney General of Hong Kong* (1993) 61 B.L.R. 41 at PC; *Permavent Ltd v Makin* [2021] EWHC 467 (Ch) at [87].

4.   APPLICATION OF THE EXTREME DISPROPORTION WITH A "LEGITIMATE INTEREST" TEST

(2)   Where there are several obligations upon the breach of which the sum becomes payable or property transferrable

(b)   Where the loss is not reasonably calculable at the time of contracting

Replace paragraph with:

16-061   The first method is to be found in *Dunlop Pneumatic Tyre Co v New Garage and Motor Co.*[228] Lord Atkinson there said that:

> "… although it may be true … that a presumption is raised in favour of a penalty where a single lump sum is to be paid by way of compensation in respect of many different events, some occasioning serious, some trifling damage, it seems to be that the presumption is rebutted by the very fact that the damage caused by each and every one of those events, however varying in importance, may be of such an uncertain nature that it cannot be accurately ascertained."[229]

The same idea had been put in more concrete form much earlier by Alderson B in *Galsworthy v Strutt,*[230] where he said in relation to a covenant in restraint of trade on the sale of a solicitor's practice:

> "The act of damage … by another's practising within 50 miles for the period of seven years, would not be the same in amount as if he were to practise within 40 miles, or next door, nor the same if he had set up in business in the first, second, or sixth year, … but the parties have agreed to a certain fixed sum, in order to prevent the necessity of being at the expense of procuring the attendance of witnesses for the purpose of giving evidence upon those matters."[231]

This method is more likely to prove efficacious if the probable damage varies in degree, and not also in kind, with each breach, a point put forward by Lord Parker of Waddington in *Dunlop Pneumatic Tyre Co v New Garage and Motor Co,*[232] and acted upon by the Court of Appeal in *Ford Motor Co v Armstrong.*[233] This approach was applied in *Eco World - Ballymore Embassy Gardens Co Ltd v Dobler UK Ltd*[233a] in which O'Farrell J held that a single liquidated damages amount for late completion of either Block A, B or C of a construction contract could lead to a variety of different losses depending on the circumstances.

228 [1915] A.C. 79.

229 [1915] A.C. 79 at 95–96.

230 (1848) 1 Ex. 659.

231 (1848) 1 Ex. 659 at 666–667.

232 [1915] A.C. 79 at 98.

233 (1915) 31 T.L.R. 267 CA.

233a [2021] EWHC 2207 (TCC); [2021] T.C.L.R. 7 at [80].

5. MAIN TYPES OF CONTRACT IN WHICH THE OLDER RULES WERE APPLIED

(1) Types of contract where the stipulated sum or property to be transferred is generally a penalty

(a) Charterparties: failure to carry out general provisions on either side

After para.16-066, add new paragraph:

On the other hand, it is not a penalty for a charterparty contract to provide for a **16-066A** right for the owner to suspend performance during periods of non-payment of hire while requiring the hire payments to continue. The right to suspend performance is a common condition in charterparties.249a Merely requiring the hire payments to continue cannot be a penalty because the continuing obligation is not contingent upon breach. That continuation "simply gives effect to the fundamental bargain".249b

249a See, for instance, *Greatship (India) Ltd v Oceanografia SA de CV (The Greatship Dhriti)* [2012] EWHC 3468 (Comm); [2013] 2 Lloyd's Rep. 359.

249b *Al Giorgis Oil Trading Ltd v AG Shipping and Energy Pte Ltd (The MT Marquessa)* [2021] EWHC 2319 (Comm) at [35].

(2) Types of contract where the stipulated sum is generally liquidated damages

(d) Building contracts: failure to complete construction on time

Replace paragraph with:

The new century has produced further decisions on delay in building contracts. **16-093** In *Alfred McAlpine Capital Projects Ltd v Tilebox Ltd,*377 a provision for payment at the rate of £45,000 for every week of delay in completion of building works was held to constitute liquidated damages. Apart from an extended review of all the leading authorities on the subject,378 the lengthy judgment is taken up with attempting to assess what losses were likely to have been foreseeable at the time of contracting in order to come to a view on whether the weekly £45,000 constituted a genuine pre-estimate of loss. In *CFW Architects v Cowlin Construction Ltd,*379 the provision for payments on delay in the construction of houses under a design and build contract was upheld as liquidated damages despite being potentially harsh on the builder.380 In *Hall v Van Der Heiden,*381 a sum to be paid for each day's delay by the builder in his work on the claimant's flat was without difficulty held to be liquidated damages. And in *Eco World - Ballymore Embassy Gardens Co Ltd v Dobler UK Ltd,*381a a clause in a contract with a price for works of £8 million that required payment of £25,000 a week for late completion, with a grace period and a cap, was held to be liquidated damages despite its application to all severable parts of the contract.

[377] (2006) 104 Con. L.R. 39.

[378] (2006) 104 Con. L.R. 39 at [35]–[49].

[379] (2006) 105 Con. L.R. 116.

[380] (2006) 105 Con. L.R. 116 at [177]–[191].

[381] [2010] EWHC 586 (TCC). Facts at para.16-032, above.

[381a] [2021] EWHC 2207 (TCC); [2021] T.C.L.R. 7 at [83].

6. RELATED SITUATIONS

(1) Limitations of liability by way of liquidated damages

16-103 *The title of this sub-section should be changed to "Limitation of liability by way of liquidated damages".*

Replace paragraph with:

16-107 Suppose that the sum stipulated in the contract turns out to be less than the actual damage in fact suffered, although, as an estimate, it was disproportionately large. Measured at the date of contract the clause is likely to be a penalty in the ordinary way. It might seem unlikely that the disproportionately large penalty clause turns out to be less than the actual damage suffered, but the situation can arise where one sum is stipulated to be paid for a number of breaches of varying importance. It is likely to be a penalty if as to one breach it is disproportionately large, and it is immaterial that, in the events that happen, another breach occurs which involves greater damage than the stipulated sum. The penalty clause would be void.[420] But it is possible that part, or all, of the penalty clause might be intended by the parties to serve a broader purpose than a penalty and intended effectively as a separate clause to operate as a limitation of liability. If that is the intention of the parties, then it is difficult to see why the clause should be void. This issue was considered in obiter dicta in *Eco World - Ballymore Embassy Gardens Co Ltd v Dobler UK Ltd*.[421] The issue was obiter dicta because the clause was not held to be a penalty. The provision required that "[l]iquidated damages will apply ... at the rate of £25,000 per week ... up to an aggregate maximum of 7% of the final Trade Contract Sum". Even if the provision had been void as a penalty, the aggregate maximum of 7%, if truly intended to apply as an aggregate maximum to *any* recovery, should be capable of being upheld as a limitation of liability.

[420] See above at para.16-029.

[421] [2021] EWHC 2207 (TCC); [2021] T.C.L.R. 7 at [111].

PART 3 VARIOUS GENERAL FACTORS IN THE ASSESSMENT OF DAMAGES

CHAPTER 18

THE INCIDENCE OF TAXATION

TABLE OF CONTENTS

I. **Income Tax** 18-002
   1.   THE RULE IN GOURLEY'S CASE 18-002
   2.   TYPE-SITUATIONS IN WHICH THE RULE IN GOURLEY'S CASE MAY
       APPLY 18-005
     (1) General considerations 18-005
     (2) Tort .... 18-025■
     (c) Contract 18-042
   3.   THE PRACTICAL APPLICATION OF THE RULE IN GOURLEY'S CASE . 18-056
     (1) Burden of proof .... 18-056■
     (1A) Mitigation .... 18-059A□
     (2) Calculation of the tax 18-060

II. **Capital Gains Tax** 18-063
   1.   GENERAL CONSIDERATIONS 18-063
   2.   TORT 18-067
     (1) Torts affecting the person 18-067
     (2) Torts affecting property 18-069
   3.   CONTRACT 18-072
     (1) Contracts of employment: wrongful dismissal 18-072
     (2) Contracts for the sale of property: failure to perform ... 18-074
     (3) Contracts for professional services: negligent advice ... 18-076

III. **Other Taxes** .... 18-078□

I. INCOME TAX

2. TYPE-SITUATIONS IN WHICH THE RULE IN GOURLEY'S CASE MAY APPLY

(2) Tort

The title of this sub-section should be changed to "Torts and equitable wrongs". **18-025**

After para.18-041, add new paragraph:

(f) Equitable wrongs Although there are few cases on the subject, the same **18-041A**
principles should apply to equitable compensation for loss where, as explained in
Ch.50 below, the same principles should apply as for compensation for loss at common law. Further, a mirror image of the same principles must apply where the

money award in equity is disgorgement of profits: since disgorgement of profits is concerned only to strip the benefit to a defendant, a defendant should only disgorge the net profits made after tax. This was conceded in *Blizzard Entertainment SAS v Bossland GmbH*[176a] in the context of disgorgement of profits for copyright infringement. And in *Lifestyle Equities CV v Ahmed*,[176b] in the context of disgorgement of profits from infringement of a trade mark, the Court of Appeal held that the concession had been correctly made.

[176a] [2019] EWHC 1665 (Ch).

[176b] [2021] EWCA Civ 675; [2021] Bus. L.R. 1020 at [95].

3. THE PRACTICAL APPLICATION OF THE RULE IN GOURLEY'S CASE

(1) Burden of proof

(a) Application of the Gourley rule

Replace paragraph with:

18-057   After a period of uncertainty the Court of Appeal eventually, in *Stoke-on-Trent City Council v Wood Mitchell*,[228] held that it was the defendant's onus to show that factor (2) is satisfied, so that their failure to do so ousts the *Gourley* rule. The court took the view that the rule could only be applied if "it is clear beyond peradventure"[229] that the sum received by the claimant—in the particular case statutory compensation rather than damages but to which the same principles apply—would not be taxable in the claimant's hands[230]; otherwise the dangers of double taxation are too great. Indeed it is of some concern that the courts do not always get the tax position right. Thus in *Pennine Raceway v Kirklees Metropolitan Council (No.2)*,[231] the compensation—again the case was one of statutory compensation rather than damages—was held to be payable net of tax on the basis that it would not be taxable in the claimant company's hands and, after the time of appealing this decision had run out, the Revenue turned round and demanded tax. Fortunately, faced with this double taxation the claimant company was able to obtain an extension of time for requiring a case to be stated and the decision was changed, the Court of Appeal by then adopting the same approach to factor (2) onus as it had done in *Stoke-on-Trent City Council v Wood Mitchell*.[232] But none of this would have happened in *Pennine Raceway v Kirklees Metropolitan Council*,[233] if the onus had firmly been on the defendant to show that factor (2) applied. These considerations suggest that it may be wise in some cases to try to join the Revenue but it may prove difficult to obtain the Revenue's consent.[234] Indeed it was said by the Court of Appeal in *Deeny v Gooda Walker*[235] that the court had been told that it was the first time that the Revenue had been joined by consent to argue the tax issue before the trial judge in relation to a dispute over damages, not being a tax appeal.[236] This law was correctly applied in *Mathieu v Hinds*[236a] where Hill J explained that the lack of evidence on the complex issues of foreign tax law, and the inappropriateness for an English court to undertake its own investigations on those issues, meant that it could not be said that it was clear beyond peradventure that the damages would not be taxed.

[228] [1980] 1 W.L.R. 254 CA; see the case at para.18-041, above.

[229] [1980] 1 W.L.R. 254 CA at 259G.

[230] See especially [1980] 1 W.L.R. 254 at 258H–259H.

[231] [1989] S.T.C. 122 CA.

232 [1980] 1 W.L.R. 254 CA.

233 [1989] S.T.C. 122 CA. As the court pointed out, the problem may be solved by the Revenue's acceptance that the compensation would not be taxable, as happened in two further cases of statutory compensation, *West Suffolk CC v Rought* [1957] A.C. 403 and *McGhie v British Transport Commission* [1963] 1 Q.B. 125 (both at para.18-041, above).

234 The CPR confirms that the Revenue is not to be added as a party to any proceedings except with their consent. They may, however, themselves apply to be joined as a party.

235 [1996] L.R.L.R. 109 CA.

236 [1996] L.R.L.R. 109 CA at 111, col.1. The burden of proof apart, where there is uncertainty whether the damages are to be taxable, it might be possible to award damages without any deduction of tax on the claimant's undertaking to return the amount of damages attributable to the tax element should the damages turn out not to be taxable. This was done in the somewhat exceptional case of *4 Eng Ltd v Harper* [2009] Ch. 91, considered at para.18-024, above.

236a [2022] EWHC 924 (QB) at [147]–[157].

After para.18-059, add a new sub-section:

(1A)   Mitigation

The same principles should apply where the issue is not whether damages should **18-059A** be reduced because they will be subject to no, or a lower level of, tax but where the issue is whether damages should be increased because money obtained in mitigation of the loss will be subject to tax, thereby reducing the extent of the mitigation and therefore increasing the loss. This was the approach correctly taken in *Comberg v Vivopower Services Ltd*240a where the claimant had been wrongfully dismissed from employment but the money received in mitigation had been by a consultancy agreement in the British Virgin Islands where no tax was paid. In light of the paucity of evidence in the case, the issue having been raised only after a draft judgment was circulated, the Court increased the damages, reducing the amount in mitigation by only £2,000 which was the tax paid by the claimant upon money remitted to the United Kingdom from the British Virgin Islands.

240a [2020] EWHC 2787 (QB); [2020] Costs L.R. 1655.

After para.18-077, add a new section:

III.   OTHER TAXES

The main circumstances into which the cases fall are those of income tax and **18-078** capital gains tax, which have been considered above. But the same principles should generally apply in relation to other taxes. For instance, in *Gosden v Halliwell Landau (A Firm)*,310 a credit was given for inheritance tax that would have been payable on the value of the land that the claimant would have received but for the negligence of the solicitors, less pre-owned asset tax that would have been paid on the land during the life of the deceased. The trial judge applied the principles in *Gourley* by analogy since without the negligence of the defendants there would have been insufficient funds in the estate to have paid inheritance tax so that the land which the claimant would have received would have been sold to pay the inheritance tax, thus reducing the value that would have been obtained by the claimant. The same general principles were applied including the onus of proof resting on the defendant.311

310 [2021] EWHC 159 (Comm); [2021] P.N.L.R. 14.

311 [2021] EWHC 159 (Comm); [2021] P.N.L.R. 14 at [38]. See paras 18-056 to 18-057 above.

CHAPTER 19

THE AWARDING OF INTEREST

TABLE OF CONTENTS

I.   **Introductory**   19-001

II. **The Position Before Sempra Metals**   19-004
     1.   INTEREST OUTSIDE STATUTE: INTEREST AS DAMAGES   19-004
          (1)   Contract: obligations to pay money   19-004
          (2)   Contract: obligations relating to property   19-012
          (3)   Contract: obligations relating to services   19-017
          (4)   Torts affecting property other than land   19-019
          (5)   Torts affecting land   19-026
          (6)   Torts affecting the person   19-028
     2.   INTEREST CONFERRED BY STATUTE: INTEREST ON DAMAGES   19-030
          (1)   Limits of the statutory provision   . . . . .19-036■
          (2)   Categories to which statutory interest applies   . . . . .19-043□

III. **The Position After Sempra Metals**   19-058
     1.   THE DECISION   19-059
     2.   THE ANALYSIS   19-063
     3.   THE RESULTS AT COMMON LAW AND IN EQUITY   19-067
          (1)   Cases where compound interest is sought   . . . . .19-067■
          (2)   Cases where statutory interest is limited to the amount for
                which judgment is given   19-069
          (3)   Cases generally   19-070

IV. **Calculation of the Amount of Interest**   19-071
     1.   PERIOD OF TIME FOR WHICH INTEREST IS AWARDED   19-071
          (1)   Time to which interest runs   19-072
          (2)   Time from which interest runs   19-076
          (3)   Application of the above principles to personal injury and
                wrongful death cases   19-087
          (4)   Effect of delay on time to and from which interest runs   .   19-096
     2.   RATE OF INTEREST AWARDED   19-103
          (1)   General overview: the various rates of interest   19-104
          (2)   Cases in the Commercial Court and analogous cases   . . .19-109□
          (3)   Cases in admiralty   19-123
          (4)   Cases of personal injury and wrongful death   19-126
          (5)   Cases of nuisance   19-134
     3.   AMOUNT ON WHICH INTEREST IS AWARDED: INTEREST AND
          TAXATION   19-135

II. The Position Before Sempra Metals

2. Interest Conferred by Statute: Interest on Damages

(1) Limits of the statutory provision

(b) Limited to interest on amount of judgment

(iii) Other amounts which go to reduce the damages award

After "… has come to the fore.", add new footnote 136a:

19-042 136a This paragraph was quoted with approval by Leech J in *Barrowfen Properties Ltd v Patel* [2022] EWHC 1601 (Ch) at [127].

(2) Categories to which statutory interest applies

(f) Torts affecting the person

(i) Personal injury and wrongful death

Replace the paragraph with:

19-053   Yet it appears that the only reason advanced before their Lordships for not awarding interest was the inflation argument and it is thought that there are other, and cogent, reasons for proscribing any interest on the damages for non-pecuniary loss. There is much to be said for regarding the purpose behind the awarding of interest as damages as being to compensate a claimant for the delay, which the process of litigation makes inevitable, in reimbursing a money loss which they have suffered as a result of the tort or breach of contract. Accordingly, interest can have no relevance where monetary damages are being awarded not as a replacement for other money but as representing the best that the law can do in the face of incommensurable loss which is not truly calculable in money. It is accepted that any award for pain and suffering and loss of amenities must be in the nature of a conventional sum,[199] and to award interest upon such a conventional sum surely becomes supererogatory. Indeed it is suspected that their Lordships' further endorsement of the reduction in the rate of interest for non-pecuniary loss to, as we shall see, two per cent in *Wright v British Railways Board*,[200] reflects an uneasiness at making any award at all. Fortunately, the Court of Appeal has now had the good sense to refuse to award any interest on the damages for non-pecuniary loss in an action for deceit[201]; it would be wise, but is probably too late, to do the same with personal injury and also wrongful death.[202] But in the absence of such a bold step, the next best solution is that adopted by the Court of Appeal in *Rees v Commissioner of Police of the Metropolis*.[202a] In that case, Davis LJ in the leading judgment recognised that s.35A of the 1981 Act confers a discretion to make or withhold the award of interest and that, in circumstances where inflation has been taken into account in the award and the non-pecuniary damages have been assessed at the date of trial, there should be a pragmatic practice to decline to award interest upon damages for losses such as loss of liberty or pain and suffering.

199 See para.40-257, below.

200 [1983] 2 A.C. 773; see para.19-127, below.

201 *Saunders v Edwards* [1987] 1 W.L.R. 1116 CA. See the case at paras 19-054 to 19-056, below.

[202] At least, however far compound interest may advance after the decision in *Sempra Metals* (which see at paras 19-058 and following), the reasoning of their Lordships in that case makes it clear that compound interest could never be awarded on the damages for non-pecuniary loss. See too the recommendation of the Law Commission in its Report on *Pre-Judgment Interest on Debt and Damages* that, should a power to award compound interest be introduced, interest on damages for non-pecuniary loss in personal injury cases should continue to be single: (2004), Law Com. No.287, paras 7.8 to 7.12.

[202a] [2021] EWCA Civ 49 at [42]–[45]. See also *Saunders v Edwards* [1987] 1 W.L.R. 1116; [1987] 2 All E.R. 651 CA and *Holtham v Commissioner of Police for the Metropolis* [1987] C.L.Y. 1154 CA, discussed above at paras 19-049 and 19-054 to 19-056.

III. The Position After Sempra Metals

3. The Results at Common Law and in Equity

(1) Cases where compound interest is sought

Replace paragraph with:

A further word should be said here about compound interest in equity today. **19-068** Equity awards compound interest as compensation for loss for the same reasons as the common law, although with one curious difference that the loss is assessed objectively based upon what a person with the general characteristics of the defendant might have done, rather than what the defendant would have done. Historically, this was justified for pragmatic reasons involving a saving of time. It is hard to justify today an approach that does not require a claimant to prove their loss. Nevertheless, in *Watson v Kea Investments Ltd*[244] the Court of Appeal approved the approach of the trial judge, Nugee J (who had referred to the earlier authorities),[245] which awarded compound interest at a rate that would have been obtained by a reasonable person with the general characteristics of the claimant. This approach continues to be applied.[246] Equity awards compound interest in order to ensure that a person does not make a profit from their own wrongdoing if that person is in a fiduciary position.[247] It also does so if compound interest is made by a dishonest recipient in breach of fiduciary duty.[248] Such a recovery of interest constitutes an accounting or is by way of disgorgement and is considered in Ch.15. Although there is high authority that appears to recognise the availability of compound interest to disgorge profits made by fraud,[249] and although this has been recognised by the High Court of Australia,[250] there may be uncertainty about whether there is jurisdiction in equity to award compound interest to disgorge profits made by those obtaining money or other benefit through fraud. This uncertainty derives from retrograde authority that purports to limit the availability of an account and disgorgement of profits for deceit.[251] It is hard to see why disgorgement of profits made as compound interest should be possible in relation to compound interest made by a dishonest recipient in breach of fiduciary duty but not in relation to actual fraud either at common law or in equity. The question was raised but left undecided by the Court of Appeal in *Clef Aquitaine SARL v Laporte Materials (Barrow) Ltd*,[252] though it was accepted that the matter will need decision one day.[253] Since Clef Aquitaine the question has reappeared more than once but with no very clear answer. In *Black v Davies*,[254] which was an action in deceit, McCombe J would have been prepared to award compound interest but for his belief that the equitable remedy of compound interest should be ancillary to an equitable cause of action. Instead, the Court of Appeal, while not sharing this belief, refused compound interest because the defendant's fraudulent representation had not caused him to obtain and retain money belonging to the claimants but had simply caused them to lose money.[255]

Subsequently, an award of compound interest was made in the complicated fraud case of *Man Nutzfahrzeuge AG v Freightliner Ltd*,[256] but it is not entirely clear whether this was based on the benefit obtained by the fraudulent defendant or on the loss to the claimant.[256a] Again, in *Glenn v Watson*,[256b] Nugee J awarded compound interest upon a claim based upon deceit but the claim, which was expressed as one for "equitable compensation" consequent upon a constructive trust of the money paid by deceit, bore a close resemblance to disgorgement of profits. And in obiter dicta in *Wood v Commercial First Business Ltd*,[256c] Mr James Pickering QC recognised a category in which compound interest could be disgorged for fraud but, curiously, considered that the compound interest needed to have been retained by the fraudster at the time of trial and not merely earned as a profit. The better view is that the power to award interest upon money that was obtained and retained by fraud, the existence of which their Lordships had "no doubt" about in 1904,[256d] extends to compound interest both at common law and in equity but that, consistently with the account of profits generally,[256e] the reference to money "retained" by fraud was to describe the alternative circumstance where the profit was not "obtained" but "retained".

[244] [2019] EWCA Civ 1759; [2019] 4 W.L.R. 145 at [14].

[245] *Glenn v Watson* [2018] EWHC 2016 (Ch) at [548]–[550].

[246] *Van Zuylen v Whiston-Dew* [2021] EWHC 2219 (Ch) at [318].

[247] See especially the treatment of the interest issue by Buckley LJ in *Wallersteiner v Moir (No.2)* [1975] Q.B. 373 CA at 397–399, and by Hobhouse J and Lord Browne-Wilkinson in *Kleinwort Benson Ltd v South Tyneside MBC* and *Westdeutsche Landesbank Girozentrale v Islington LBC* at, respectively, [1994] 4 All E.R. 972 at 990–995 and [1996] A.C. 669 at 701D. See too *O'Sullivan v Management Agency and Music* [1985] Q.B. 428 CA and see *Miliangos v George Frank (Textiles) (No.2)* [1977] Q.B. 489 at 495A–D, per Bristow J.

[248] *FM Capital Partners Ltd v Marino* [2019] EWHC 725 (Comm) at [33]. See also *Central Bank of Ecuador v Conticorp SA* [2015] UKPC 11 at [185] referring to *Novoship v Nikitin* [2014] EWCA Civ 908; [2015] Q.B. 499.

[249] *President of India v La Pintada Compania Navigacion SA* [1985] A.C. 104 at 116.

[250] *Northern Territory v Mr A. Griffiths (deceased) and Lorraine Jones on behalf of the Ngaliwurru and Nungali Peoples* [2019] HCA 7; (2019) 93 ALJR 327 at [131], [340].

[251] See paras 15-039 to 15-044 above.

[252] [2001] Q.B. 488 CA.

[253] [2001] Q.B. 448 CA at 503H–506B.

[254] [2004] EWHC 1464 (QB).

[255] See [2005] EWCA Civ 531 CA, especially at [87]–[89].

[256] [2006] EWHC 2347 (Comm).

[256a] See [2006] EWHC 2347 (Comm) at [318]–[321]. The claim in deceit, and therefore the issue of interest, does not appear in the appeal at [2008] P.N.L.R. 6 at 117.

[256b] [2018] EWHC 2483 (Ch).

[256c] [2021] EWHC 1403 (Ch) at [21].

[256d] *Johnson v The King* [1904] A.C. 817 PC (SL) at [822].

[256e] *Central Bank of Ecuador v Conticorp SA* [2015] UKPC 11; [2016] 1 B.C.L.C. 26 at [9].

IV. CALCULATION OF THE AMOUNT OF INTEREST

2. RATE OF INTEREST AWARDED

(2) Cases in the Commercial Court and analogous cases

(a) Development over the years

Replace the paragraph with:

19-113 For quite some years interest at base rate plus 1% continued to be the norm.[491] Thus Webster J in *Shearson Lehman v Maclaine Watson (No.2)*[492] applied what he regarded as the general rule and awarded 1% over base rate. In the familiar negligence claims by mortgage lenders against valuers and solicitors, base rate plus 1% has from time to time been awarded, as in *Banque Bruxelles Lambert v Eagle Star Insurance Co*[493] and on the consequential loss in *Hartle v Laceys*.[494] Base rate plus 1% was also awarded in *Martini Investments v McGinn*,[495] and in *Adcock v Co-operative Insurance Society*,[496] while, with foreign interest rates involved, in *Kuwait Airways v Kuwait Insurance*[497] and in *Hellenic Industrial Development Bank SA v Atkin, The Julia*,[498] United States prime rate was awarded because it was the nearest equivalent to base rate plus 1%.[499] Interest was awarded at 2% over base rate in *Brown v K.M.R. Services*[500] and *Deeny v Gooda Walker (No.3)*,[501] claims in the Commercial Court in the litigation by Lloyd's Names against their agents. The reason given was that this "represented what individual Names were likely to have to pay when borrowing money".[502] It was also awarded at 2% above base rate in *Maloney v Mundays LLP*[502a] since this was the likely borrowing cost of a claimant with the general attributes of the assignor to the claimant, namely a relatively small business.

[491] Interest at base rate less 1% was all that was awarded in *University of Keele v Price Waterhouse* [2004] P.N.L.R. 8 at 112 but that was because the claimant had conceded that this was the rate it would have earned on the moneys; see at [70] and [71]. No issue on interest appears in the appeal: [2004] P.N.L.R. 43 CA at 888.

[492] [1990] 3 All E.R. 723.

[493] [1995] 2 All E.R. 769 at first instance; not in issue on appeal.

[494] [1999] Lloyd's Rep. P.N. 315 CA; for interest on the main award, see para.19-017, above.

[495] [2001] Lloyd's Rep. I.R. 374.

[496] [2001] Lloyd's Rep. I.R. 657.

[497] [2001] Lloyd's Rep. I.R. 678; see the case at para.19-120, below.

[498] [2003] Lloyd's Rep. I.R. 365.

[499] These last cases were claims on an insurance policy, not claims for damages.

[500] [1995] 2 Lloyd's Rep. 513. This does not appear from this report but from the report of the second case; see fn.501.

[501] [1996] L.R.L.R. 168.

[502] [1996] L.R.L.R. 168 at 175, col.1.

[502a] [2021] EWHC 1324 (Ch) at [105]–[107].

CHAPTER 22

BREACH OF UNDERTAKINGS AS TO DAMAGES

TABLE OF CONTENTS
1. THE ISSUE 22-001
2. THE GIVING OF AN UNDERTAKING AND WHETHER IT WILL BE
    ENFORCED .... 22-002□
3. THE ASSESSMENT OF DAMAGES UPON AN ENFORCED UNDERTAKING . 22-004□
    (A1) Non-pecuniary loss .... 22-006A□
    (1) Loss of a chance .... 22-007■
    (2) Causation and remoteness .... 22-008■
4. EXEMPLARY DAMAGES 22-011

2. THE GIVING OF AN UNDERTAKING AND WHETHER IT WILL BE ENFORCED

After para.22-002, add a new paragraph:

This principle comes, however, with a caveat. In drawing the analogy with breach   **22-002A**
of contract it should not be forgotten that the court is not compensating for a breach
of contract but for loss caused by an interlocutory injunction that, as it turns out,
was not justified. As McCombe LJ said, although the court will usually apply rules
such as remoteness by analogy with breach of contract, "because in truth there is
no contract there has to be room for exceptions". In this respect labels such as "common law damages" or "equitable compensation" can distract.[1a]

[1a] *Abbey Forwarding Ltd v Hone (No.3)* [2014] EWCA Civ 711; [2015] Ch. 309 at 333 [63]. See also
PJSC National Bank Trust v Mints [2021] EWHC 1089 (Comm) at [25].

3. THE ASSESSMENT OF DAMAGES UPON AN ENFORCED UNDERTAKING

Replace footnote 10 with:

[10] [2016] EWHC 2163 (Comm); [2017] 2 All E.R. 570 at [51]. See also *Alta Trading UK Ltd v Bosworth*   **22-006**
[2021] EWHC 1126 (Comm) at [25].

After para.22-006, add a new sub-section:

(A1) Non-pecuniary loss

In principle there is no reason why non-pecuniary loss, such as for the   **22-006A**
consequences of loss of reputation, cannot be recovered on enforcement of an
undertaking as to damages. In this respect there is little difference in principle
between the loss of reputation suffered as a result of publicity surrounding an
injunction or freezing order that, it turns out, was not justified and the loss of reputation arising from the stopping of a cheque that should not have been stopped.[11a] But,

as Calver J observed in *PJSC National Bank Trust v Mints*,[11b] the defendant will usually be unable to show the element of causation: the same reputational loss would often have been suffered from the bringing of the litigation against the defendant despite the freezing order or injunction upon which the undertaking was given. In the few cases where causation is satisfied and an award is made, the award has been modest, ranging from £1,000 to £15,000, because any additional or "pure" reputational effect is likely to have limited future consequences.[11c]

[11a] *Al Rawas v Pegasus Energy Ltd* [2008] EWHC 617 (QB); [2009] 1 All E.R. 346 at [35], [39].

[11b] [2021] EWHC 1089 (Comm) at [27]. See also *Tharros Shipping v Bias* [1994] 1 Lloyd's Rep. 577 at 581–583.

[11c] [2021] EWHC 1089 (Comm) at [27(l)] referring to *Al Rawas v Pegasus Energy Ltd* [2008] EWHC 617 (QB); [2009] 1 All E.R. 436 at [48]; *Columbia Picture Industries Inc v Robinson* [1987] Ch. 38 and *Abbey Forwarding Ltd v Hone (No.3)* [2014] EWCA Civ 711; [2015] Ch. 309 at [129] respectively for these amounts.

(1) Loss of a chance

After para.22-007, add new paragraph:

22-007A   A loss of chance approach was recognised by the Privy Council as rightly not applied in *Ennismore Fund Management Ltd v Fenris Consulting Ltd*.[12a] In that case, it had been held that but for the freezing order, supported by the undertaking, the party giving the undertaking would, on the balance of probabilities, have made a less risky investment than that which it alleged. No discount was made for any uncertainty.

[12a] [2022] UKPC 27 at [64]–[65].

(2) Causation and remoteness

After para.22-008, add new paragraph:

22-008A   The application of the but for approach to causation arose in *Dr Reddy's Laboratories (UK Ltd) v Warner-Lambert Co LLC*.[16a] The dispute in that case concerned the matters that should be ignored in assessing the loss that would have been suffered but for various orders that were issued, subject to undertakings as to damages, on the assumption of the validity of a patent. As Zacaroli J said, and consistently with the application of the "but for" test generally in the law of torts,[16b] in constructing the counterfactual it is always necessary to remove the very undertaking that was wrongly made.[16c] This meant that it was not appropriate on the counterfactual analysis to assume that everyone knew at all times that the patent was invalid.[16d] More difficult was the question of the precise counterfactual assumption to be made in the absence of the orders. Was it that: (1) the order was refused by the court; (2) the order was applied for but not pursued before the court; or (3) the order was not sought in the first place?[16e] Zacaroli J followed an Australian authority[16f] in concluding that the correct answer was (2). That approach has the benefit of making the smallest change from the real world, since a counterfactual involving the refusal of an order or the lack of an application would have larger consequences in the real world than a counterfactual that preserved the signal of making the application, although withdrawing it, and did not involve the false signal that the court had refused the application.

[16a] [2021] EWHC 2182 (Ch); [2021] Bus. L.R. 1496.

[16b] See above paras 8-005 to 8-006.

[16c] [2021] EWHC 2182 (Ch); [2021] Bus. L.R. 1496 at [58].

[16d] [2021] EWHC 2182 (Ch); [2021] Bus. L.R. 1496 at [60].

[16e] [2021] EWHC 2182 (Ch); [2021] Bus. L.R. 1496 at [87].

[16f] [2021] EWHC 2182 (Ch); [2021] Bus. L.R. 1496 at [85]–[93], citing *Sigma Pharmaceuticals (Australia) Pty Ltd v Wyeth* [2018] FCA 1556.

After para.22-010, add new paragraph:

The principles of remoteness of damage also illustrate why the period over which **22-010A** the damage flowing from the undertaking is usually limited to the period from the date of the undertaking until the date of final judgment, even if the undertaking was only later shown on a successful appeal to have been without basis. As Dame Kate Thirlwell put it, for the Privy Council in *Ennismore Fund Management Ltd v Fenris Consulting Ltd*[23a] although it was later overturned, the final judgment "totally eclipsed" the interim relief upon which the undertaking had been given.

[23a] [2022] UKPC 27 at [50].

CHAPTER 25

SALE OF GOODS

Table of Contents

I. **Breach by Seller** 25-002
    1.   Non-delivery 25-002
        (1)   Normal measure 25-004
        (2)   Consequential losses ....25-023■
    2.   Delayed Delivery 25-038
        (1)   Normal measure 25-039
        (2)   Consequential losses 25-044
    3.   Breach of Condition: Goods Properly Rejected 25-058
    4.   Breach of Condition or Warranty as to Quality, Fitness or
         Description: Goods Accepted 25-059
        (1)   Normal measure ....25-061■
        (2)   Consequential losses ....25-071■
    5.   Breach of Condition as to Title or of Warranty of Quiet
         Possession 25-110
    6.   Breach of Condition: Loss of the Right to Reject the Goods . 25-112

II. **Breach by Buyer** 25-114
    1.   Non-acceptance 25-115
        (1)   Normal measure 25-117
        (2)   Consequential losses 25-128
    2.   Failure to Procure the Opening of a Letter of Credit 25-132
    3.   Other Breaches 25-134

I. Breach by Seller

1. Non-delivery

(2) Consequential losses

(b) Loss on a resale

(i) Loss of profit on a resale

Replace the paragraph with:

Where damages are allowed for loss of profit on a resale of which the seller knew **25-030**
the actuality or the probability, the seller will not be liable for an exceptional loss

of profits unless the seller has been informed of the details of the sub-contracts and only then if the seller can be said to have taken the risk of such loss. This appears from the speeches in *Hall v Pim*.[143] Lord Dunedin said: "The contracts ... must be contracts in accordance with the market, not extravagant and unusual bargains".[144] And Lord Shaw said:

> "It is not suggested that these prices were out of the ordinary course of business. Had this been so, different considerations might quite well have arisen."[145]

Thus in *Household Machines v Cosmos Exporters*,[146] where the seller knew of the claimant's intention to resell but did not know the details of the sub-contract, Lewis J did not award the claimant the 12 per cent by which the sub-contract price was higher than the contract price, but gave only 10 per cent. Similarly, in *Coastal International Trading v Maroil*,[147] where the sub-contract, of which the defendants were fully aware, contained unusual terms rendering the claimants' profit under it unreasonable and such as would not have been within the contemplation of the parties, the profit awarded to the claimants was arrived at after eliminating the extravagant effect of the unusual terms. On the other hand, and without reference to any of the authorities above, a loss of profit from a resale contract was awarded in *F&T Terrix Ltd v CBT Global Ltd*.[147a] In that case, the claimant agreed to purchase 100,000 pairs of protective gloves for £800,000. Before delivery, the claimant sought assurances of delivery, telling the defendant that it had entered a resale contract for £960,000. In breach of contract, the defendant failed to deliver the gloves. The claimant sought recovery of its deposit and £160,000 profit that it would have made on the resale contract. HH Judge Stephen Davies, sitting as a judge of the High Court, held that the claimant was entitled to recovery of its deposit, but damages were limited to £50,000 because of expenses on the primary contract and because the claimant had unreasonably refused a later alternative offer by the defendant to supply the gloves for £870,000, which would still have permitted it a profit on resale of £70,000.

[143] (1928) 33 Com. Cas. 324 HL.

[144] (1928) 33 Com. Cas. 324 HL at 330.

[145] (1928) 33 Com. Cas. 324 HL at 331. See *Victoria Laundry v Newman* [1949] 2 K.B. 528 CA in relation to loss of user profits at para.25-046, below.

[146] [1947] 1 K.B. 217.

[147] [1988] 1 Lloyd's Rep. 92.

[147a] [2021] EWHC 3379 (Comm).

4. BREACH OF CONDITION OR WARRANTY AS TO QUALITY, FITNESS OR DESCRIPTION: GOODS ACCEPTED

(1) Normal measure

Replace the paragraph with:

25-062 That the time and place taken for assessing the value of the goods is the time and place of delivery is, however, only a prima facie rule and in *Choil Trading SA v Sahara Energy Resources Ltd*,[265] the rule was held displaced. Delivery to the buyer of a cargo of contaminated naphtha took place at the time of its shipment, but it was not until tests carried out on board the ship had revealed the contamination some two weeks later that there was rejection of the cargo by the buyer's sub-buyer. It was held that the difference between the values of sound and contaminated naphtha fell to be assessed as at the later date.[266] Similar is *Bominflot Bunkergesellschaft für Mineralole mbH Co v Petroplus Marketing AG*.[267] The defect in gasoil sold to the claimant buyer did not become patent until some time after it had been delivered from the ship transporting it, whereupon the buyer promptly proceeded to find for the unsound gasoil a sub-buyer who as part of the arrangement sold to the buyer a cargo of replacement, sound gasoil. It was held that the time to ascertain the value of both sound and unsound gasoil was the time of the later sale and repurchase.[268] So too in *Deutsche Bank AG v Total Global Steel Ltd*,[269] a time later than that of delivery was taken as the buyer of the carbon emission units had delayed in order to give the seller a chance to put things right.[270] The same approach was taken in *BP Oil International Ltd v Glencore Energy UK Ltd*[270a] where defective oil was supplied by the seller and sold by the buyer to a sub-buyer who then resold it to the buyer at a lower value reflecting its defects. The buyer then resold to a second sub-buyer at the same price. Since the oil had no market value at the time of supply but did have a later market value when the buyer resold the defective oil in a sub-sale, the later date of resale was used for valuation of the difference between the sale price and the market value of oil obtained.[270b]

[265] [2010] EWHC 374 (Comm).

[266] See [2010] EWHC 374 (Comm) at [115] and following, together with [131].

[267] [2012] EWHC 3009 (Comm).

[268] See the discussion at [2012] EWHC 3009 (Comm) at [60]–[66].

[269] [2012] EWHC 1201 (Comm).

[270] See [2012] EWHC 1201 (Comm) at [166].

[270a] [2022] EWHC 499 (Comm).

[270b] [2022] EWHC 499 (Comm) at [270], [401].

(b) Relevant and irrelevant prices in ascertaining the value of the goods as they are

Replace the paragraph with:

The price at which the buyer has resold the defective goods may be taken as **25-065** evidence of their value where this is difficult to assess.[283] Such evidence can play a more important part here than in other situations since, where goods are defective, it is likely that there will be no market for them.[284] Devlin J, dealing with a case of such goods in *Biggin v Permanite*,[285] there said:

"It seems to me that one can rarely arrive at an accurate figure of unsound value. Where the breach is non-delivery, there is often a market price which can be quoted, or evidence can be given of the price at which at the relevant date similar goods were changing hands, but there is rarely any market price for damaged goods, since their value depends on the extent of the damage. If the actual damaged goods are sold with all faults, good evidence can be obtained of the difference in value, but such a sale is not always possible, and a claim for substantial damages cannot be limited to goods which have been sold."[286]

In *Choil Trading SA v Sahara Energy Resources Ltd*,[287] where the buyer had sold the cargo of naphtha in its contaminated condition to a third party, Christopher Clarke J held that the price at which this sale was made could be taken as the value of the naphtha in its contaminated condition at the date, two weeks earlier, on which contaminated value had to be assessed.[288] Similarly, in *Bominflot Bunkergesellschaft für Mineralole mbH Co v Petroplus Marketing AG*,[289] the best evidence of value of the unsound gasoil was held to be the price paid for it to the buyer under the contract made at the very time value was to be assessed.[290] And in *BP Oil International Ltd v Glencore Energy UK Ltd*,[290a] Moulder J held that the value of defective oil was to be assessed by reference to the later price of a sub-sale.

[283] See *Slater v Hoyle & Smith* [1920] 2 K.B. 11 CA at 17 per Warrington LJ.

[284] In the absence of an available market it was difficult to assess the value of the carbon emission units sold in *Deutsche Bank AG v Total Global Steel Ltd* [2012] EWHC 1201 (Comm): see at [167] and following.

[285] [1951] 1 K.B. 422, reversed on a ground not affecting the present issue: [1951] 2 K.B. 314 CA.

[286] [1951] 1 K.B. 422 at 438. In the case itself there was no resale to assist Devlin J in assessing the depreciated value of the goods. Evidence of hypothetical sub-buyers as to what they would have been prepared to pay for the goods at the date of breach, goods "which they never saw and of whose defects they have learnt only at second-hand" (at 439), would, he said, have been of no use to him. He thought that in these circumstances a method of calculation which could be legitimately followed by the court was by way of a price allowance. This was "a common practice of the commercial world to deal with this type of case ... and claims for damaged goods are constantly met to the satisfaction of both parties by the fixing of an allowance by an adjuster or some person skilled in the trade": at 439.

[287] [2010] EWHC 374 (Comm).

[288] See [2010] EWHC 374 (Comm) at [151]–[155]. Contrast Christopher Clarke J's holding on value as warranted at para.25-064, above. Facts of the case at para.25-062, above.

[289] [2012] EWHC 3009 (Comm).

[290] See [2012] EWHC 3009 (Comm) at [61]. Facts at para.25-062, above.

[290a] [2022] EWHC 499 (Comm). Facts at para.25-062, above.

(2)   Consequential losses

(c)   Loss on a resale

(vi)   Loss of profit on further sales

After "... have brought an entitlement to damages.[489]", add:

25-107   The Court of Appeal has also expressly acknowledged, including by reference to this paragraph, that losses of goodwill, and by analogy reputation, are species of loss of profit claims.[489a]

[489a] *Soteria Insurance Ltd v IBM United Kingdom Ltd* [2022] EWCA Civ 440; (2022) 202 Con. L.R. 1 at [67].

PART 4A CONTRACT

CHAPTER 28

LEASE OF LAND

TABLE OF CONTENTS

I. **Breach by Lessor** 28-001
    1. FAILURE TO COMPLETE 28-003
        (1) Normal measure 28-004
        (2) Consequential losses 28-006
    2. DELAY IN COMPLETION 28-007
        (1) Normal measure 28-008
        (2) Consequential losses 28-009
    3. BREACH OF COVENANTS 28-010
        (1) Covenant for quiet enjoyment and covenant against
             incumbrances 28-012
        (2) Covenant to repair ....28-024■
        (3) Covenant of fitness for habitation 28-034
        (4) Covenant to renew and option to purchase 28-035

II. **Breach by Lessee** 28-038
    1. FAILURE TO ACCEPT 28-039
    2. BREACH OF COVENANTS 28-041
        (1) Covenant to repair ....28-043■
        (2) Other covenants on the condition and use of the premises .28-084■
        (3) Covenant Against Assignment or Underletting 28-094
        (4) Covenant to Deliver up Possession 28-098

I. BREACH BY LESSOR

3. BREACH OF COVENANTS

(2) Covenant to repair

(c) Non-pecuniary loss

Replace paragraph with:

Where the claimant is a company rather than an individual there is no require- **28-033**
ment to award damages in the form of a sum for distress, inconvenience and disrup-
tion; a company can only suffer financial loss.[162] Thus in *Electricity Supply
Nominees v National Magazine Co*,[163] no non-pecuniary award was made to the
trading company tenant. The court was thus forced back upon an assessment of
diminution in value.[164] By contrast, as an award for non-pecuniary loss arising from

breach of a repair covenant, the general damages awarded to an individual for distress and inconvenience have been held to fall "squarely" within the purpose of the 10% *Simmons v Castle* uplift.[164a]

[162] See para.18-031, per Lord Reid; also para.5-014, above.

[163] [1999] 1 E.G.L.R. 130. The breach was not of a covenant to repair but of a covenant to provide certain services, including the installation of lifts and air-conditioning; but the principles are the same.

[164] See the case at para.28-027, above.

[164a] *Khan v Mehmood* [2022] EWCA Civ 791; [2022] H.L.R. 34 at [58].

II.   BREACH BY LESSEE

2.   BREACH OF COVENANTS

(1)   Covenant to repair

(c)   Measure of damages in action at determination of tenancy

(i)   At common law: pre-1927

At the end of the first sentence ending "to leave them", add new footnote 249a:

28-055   [249a] This paragraph was approved in *Pullman Foods Ltd v Welsh Ministers* [2020] EWHC 2521 (TCC).

After para.28-057, add new paragraph:

28-057A   Despite these inroads into containing the principle in *Joyner v Weeks*, the principle itself remains intact. Thus, when it was argued, relying upon *Ruxley Electronics Construction Ltd v Forsyth*,[269a] that a defendant lessee should not be required to pay damages representing the cost of repair where a repair was unreasonable, Veronique Buehrlen QC, sitting as a Deputy High Court judge in *Coldunell Ltd v Hotel Management International Ltd*,[269b] would have followed *Joyner* even if the repair was unreasonable.

[269a] [1996] A.C. 344; [1995] 3 W.L.R. 118 HL, at para.31-014, below.

[269b] [2022] EWHC 1290 (TCC) at [36].

(ii)   As limited by statute: post-1927

Replace paragraph with:

28-068   Where the covenanted repairs were to be carried out in full although not by the lessor, the cost of repairs was held to be recoverable in *Haviland v Long*.[323] The defendant being in breach of his repairing covenants, the claimant lessor shortly before the end of the lease entered into a fresh lease with a third party who, while paying a full economic rent, agreed to carry out the repairs, the claimant undertaking to reimburse him out of any sum recovered from the defendant by way of dilapidations. It was contended for the defendant that having regard to the terms of the new lease the value of the reversion had not been diminished and that the lessor had therefore suffered no loss. The court, however, held that at the time of the new lease the claimant had a contingent right to recover damages should the defendant eventually be in breach, that he did not lose that right by reason of the new bargain with the third party, and allowed the cost of repairs as the measure of damages. Somervell LJ said:

"The damage to the reversion would be measured by the cost of the repairs, because it was everybody's intention to go on using the building as it was before, and it was economic to do so. I cannot see why that right should be lost because it is made a term in a bargain."[324]

In this case the claimant had arranged to pay over to the third party any sum that he obtained on this account from the defendant, and if there had been no such arrangement it is unlikely that the third party would have been prepared to pay the full economic rent for the property. Nevertheless, even if the lessor stood to benefit by dint of an advantageous bargain with the third party, it would seem from the reasoning of all three members of the Court of Appeal in *Haviland v Long*,[325] that the cost of repairs would still be recoverable. Thus Somervell LJ, quoting the judge below, said:

"It is the fact that ... the repairs require to be done and not the circumstances in which the landlord and his new tenant agree upon the manner of meeting the charge, which is the governing consideration."[326]

Denning LJ said quite categorically:

"The fact that the landlord has an undertaking from a new tenant to do the repairs does not go in diminution of damages. It is res inter alios acta."[327]

And Roxburgh J said[328] that to decide otherwise would be contrary to the principle which Lawrence LJ had enunciated in *Hanson v Newman*,[329] that reversionary leases must be disregarded.[330] In the light of this, ironically enough, *Joyner v Weeks*,[331] could be decided the same way today.[332] Yet in view of the decision in *Ruxley Electronics Construction Ltd v Forsyth*,[333] it has been suggested by Judge Toulmin in *Pgf II SA v Royal & Sun Alliance Insurance Plc*,[334] that it would now not be followed.[335] Without reference to that case, a similar submission was, however, rejected in *Coldunell Ltd v Hotel Management International Ltd*.[335a] Unless, and until *Joyner* is overruled, the approach in *Coldunell* is to be preferred as one that avoids increased uncertainty and respects the premise upon which the legislation was based.

[323] [1952] 2 Q.B. 80 CA.

[324] [1952] 2 Q.B. 80 CA at 83.

[325] [1952] 2 Q.B. 80 CA.

[326] [1952] 2 Q.B. 80 CA at 83.

[327] [1952] 2 Q.B. 80 CA at 84.

[328] [1952] 2 Q.B. 80 CA at 84.

[329] [1934] Ch. 298 CA; see para.28-059, above.

[330] It had already been held in *Terroni v Corsini* [1931] 1 Ch. 515 that reversionary leases must be disregarded, but that case was more concerned with the moment in time at which the value of the reversion had to be taken in assessing damages: see the footnote reference to the case at para.28-059, above.

[331] [1891] 2 Q.B. 31 CA; see para.28-057, above.

[332] Despite Denning J's dictum in *Westminster v Swinton* [1948] K.B. 524 at 534 that s.18 was enacted "in order to remedy *Joyner v Weeks*".

[333] [1996] A.C. 344, at para.31-014, below.

[334] [2010] EWHC 1459 (TCC).

[335] See his discussion at [2010] EWHC 1459 (TCC) at [23] and following, and see too para.9-187, above.

[335a] [2022] EWHC 1290 (TCC) at [36].

(2)   Other covenants on the condition and use of the premises

(b)   Measure of damages in action at determination of tenancy

After "… assessed by taking the cost of reinstatement.", add:

28-090   The principles that derive from *Joyner v Weeks* in relation to covenants to repair therefore do not apply to other covenants.

CHAPTER 29

SALE OF SHARES AND LOAN OF STOCK

TABLE OF CONTENTS

I. **Breach by Seller** 29-003
    1. NON-DELIVERY ....29-003□
    2. OTHER BREACHES 29-007

II. **Breach by Buyer** 29-010
    1. NON-ACCEPTANCE 29-010
    2. OTHER BREACHES 29-012

III. **Breach by Lender** 29-013

I. BREACH BY SELLER

1. NON-DELIVERY

Replace the paragraph with:

The time at which the market price is to be assessed is the contractual time for **29-005** delivery. In general the principles worked out in the sale of goods cases apply here: of the several possible situations,[15] few have been adjudicated upon in relation to the sale of shares, but the cases that there are indicate an application of common principles while at the same time bringing out small differences. (1) Where the market price has risen between the date of breach and the date of judgment in the action, it was held in *Shaw v Holland*[16] that the time of judgment was not to be taken in preference to the time of breach by non-delivery. Parke B said that the action was more akin to one for non-delivery of goods than to one for not replacing stock,[17] since:

"... the plaintiff had his money in his own possession, and might have gone into the market and bought other shares as soon as the contract was broken."[18]

This rationale disappears where the purchase price has been paid in advance; and it has been submitted that in the case of goods the buyer should then be entitled to recover for any increase in the market price between breach and judgment.[19] Here, however, it is submitted that there is no call for such a rule, as the buyer of shares has in their own hands the power to right their position by suing for specific performance which will give the buyer the shares themselves.[20] (2) Where the buyers in *Bear Stearns Bank Plc v Forum Equity Ltd*[21] had acted reasonably in initially pursuing a claim for specific performance, abandoned for a damages claim upon knowledge that the sellers had disposed of the shares elsewhere, they were held

[109]

entitled to have the market price taken at a date many months later than the contractual time of delivery, by which date the market price had risen.[22] (3) Where the time fixed for delivery is postponed at the request of the seller, it has been held in *Wilson v London and Globe Finance Corp*[23] that the date of the breach is postponed until the buyer no longer will grant indulgence and the market price on that date will therefore be the relevant one.[24] This is the same as with sale of goods.[25] (4) Where the contract is for the sale of shares not yet in existence at the time of the contract, the delivery required by the contract may be not the shares when issued but the earlier letter of allotment. In such a case it was held in *Tempest v Kilner*[26] that, for the failure to deliver the letter of allotment constituting the breach, the damages were to be calculated at the market price on that date and the buyer could not claim on the basis of the rise in price at the time of the later issue of the shares themselves. (5) Where the damages claimed are in the nature of Lord Cairns' Act damages,[26a] then provided that the claimant has not unreasonably delayed in selling the shares the court will usually assess damages by reference to the date at which specific performance or an injunction would have been ordered since the damages are to be in substitution for that order.[26b]

[15] See paras 25-015 to 25-022, above.

[16] (1846) 15 M. &. W. 136.

[17] See paras 29-013 to 29-015, below.

[18] (1846) 15 M. & W. 136 at 146. He relied on *Gainsford v Carroll* (1824) 2 B. & C. 624, which gave the same reason for goods: see para.25-015, above.

[19] See para.25-015, above.

[20] And, in damages, the dividends paid between breach and judgment: *Sri Lanka Omnibus Co v Perera* [1952] A.C. 76 PC at para.29-007, below.

[21] [2007] EWHC 1576 (Comm); facts in the preceding paragraph.

[22] See [2007] EWHC 1576 (Comm) at [210]–[216]. In the different context of sale of land the important *Johnson v Agnew* [1980] A.C. 367 (at para.27-041, above) is along the same lines.

[23] (1897) 14 T.L.R. 15 CA. This ratio decidendi was on the facts adopted by only a majority of the Court of Appeal; there was a second ratio in which all concurred.

[24] It had previously been recognised in *Shaw v Holland* (1846) 15 M. & W. 136 at 146 that the buyer's indulgence at the seller's request postpones the breach, but the point had not been argued.

[25] The equivalent sale of goods case, *Ogle v Vane* (1867) L.R. 2 Q.B. 275, was indeed applied in *Wilson v London and Globe Finance Corp* (1897) 14 T.L.R. 15 CA.

[26] (1845) 3 C.B. 249.

[26a] See above at paras 1-015 and 27-041.

[26b] *Rahman v Rahman* [2020] EWHC 2392 (Ch) at [68].

Chapter 34

CONTRACTS FOR PROFESSIONAL AND OTHER SERVICES

Table of Contents

I. **Breach by the Party Engaging the Services** 34-002

II. **Breach by the Party Rendering the Services** 34-003
    1.   IN GENERAL 34-003
    2.   PARTICULAR CATEGORIES 34-008
      (1) Solicitors . . . . 34-009□
      (2) Surveyors, valuers and progress monitors . . . . 34-053■
      (3) Accountants . . . . 34-088□
      (4) Bankers 34-090
      (5) Stockbrokers 34-095
      (6) Estate agents 34-098
      (7) Travel agents 34-099

II. BREACH BY THE PARTY RENDERING THE SERVICES

2. PARTICULAR CATEGORIES

(1) Solicitors

Replace the paragraph with:

Solicitors can be negligent in a variety of ways as the cases on damages show; **34-009** indeed cases against solicitors are becoming legion, thereby making it difficult to deal with them in an organised fashion and to categorise them satisfactorily. An attempt is here made to place the decisions into various categories but this is intended purely for the purposes of exposition, and decisions appearing in one category may well prove useful in relation to another category.[31] Moreover, many of the decisions are dealt with again in other parts of this book, as they tend to give rise to general problems on damages, particularly on questions of certainty[32] and of recovery for non-pecuniary loss in contract.[33] Two general principles of particular relevance are a general distinction, in assessing the extent of loss, between whether (i) the claimant would not have entered the transaction at all but for the negligence (a "no transaction case") or (ii) the claimant would have entered a better, yet still flawed transaction but for the negligence (a "flawed transaction case"). Since the *SAAMCO* decision in 1997, this distinction has been rejected in the context of the separate question, considered in detail in Ch.8,[33a] of whether the loss falls within the scope of the duty assumed. But, subject to the question of scope of duty, the distinction can still be used to assess the extent of loss suffered. Cases have continued to rely upon the distinction on that basis.[33b]

[31] There may also be claims in tort where there is no contractual relationship between the claimant and the solicitor, as in *Al-Kandari v Brown & Co* [1988] Q.B. 665 CA and *White v Jones* [1995] 2 A.C. 207 CA.

[32] See Ch.10, above.

[33] See Ch.5, above.

[33a] See paras 8-032 to 8-033 and 8-047 to 8-055 above.

[33b] *Maharaj v Johnson* [2015] UKPC 28; [2015] P.N.L.R. 27 at [19]; *Elliott v Hattens Solicitors (a firm)* [2021] EWCA Civ 720 at [12]–[13], [27].

(a) Pecuniary loss

(v) Rights to property lost by negligence

Replace the paragraph with:

34-035   In quite a number of cases the negligence of the solicitor has consisted of a failure to take steps, timeously or otherwise, to protect the property rights of their client and has led to some substantial awards.[123] In *Hodge v Clifford Cowling & Co*[124] and again in *Ricci v Masons*,[125] in *Matlock Green Garage Ltd v Potter Brooke-Taylor & Wildgoose*[126] and in *Nahome v Last Cawthra Feather Solicitors*,[127] it was the claimant lessee's right to apply for a new tenancy that was lost. This was because the application was not made within the statutory time limit or, in the *Nahome* case, was not made in proper form. In *Ricci*, the claimant, who ran the business of a restaurant on the premises, had succeeded in agreeing a new but, of course, less satisfactory tenancy with the landlord. Nevertheless he had lost the opportunity, which he had been minded to take, of selling the restaurant together with the lease. It was held that to take a date later than the date of breach for the assessment would be an injustice to the claimant; he recovered in damages, inter alia, the difference between the value of the lease he would and should have acquired and the value of the one that he was able to negotiate with loss of statutory protection. In *Nahome* the claimants maintained that their jewellery business which they ran from the leasehold premises would have developed into a highly successful, largely internet-based business, and claimed the very large profits they allegedly would have made had the business not had to close down. The trial judge came to the somewhat uncertain conclusion that the appropriate way to compensate the claimants was by reference to the value of the business of which they had been deprived[128] and held profits from the internet business to be too remote as the defendants had not been made aware either of its existence or of its dependence on the leasehold premises.[129] In *Murray v Lloyd*,[130] the claimant's right to apply for a statutory tenancy was again lost but for a rather different reason. The loss of the opportunity for the claimant, who had purchased a leasehold property, to acquire a statutory tenancy was as a result of her solicitor's negligence in allowing her to take the lease in the name of an offshore company for tax purposes, so that an assignment of the leasehold interest to her required the landlord's consent which was refused. In these circumstances she was held entitled to damages assessed by reference to what it would cost her to acquire what she had lost, that is to the cost of acquiring similar rights of occupation on similar terms in similar alternative accommodation. This was assessed at the amount by which the effect of a lease on terms similar to those which the claimant would have enjoyed as a statutory tenant would depreciate the value of a similar freehold property.[131] In *Snipper v Enever Freeman & Co*,[132] the claimant lessee lost her enfranchisement rights to purchase the freehold. She nevertheless achieved an extension to her lease four years later and it was held that, while this was a benefit to be taken into account, it was only fair that the values of the enfranchisement right lost and of the extended lease gained should be taken as at the same date and that the date should be that of the lease extension. In *Layzell v Smith Morton & Long*,[133] the claimant lost his succession rights on the death of his father to the farm on which they had worked. The assessment of the damages was based upon the cost of his acquiring the freehold of a similar farm and then selling that freehold and entering into a tenancy agreement similar to the one he had lost. There was held to be no significant chance that the claimant would have been held ineligible or unsuitable to succeed his father to the farm and therefore no discount fell to be made from these damages. Finally, in *Gosden v Halliwell Landau (A Firm)*,[133a] the claimant lost an expected entitlement, upon the death of the trustee, to an estate in land which was held on trust. The land was sold by the trustee in breach of trust. The sale was possible because the defendant firm of solicitors failed to protect the interest in land by registering a restriction with HM Land Register. The central question for the assessment of damages was whether the land should be valued at (i) the date when the property was sold in breach of trust, (ii) the date of death, or (iii) the date of trial. The trial judge held that the correct date was the date of death because that is the date at which the claimant would have been entitled to the land. These are multifarious cases. Not only do they need to be scrutinised for the detail and the reason of the recovery allowed in each but also it is difficult to say that they present any clear common principle other than the grand overriding one of the claimant being put in the position they would have been in had no breach of contract occurred. Moreover, factual changes can easily change the damages to be awarded; in particular, there may be relevance in identifying the time when the claimant became aware of their loss of rights.[134]

[123] *Clark v Kirby-Smith* [1964] Ch. 506, at para.34-031, above can also be put into this category but the award there was of nominal damages only.

[124] [1990] 2 E.G.L.R. 89 CA.

[125] [1993] 2 E.G.L.R. 159.

[126] [2000] Lloyds's Rep. P.N. 925.

[127] [2010] EWHC 76 (Ch).

[128] [2010] EWHC 76 (Ch) at [71]; after a lengthy analysis in which many of the cases in the text of this work were cited.

[129] See [2010] EWHC 76 (Ch) at [91] and following.

[130] [1989] 1 W.L.R. 1060.

[131] This came to £115,000; the lease had been purchased, some eight years earlier, for £50,000. It may be that a discount should have been made to take into account the seven years of the lease which remained to run at the time of judgment.

[132] [1991] 2 E.G.L.R. 270.

[133] [1992] 1 E.G.L.R. 169.

[133a] [2021] EWHC 159 (Comm); [2021] P.N.L.R. 14.

[134] See the discussion in the analogous context of surveyors and valuers at para.34-063, below.

(2)   Surveyors, valuers and progress monitors

(a)   Purchasers of property negligently surveyed or valued

(ii)   Pecuniary loss: consequential losses

Replace the paragraph with:

34-064   Further cases have appeared where, at first instance, *SAAMCO* has been invoked successfully by surveyor and valuer defendants with purchaser claimants. In *Capita Alternative Fund Services (Guernsey) Ltd v Drivers Jonas,*[303] where surveyors had negligently advised the purchasers of a shopping centre development as to its value and commercial prospects, the trial judge applied *SAAMCO*, limiting the damages to the difference between what the purchasers had paid and what they should have paid on the basis of correct advice and not extending the damages to all the business losses that followed purchase.[304] In the affirming decision of the Court of Appeal,[305] the *SAAMCO* issue was not appealed.[306] The trial judge also in *Scullion v Bank of Scotland Plc,*[307] applied *SAAMCO*, where there was an overstatement by the defendant valuer of the capital value of, and the potential income from, the flat that the claimant was buying,[308] so as not to allow recovery for loss caused by a collapse in the market. In the Court of Appeal, reversing on liability,[309] this point was not touched on. But in *Large v Hart,*[309a] the Court of Appeal declined to apply *SAAMCO* where the negligence of the surveyor was the reason for the purchase of the property; although the negligence did not extend to some latent defects concerning damp-proofing, other defects concerning damp-proofing were negligently not noted. If they had been noted, the surveyor would have given advice which would have avoided the purchase of the property and the subsequent expense of knocking down the building and reconstructing it.[309b] It was not in dispute, however, that *SAAMCO* applied to prevent recovery of funding costs, or any increase in funding costs, or for any fall in property values.[309c]

[303] [2011] EWHC 2336 (Comm).

[304] See [2011] EWHC 2336 (Comm) at [298]–[309].

[305] [2012] EWCA Civ 1417 CA.

[306] [2012] EWCA Civ 1417 CA at [20]. The Court of Appeal reversed only on a question of tax deduction which, as pointed out in the footnote at the end of para.18-003, above, is not of relevance to the damages issues involving tax dealt with in Ch.18, above.

[307] [2010] EWHC 2253 (Ch).

[308] Full facts at para.49-071, below. With no contract between valuer and buyer the claim lay only in tort, but this does not affect the result.

[309] [2011] 1 W.L.R. 3212 CA.

[309a] [2021] EWCA Civ 24; [2021] B.L.R. 189.

[309b] [2021] EWCA Civ 24; [2021] B.L.R. 189 at [52]–[53].

[309c] [2021] EWCA Civ 24; [2021] B.L.R. 189 at [56].

(b)   Mortgagees of property negligently surveyed or valued

(iii)   Consequential losses: what is generally irrecoverable

Losses from fall in market

Replace paragraph with:

An application of *SAAMCO* which also confined the lender to the shortfall in **34-078** value between the amount of the loan and the true value of the property was *Charles B Lawrence & Associates v Intercommercial Bank Ltd*.[358] In that case, the extraneous event that was disregarded by the Privy Council for the purpose of damages was a separate, negligent failure to identify that the person providing security had no title to it. It is, however, equally important to notice that there are two situations when recovery will not be denied a lender claimant for the consequential loss arising from the collapse in the property market. Both situations are adverted to by Lord Hoffmann in *SAAMCO*.[359] The first is easy, being where the information is provided fraudulently.[360] The imposition of liability here is no more than a reflection of what Lord Lindley said long ago in *Quinn v Leathem*,[361] that "the intention to injure the plaintiff ... disposes of any question of remoteness of damage".[362] The second is more difficult, being where the duty is not just to provide information to enable someone to decide on a course of action but to advise someone as to what course of action to take.[363] The difficulty is not in stating the distinction, which is simply that between giving information and giving advice, but in deciding within which category a particular case falls. Cases, after *SAAMCO*, have sometimes had to grapple with this problem. The difficulty has now been removed by the decision of the Supreme Court in *BPE Solicitors v Hughes-Holland*,[364] in which Lord Sumption, with whom the others agreed, explained that the crucial distinction is not between the labels of "information" or "advice" but, rather, whether the person providing the service has assumed responsibility for the risk of the whole transaction (as is usually the case where advice is sought generally) or just for part of it (as is usually the case where only information is sought and not advice about the entry into the transaction).[365]

[358] [2021] UKPC 30; [2022] P.N.L.R. 7. See above at para.8-052A.

[359] [1997] A.C. 191.

[360] [1997] A.C. 191 at 215E–F.

[361] [1901] A.C. 495.

[362] [1901] A.C. 495 at 537.

[363] [1997] A.C. 191 at 214E–F.

[364] [2017] UKSC 21; [2018] A.C. 599. See also *AssetCo Plc v Grant Thornton UK LLP* [2020] EWCA Civ 1151, which reaffirms this principle.

[365] [2017] UKSC 21; [2018] A.C. 599 at [40]–[41]. See also *Lloyds Bank Plc v McBains Cooper Consulting Ltd* [2018] EWCA Civ 452 at [33].

Losses from non-payment of interest

After "Such a case is likely to be rare.", add:

The same principles have, however, been held not to apply to a lender's duty to **34-080** give credit in the assessment of damages for interest that would have been earned from investments which would have had funds diverted to the lost opportunity.[373a]

[373a] *Barrowfen Properties Ltd v Patel* [2022] EWHC 1601 (Ch) at [75]–[76].

(3) Accountants

Replace the paragraph with:

Ultimately, as with lawyers, the scope of liability of accountants for negligent **34-089** advice will depend upon the subject-matter for which the accountants have assumed responsibility. Although the labels of "advice" and "information" have been used in the past as means to distinguish between the different types of assumption of responsibility, those labels are descriptively inadequate,[415] "should not be treated as a rigid straitjacket",[416] and can "be a conclusion to be drawn" rather than part of the process of reasoning.[417] The point of the contrast is commonly to try to ascertain whether the adviser guided the "whole decision making process" including entry into the transaction,[418] and hence is responsible for the consequences of entry into the transaction, or whether the transaction is one (commonly involving no more than provision of "information") where the defendant does not take responsibility for the decision to enter the transaction.[419] In the latter circumstance, a useful cross-check, which can establish a cap on liability, can be to ask what loss would have been suffered if the information had been correct.[419a]

[415] *BPE Solicitors v Hughes-Holland* [2017] UKSC 21; [2018] A.C. 599 at [39].

[416] *Manchester Building Society v Grant Thornton UK LLP* [2021] UKSC 20; [2021] 3 W.L.R. 81 at [4].

[417] *Manchester Building Society v Grant Thornton UK LLP* [2021] UKSC 20; [2021] 3 W.L.R. 81 at [19].

[418] *BPE Solicitors v Hughes-Holland* [2017] UKSC 21; [2018] A.C. 599 at 623 [40]. See *AssetCo Plc v Grant Thornton LLP* [2020] EWCA Civ 1151; [2021] 3 All E.R. 517 at [76] and *LIV Bridging Finance Ltd v EAD Solicitors LLP (In Administration)* [2020] EWHC 1590; [2020] P.N.L.R. 24 at [35].

[419] [2017] UKSC 21 at [41]; [2018] A.C. 599 at 623.

[419a] *Manchester Building Society v Grant Thornton UK LLP* [2021] UKSC 20; [2021] 3 W.L.R. 81 at [23], [195]–[203].

After para.34-089, add a new paragraph:

34-089A　　The leading case that applies these principles in relation to accountants is *Manchester Building Society v Grant Thornton UK LLP*,[419b] which is considered above in Ch.8.[419c] In that case, the Supreme Court unanimously held that the respondent accountants were liable, subject to a reduction for contributory negligence, for the losses from break costs incurred by the appellant building society in closing out swap transactions that had been entered after advice from the accountants concerning their accountancy treatment. Although general commercial risks from swap agreements were not within the scope of the duty assumed by the respondent accountants, the losses suffered from breaking the swaps were within the risks which arose from adopting a business model which, as the accountants knew, depended upon the accountancy advice that the accountants gave.[419d] Again in *AssetCo Plc v Grant Thornton LLP*,[419e] the Court of Appeal held auditors liable for losses (subject to 25% contributory negligence reduction) arising from two years of group trading after the auditors had failed to detect fraud by the managers of the holding company in accounts which concealed the insolvency of the group. Although the reasoning of David Richards LJ in the leading judgment had been based mainly on causation only and had not clarified why the losses were within the scope of the auditors' duties, Lord Leggatt later explained that the losses were within the scope of the auditors' duties because the negligence of the auditors was in failing to identify two heavily loss-making contracts and it was those continuing losses that occurred.[419f]

[419b] [2021] UKSC 20; [2021] 3 W.L.R. 81 at [4].

[419c] At para.8-050.

[419d] [2021] UKSC 20; [2021] 3 W.L.R. 81 at [34].

[419e] [2020] EWCA Civ 1151; [2021] 3 All E.R. 517.

[419f] *Manchester Building Society v Grant Thornton UK LLP* [2021] UKSC 20; [2021] 3 W.L.R. 81 at [122]–[123].

PART 4B TORT

CHAPTER 37

TORTS AFFECTING GOODS: DAMAGE AND DESTRUCTION

TABLE OF CONTENTS

I. **Damage** 37-003
   1. NORMAL MEASURE 37-003
   2. CONSEQUENTIAL LOSSES 37-013
     (1) Expenses other than the cost of repair ....37-013■
     (2) Loss of profits of profit-earning chattels 37-030
     (3) Expenses and loss of profits where other repairs have been
        effected concurrently 37-040
     (4) Loss of use of chattels which are not profit-earning 37-045

II. **Destruction** 37-063
   1. NORMAL MEASURE 37-063
   2. CONSEQUENTIAL LOSSES 37-069
     (1) Expenses 37-069
     (2) Loss of profits of profit-earning chattels 37-070
     (3) Loss of use of non-profit-earning chattels 37-078

I. DAMAGE

2. CONSEQUENTIAL LOSSES

(1) Expenses other than the cost of repair

(a) Expenses made necessary

(ii) Hire of substitute vehicles

Conventional car hiring

Replace paragraph with:
    The earliest issue that arose in this field was as to whether the claimant is entitled **37-016**
to hire a car of equally high quality to the one damaged and being repaired. In
Watson Norie v Shaw,[82] a Jensen car was supplied by the claimant company, with
an eye to prestige, to its managing director. The car was damaged by the defendants' negligence, and the company hired first a Rover and then a Jaguar during the
period when the Jensen was being repaired. It was held that the full cost of hire
should not be allowed but only the amount that it would have cost to hire a Ford
Zephyr. As Sellers LJ observed, it would not have been unreasonable for the

company to have hired those cars at a reasonable price, but the company acted unreasonably by hiring the cars from a company that was not in the habit of hiring cars, without making any real enquiry as to price, and failing to obtain a 20% discount by paying cash.[82a] The decision in *Watson Norie* was distinguished in *HL Motorworks v Alwahbi*,[83] where the claimant company was repairing a Rolls Royce for its owner and became involved in a collision when taking the car out for a trial run, damages were awarded in respect of the claimants' reimbursement of the owner's cost in hiring a substitute Rolls Royce until his own could be made available to him. Cairns LJ said:

> "It is essential to bear in mind that this was not the plaintiff company's own car ... It does not seem to me that there was imposed on them a duty of querying the amount of [the owner's] claim unless it was plainly an excessive one. ... On the face of it, the customer was entitled to have ... another Rolls Royce. ... It might have been very damaging to the relationship of the plaintiff company as car repairers and the owner as their customer if they had endeavoured to cut down the amount of his claim ... *Watson Norie v Shaw* ... was quite a different case, among other things, because there the car in question was the plaintiff company's own car."[84]

Where, as is usual, the damaged car is owned by the claimant, it has therefore been held, as in *Daily Office Cleaning Contractors v Shefford*,[85] to be reasonable to hire another prestige car, and indeed it has now been said in *Brain v Yorkshire Rider Ltd*,[86] where the cost of the car hired by the claimant was eventually held recoverable on an appeal because he had acted reasonably in hiring the particular car, that which was called the ill-reported *Watson Norie v Shaw*,[87] was not authority for refusing the cost of a prestige car where a more modest vehicle is adequate for the claimant's needs.

[82] [1967] 1 Lloyd's Rep. 515 CA.

[82a] [1967] 1 Lloyd's Rep. 515 CA at 516–517.

[83] [1977] R.T.R. 276 CA.

[84] [1977] R.T.R. 276 CA at 280G–281D; and see similarly at 282F–J, per Roskill LJ.

[85] [1977] R.T.R. 361 DC.

[86] [2007] Lloyd's Rep. I.R. 564 CC (Leeds).

[87] [1967] 1 Lloyd's Rep. 515 CA.

After para.37-016, add new paragraph:

37-016A   The underlying point is that it will usually be reasonable for a claimant to hire an equivalent car. The reason for this was explained by the High Court of Australia in *Arsalan v Rixon*.[88] The claimant will usually have suffered both physical inconvenience and a loss of the amenity value of using the luxury car, so it is reasonable for the claimant to mitigate those losses by hiring an alternative which is a substitute in terms of quality. But, as the High Court also pointed out in that case, a mere loss of use, with no adverse consequences, does not entitle the claimant to recover the value of hiring an alternative. The reasoning of the High Court explains why the hire costs are not recoverable for a substitute vehicle owned by a business that suffers no inconvenience and, being a business, has no amenity value. Thus, in *Singh v Yakubi*,[89] where the claimant's Rolls Royce having been damaged, he hired first a Bentley and then another Rolls Royce for use in a business partnership and claimed as much as £99,000 by way of hire charges, the trial judge refused the claim as need by the business partnership, which had a fleet of other cars, had not been shown. He was upheld by the Court of Appeal, which decreed that such high claims should be scrutinised carefully by the court to see whether need existed.[90] A further consequence of the reasoning of the High Court of Australia is that a claimant's expenses incurred in mitigation will not be recoverable where those expenses are unreasonable. Hence, in *Hussain v EUI Ltd*,[91] Pepperall J held that the claimant could not recover the additional cost of 18 days of hire of a Mercedes E220 car to replace a vehicle worth £7,450 which was used to earn income over that period of around £423.

[88] [2021] HCA 40; (2021) 96 ALJR 1.

[89] [2013] EWCA Civ 23; [2013] C.P. Rep. 22.

[90] [2013] EWCA Civ 23; [2013] C.P. Rep. 22 at [39].

[91] [2019] EWHC 2647 (QB); [2020] R.T.R. 7.

Replace the paragraph with:

Next come cases dealing with the period of hire for which the claimant is entitled **37-017** to claim. It was held in *Martindale v Duncan*[93] by the Court of Appeal that the claimant was not debarred by mitigation principles from claiming for the full 22 weeks that he had hired a substitute car although, being impecunious, he had delayed having repairs done pending approval of them by the defendant's and his own insurers. Similarly in *Mattocks v Mann*,[94] the Court of Appeal allowed the claimant hire charges not only during the period of repair, which itself took place a little short of a year from the damage,[95] but for some months thereafter until her repossession of the car; the delay in repossession was due to the claimant's inability to pay from her own resources and consequent need to await payment by the insurers.[96] By contrast, in *McKibbin v UK Insurance Ltd*[96a] the claimant was disentitled to four days of the claimed 37 days of hire because the insurer, who was acting for the claimant, delayed for four days in contacting the motor assessor to assess the repairs needed for the car. That assessment should have been done immediately.

[93] [1973] 1 W.L.R. 574 CA.

[94] [1993] R.T.R. 13 CA.

[95] Contrast [1993] R.T.R. 13 CA at 18L: "The plaintiff had put the car with reputable and well known repairers. She was not … to be criticised because they were overworked or had taken on too much work."

[96] Contrast *Ramwade v W.J. Emson & Co* [1987] R.T.R. 72 CA, where the basic reason for the vehicle hire charges there being held not recoverable was remoteness; it was unnecessary for Parker LJ to have invoked, at 75L to 76A, impecuniosity and *The Liesbosch* (now departed from) to support the court's conclusion. Also there was no recovery of hire charges in *Agheampong v Allied Manufacturing (London) Ltd* unreported 30 June 2008 CC Circuit Judge, where the claimant had been driving his car illegally because uninsured and, but for the damage to it, would have continued to do so throughout the period of hire for which he was claiming; it was held that the case fell squarely within the ambit of the ex turpi causa principle as applied, in a different context, in *Hewison v Meridian Shipping Services PTE Ltd* [2003] I.C.R. 766 CA (at para.40-079, below).

[96a] [2021] NIQB 27 at [115].

Car hiring on credit: the credit car hire imbroglio

After para.37-038, add new paragraph:

The negligently caused damage to a chattel can sometimes give rise to a **37-028A** contractual liability to a third party. This contractual liability may be too remote to be recovered. In *Armstead v Royal and Sun Alliance Insurance Co Ltd*,[149a] Mrs Armstead's hire car was damaged due to negligence, for which the respondent insurer was responsible. She returned the hire car at the end of the hire and it was then repaired by the hire company. The Court of Appeal held that Mrs Armstead would have been entitled to recover for the value of the loss of use suffered by the hire company on the basis that the losses of the bailee and bailor could be treated "as one".[149b] But Mrs Armstead did not seek to recover such a loss. She sought to recover the amount for which she was liable under a clause in the contract between her and the hire company, namely a higher daily rental rate for each day that the hire car was being repaired. In the lead judgment of Dingemans LJ, various reasons were given for refusing recovery to Mrs Armstead. The key reason, however, should be that the expense to Mrs Armstead arose from the "internal agreement" between the hire company and Mrs Armstead.[149c] As Singh LJ expressed the point, Mrs Armstead's loss flowed from her contractual liability rather than from the physical damage.[149d] The loss was too remote.

[149a] [2022] EWCA Civ 497; [2022] R.T.R. 23.
[149b] [2022] EWCA Civ 497; [2022] R.T.R. 23 at [52], [60].
[149c] [2022] EWCA Civ 497; [2022] R.T.R. 23 at [56], [59].
[149d] [2022] EWCA Civ 497; [2022] R.T.R. 23 at [66].

CHAPTER 38

TORTS AFFECTING GOODS: MISAPPROPRIATION

TABLE OF CONTENTS

I. **Introductory and the Demise of Detinue** 38-001

II. **Conversion** 38-006
   1. NORMAL MEASURE 38-006
     (1) In general 38-006
     (2) The particular case of conversion by infringement of
        copyright 38-010
   2. TIME AT WHICH VALUE IS TO BE TAKEN: CHANGES IN THE VALUE OF
      THE GOODS 38-011
     (1) Market fluctuations 38-014
     (2) Value increased through acts of defendant or third parties . 38-023
   3. PLACE AT WHICH VALUE IS TO BE TAKEN 38-042
   4. SOME SPECIAL CASES OF VALUE 38-043
     (1) Value of bills of exchange, promissory notes and similar
        instruments 38-043
     (2) Value of title deeds 38-047
     (3) Value of goods which the claimant must sell in any event . 38-048
     (4) Value of goods where the defendant fails to produce them . 38-049
   5. CLAIMANT WITH A LIMITED INTEREST IN THE GOODS 38-050
     (1) Defendant a stranger with no interest in the goods, but a
        jus tertii 38-051
     (2) Defendant the person holding the remaining interest in the
        goods, and no jus tertii 38-058
   6. LICENCE FEES AND CONSEQUENTIAL LOSSES . . . . 38-066□
   7. EFFECT ON DAMAGES OF REDELIVERY OF THE GOODS OR THEIR
      EQUIVALENT 38-075
     (1) Where the claimant accepts redelivery 38-075
     (2) Where the claimant refuses to accept redelivery 38-081
   8. EXEMPLARY DAMAGES . . . . 38-082□

III. **Trespass** 38-084

IV. **Wrongful Distress** 38-089

V. **Replevin** 38-090

II. Conversion

6. Licence Fees and Consequential Losses

Replace the paragraph with:

38-071   *Kuwait Airways Corp v Iraq Airways Co*,[378] affirmed by the House of Lords,[379] is a decision of enormous complexity—the judgment of the Court of Appeal runs to over 100 pages and to just short of 700 paragraphs—raising many issues of damages among which is that of recovery for lost profits. After the invasion and occupation of Kuwait by Iraq in 1990, 10 aircraft of the Kuwait airline were converted by the Iraqi airline. Four of the planes were subsequently destroyed in a bombing attack by international forces; the other six were taken out of Kuwait and detained until their eventual return to the Kuwait airline in 1992. The Court of Appeal rightly considered that a claim for loss of profits was appropriate for the destroyed aircraft, and could have succeeded[380] but for the fact that the claim failed for other reasons,[381] and that a claim in respect of the detained aircraft was also appropriate in principle but remained subject to proof.[382] While reliance was placed upon the many cases concerning destruction of ships,[383] including in particular *The Liesbosch*,[384] the *Kuwait* case properly seems to go beyond them in its preparedness to allow loss of profits.[385] However, the period for which the loss of profit would be allowable did not extend beyond the time when the destroyed four aircraft could have been replaced and when the detained six were returned. The House of Lords affirmed[386] this award for loss of profits in respect of the detained aircraft[387] without, however, any reference to the authorities on the destruction of ships.[388] A more recent, and much simpler, application of *Kuwait* came in *R. (on the application of Linse) v Chief Constable of North Wales*.[388a] In that case, it was not reasonably foreseeable to a person in the position of the defendant that a consequence of the conversion of the claimant's car was that the claimant would lose income that would have been obtained from the sale of artwork in European countries.

[378] [2002] 2 A.C. 883 CA.

[379] [2002] 2 A.C. 883 HL.

[380] See [2002] 2 A.C. 883 at CA at [627].

[381] See [2002] 2 A.C. 883 at CA at [404].

[382] See [2002] 2 A.C. 883 at CA at [652].

[383] [2002] 2 A.C. 883 at CA at [587]–[598] and [621]–[626]. These cases are at paras 37-070 to 37-076, above.

[384] [1933] A.C. 449.

[385] See, especially, [2002] 2 A.C. 883 CA at [623].

[386] [2002] 2 A.C. 883 HL.

[387] [2002] 2 A.C. 883 HL at [95] and [130], per Lord Nicholls and Lord Hoffmann, respectively.

[388] Damages for lost profits, user damages and damages to cover the cost of replacement aircraft were eventually assessed and awarded in this very long-running case: *Kuwait Airways Corp v Iraqi Airways Co* [2007] EWHC 1474 (Comm).

[388a] [2020] EWHC 3403 (Admin) at [33].

After para.38-074, add a new paragraph:

38-074A   A final, although unusual, category of consequential loss for misappropriation of chattels is for injury to feelings. There is limited authority that injury to feelings is recoverable, seemingly even if it is not too remote, for unlawful interference with chattels.[402a] Neither of the cases that have asserted this conclusion have supported it by anything other than the absence of any authority to which the court was referred. As a matter of principle this head of damages should be available, although the quantum might be expected to be small even where such injured feelings are proved. In any event compensatory damages can be aggravated by injury to feelings so the injury to feelings can be recovered where aggravated damages are available.[402b]

[402a] *Cash & Brown v Chief Constable of Lancashire* [2008] EWHC 396 (Ch); [2008] Po. L.R. 182 at [57]; *R. (on the application of Linse) v Chief Constable of North Wales* [2020] EWHC 3403 (Admin) at [38]. See also para.5-013 above.

[402b] See above at para.5-014.

8.   EXEMPLARY DAMAGES

Replace the paragraph with:

The tort of conversion also provides the only clear example of the category of **38-083** exemplary damages authorised by statute: the Reserve and Auxiliary Forces (Protection of Civil Interests) Act 1951, which by Pt I gives protection to servicemen against remedies involving interference with goods, such as execution, distress and the like, provides by s.13(2) that in any action for damages for conversion in respect of such goods the court may take into account the defendant's conduct and award exemplary damages. But Lord Kilbrandon in *Broome v Cassell & Co*[445] sought to interpret the "exemplary" in the subsection as referring to aggravated damages. Exemplary damages of £6,000 were, however, awarded in Lord Devlin's first category for arbitrary conduct by the Chief Constable in *R. (on the application of Linse) v Chief Constable of North Wales.*[445a]

[445] [1972] A.C. 1027 at 1133G.

[445a] [2020] EWHC 3403 (Admin) at [43].

CHAPTER 39

TORTS AFFECTING LAND

TABLE OF CONTENTS

I. **Damage** 39-003
   1. NORMAL MEASURE 39-003
     (1) In general 39-003
     (2) The particular case of trespass by unauthorised mining . 39-015
     (3) The particular case of nuisance . . . . 39-017■
     (4) The particular case of infringement of human rights 39-023
   2. PROSPECTIVE LOSS 39-024
   3. CONSEQUENTIAL LOSSES 39-026
     (1) Loss of profits and expenses incurred . . . . 39-026□
     (2) Losses grounding a separate cause of action 39-033
     (3) The special case of trespass by livestock 39-037
   4. CLAIMANT WITH A LIMITED INTEREST 39-039
     (1) Persons in occupation 39-040
     (2) Persons not in occupation 39-041
   5. AGGRAVATION AND MITIGATION; EXEMPLARY DAMAGES 39-045

II. **Occupation and User** 39-047
   1. NORMAL MEASURE 39-049
     (1) Where the occupation or user has come to an end 39-049
     (2) Where the occupation or user is continuing 39-057
   2. PROSPECTIVE LOSS 39-062
   3. CONSEQUENTIAL LOSSES 39-069
   4. CLAIMANT WITH A LIMITED INTEREST 39-071
   5. AGGRAVATION AND MITIGATION; EXEMPLARY DAMAGES 39-074
   6. THE STATUTORY ACTION 39-079
     (1) The statutory measure of damages 39-079
     (2) The interrelation of common law and statutory damages . 39-084
     (3) The lack of a need for exemplary damages 39-088

I. DAMAGE

1. NORMAL MEASURE

(3) The particular case of nuisance

Replace paragraph with:
Beyond physical and other damage to the land leading to pecuniary loss,[109] a **39-020**

nuisance may cause annoyance, inconvenience, discomfort, or even illness to the claimant occupier. Recovery in respect of these principally non-pecuniary losses is allowable[110] and may be regarded as part of the normal measure of damages[111] in the cases the claimant has been disturbed in the occupation of their home. In *Hunter v Canary Wharf Ltd*,[111a] Lord Hoffmann (Lord Hope agreeing) provided a rationalisation of the cases concerning damages for nuisance. Damages can be recovered if the nuisance reduces the capital value of the land or if it reduces the amenity value of the land. A possessor or occupier of land is entitled to compensation for any diminution of utility in the use of land. And separately from the normal loss of capital or amenity value, an owner or occupier is entitled to recover consequential losses, such as loss of profits. Early illustrations must be understood in light of this taxonomy of damages for nuisance. Early illustrations are afforded by *Halsey v Esso Petroleum Co*,[112] where the claimant suffered noise and smell from an oil-distributing depot, *Bone v Seale*,[113] where the claimant had to endure persistent smells emanating from a pig farm, and *Bunclark v Hertfordshire CC*,[114] where the spreading of tree roots inflicted upon the claimant cracked walls, dust and general anxiety.[115] *Bone v Seale*[116] was taken to appeal, and the Court of Appeal reduced the award for 12 years of discomfort from £6,000 to £1,000, Stephenson and Scarman LJJ considering that the award below must be too high in the light of awards for loss of the sense of smell in personal injury cases.[117] In *Ward v Cannock Chase DC*,[118] a case of negligence rather than nuisance,[119] the court held the claimant entitled to damages for the discomfort, and any attendant anxiety and distress, experienced by himself and his large family, first in living in a house which the defendant council had failed to repair and later in living in temporary, and unsatisfactory, accommodation while the house was being rebuilt.[120] In *Scutt v Lomax*[121] and *Bryant v Macklin*,[122] cases of trespass rather than nuisance, awards were made to the claimants to compensate them for their unhappiness at the loss, for a time, of the amenity of trees to look out upon.[123] The Court of Appeal's award in *Scutt* was of £3,000 but in *Bryant* the trial judge's award was increased by the Court of Appeal to £12,000 as the loss of the amenity of the trees affected the enjoyment of the claimants' home very directly and more severely than in the earlier case.[124] In *Alcoa Minerals of Jamaica Plc v Broderick*,[125] where the defendant's smelting plant affected the claimant's nearby house, the general damages of Jamaican $30,000 awarded below went unchallenged in the appeal to the Privy Council,[126] but this amount related mainly to the injury to health and, although looking very large, was the equivalent at the time of the award of under £600.[127] In *Barr v Biffa Waste Services Ltd*,[128] damages were claimed in nuisance by over 150 households on account of the smell from pre-treated waste coming from the defendant's landfill site. While the claims all failed as the defendant's use was held to be reasonable and therefore not a nuisance[129] and, this apart, while practically all of the household claims would have failed as the smell was not shown to have exceeded a permissible threshold,[130] any household which could prove that for it the threshold had been exceeded would have been held entitled to £1,000 per annum for loss of enjoyment of the property,[131] there being no diminution in value of any of the properties. Similarly, in *Anslow v Norton Aluminium Ltd*,[132] 132 households largely succeeded in claiming nuisance damages on account of odours emanating from an aluminium foundry operated by the defendant but did not succeed on account of dust, smoke and noise as there had been an insufficiency of interference. Awards were to be of modest amounts ranging from £750 to £2,000 per annum.[133] All these amounts of course need to be updated to current prices in order to appreciate the level of the awards; in particular, the ruling in the ultimate Court of Appeal hearing of *Simmons v Castle*,[134] that damages for all types of non-pecuniary loss in all civil claims should be increased by 10 per cent needs to be kept in mind.[135]

[109] At para.39-017, above.

[110] Recovery for the non-pecuniary loss should be in addition to any damages awarded for any pecuniary loss should, for instance, reinstatement of the premises to its former condition be required. To the extent that Stuart-Smith J in *Arroyo v Equion Energia Ltd* [2013] EWHC 3150 (TCC) may say to the contrary at [67] of a judgment dealing wholly with procedure and amendment of pleadings, it should not be accepted. *Arroyo* was a claim in England by farmers in Colombia for damage to their farmlands against an offshoot of a company involved in the construction of a pipeline which passed over their lands. Colombian law applied to the heads of damage, though English to their quantification, and the damages claimed in the pleadings included "moral damages" and for "loss of amenity/quality of life": see at [4]. As for moral damages, these have already come into English law, through the European Union, in the field of intellectual property, there called moral prejudice: see para.48-071 and, for an explanation of the term, para.48-075, below.

[111] See *Bone v Seale* [1975] 1 W.L.R. 797 CA at 804F, where Scarman LJ adopted this statement from the 13th edition (1972) of this work. Damage by way of profits lost or expenses incurred falls within consequential losses: see para.39-026, below.

[111a] [1997] A.C. 655 at 706; [1997] 2 W.L.R. 684 HL. See also Lord Goff at 696.

[112] [1961] 1 W.L.R. 683; see especially at 702–703.

[113] [1975] 1 W.L.R. 797 CA.

[114] (1977) 243 E.G. 381 and 455.

[115] *Bunclark* has, a good deal later in time, found itself a progeny. In *Berent v Family Mosaic Housing* [2012] EWCA Civ 961 CA, the Court of Appeal considered the level of awards for distress and inconvenience caused by tree root damage, regarding *Eiles v London Borough of Southwark* [2006] All E.R. (D) 237 as establishing the benchmark for such damages and confirming that, as was said in *Eiles*, the general damages for having to live in a house structurally damaged by tree roots should provide modest, not generous, compensation: at [39] and [40]. Following these decisions a modest amount was awarded in the further tree roots case of *Khan v Harrow Council* [2013] EWHC 2687 (TCC): see at [100].

[116] [1975] 1 W.L.R. 797 CA.

[117] [1975] 1 W.L.R. 797 CA at 803G–804A and 805A–C respectively. But Ormerod LJ was not impressed by the analogy: at 806A.

[118] [1986] Ch. 546.

[119] Facts at para.39-009, above.

[120] [1986] Ch. 546 at 579B–H. A degree of the anxiety and distress suffered was held too remote.

[121] (2000) 79 P. & C.R. D31 CA.

[122] [2005] EWCA Civ 762 CA.

[123] In a further case of trespass, *Cash and Brown v Chief Constable of Lancashire* [2008] EWHC 396 (Ch), only a modest award of £150 was made to the second claimant as the temporary trespass by the police had caused minimal injury to his feelings.

[124] See [2008] EWHC 396 (Ch) at [27]; facts of both cases at para.39-013, above. Tree roots damage on its own commands far smaller awards: see the cases earlier in this paragraph.

[125] [2002] 1 A.C. 371 PC.

[126] See [2002] 1 A.C. 371 PC at 376H; facts at para.39-019, above.

[127] See, too, *Jan de Nul (UK) v NV Royale Belge* [2000] 2 Lloyd's Rep. 700, where the court recognised that in both public nuisance and private nuisance—silt had been deposited in an estuary through dredging operations—damages might be awarded for infringement of a claimant's rights even where the effects of the infringement could not be assessed with any precision in monetary terms: at 716.

[128] [2011] 4 All E.R. 1065.

[129] [2011] 4 All E.R. 1065 at [582].

[130] [2011] 4 All E.R. 1065 at [583].

[131] [2011] 4 All E.R. 1065 at [584] as explained at [542]–[559].

[132] [2012] EWHC 2610 (QB).

¹³³ [2012] EWHC 2610 (QB) at [476]. The damages in *Dennis v Ministry of Defence* [2003] 2 E.G.L.R. 121, where the level of aircraft noise created by the airfield operated by the defendant constituted a very serious interference with the claimant's enjoyment of his property, were dealt with curiously and it is thought improperly by the trial judge who awarded an "overview" figure of £950,000 for loss of use, loss of capital value and loss of amenity, saying enigmatically that his total was not just simply an addition of the three elements (see at [88]) and adding that for the noise there would have been needed to be "not less than £50,000 to do justice to this loss of amenity if this aspect stood alone" (see at [89]). The cases in the text show that no other nuisance case has come anywhere near so high a non-pecuniary award, and the £50,000 is in stark contrast to the £10,000 for aircraft noise in the important *Farley v Skinner* [2002] 2 A.C. 732 (*Farley* is at para.34-066, above) which their Lordships there considered to be at the very top end of the scale. The judge did not consider *Farley* an apt comparison, the noise nuisance in *Dennis* "testing the limits of tolerance" ([85]), but this can hardly justify the level of his damages increase.

¹³⁴ [2013] 1 W.L.R. 1239 CA at 1243 and following.

¹³⁵ For the procedural history and reasons for this development, stemming from the package of reforms appearing in the *Jackson Report on Civil Litigation Costs*, see para.40-285, below. In the first Court of Appeal hearing of *Simmons v Castle* [2013] 1 W.L.R. 1239 CA at 1240, where the ruling was confined to torts causing suffering, inconvenience or distress, two torts were specifically mentioned of which nuisance was one: see at [20].

After para.39-022, add new paragraph:

39-022A   The consequence of Lord Hoffmann's taxonomy of normal damages for nuisance in *Hunter v Canary Wharf* is that care must be taken to avoid double recovery. Loss of capital value of the land cannot usually be accumulated with loss of the amenity value of the land because, apart from exceptional cases such as transitory nuisances, the capital value of the land will commonly reflect its amenity value. Thus, in *Raymond v Young*,^{144a} the Court of Appeal held that the trial judge had erred in accumulating damages for past loss of amenity and distress with the lost capital value of the land. Nor could the claimant recover for the lost amenity and distress under s.3(2) of the Protection from Harassment Act 1997 because that loss had already been compensated by the loss of capital value. This conclusion has also been followed in subsequent decisions concerning harassment, where the consequence of the harassment was to diminish the capital value of the land concurrently with the distress that it caused.^{144b}

^{144a} [2015] EWCA Civ 456; [2015] H.L.R. 41.

^{144b} *Manson-Smith v Arthurworrey* [2021] EWHC 2137 (QB).

3.   CONSEQUENTIAL LOSSES

(1)   Loss of profits and expenses incurred

Replace the paragraph with:

39-026   Damages for loss of user profits, as consequential loss in the alternative to damages for the value of a lost use, have over the years been allowed as damages by way of consequential loss in several cases.^{162a} In the early case of *Rust v Victoria Graving Dock Co*,¹⁶³ the claimant, suing the defendant in respect of the flooding of his building estate, recovered for the loss of rental on the houses in his possession for the period that they were being repaired and also for the delay in letting that part of the land in his possession which was vacant. In *Dodd Properties (Kent) v Canterbury City Council*,¹⁶⁴ recovery was allowed in respect of the dislocation of the business of the second claimants, who were the tenants of the land, during the execution by the first claimants, who were the owners, of the repairs necessitated by the nuisance committed by the defendants. The computation was based upon the assumption that the repairs were carried out not at or soon after the accrual of the cause of action, which they had not been, but at the much later date to which the court considered that it had been reasonable for the first claimants to defer carrying out the repairs and at which the figure of the second claimants' loss of profits through the dislocation of their business was nearly three times as great.[165]

[162a] *Bockenfield Aerodome Ltd v Clarehugh* [2021] EWHC 848 (Ch) at [122]. As to loss of use claims see para.14-027 above and para.39-047 below.

[163] (1887) 36 Ch. D. 113 CA.

[164] [1980] 1 W.L.R. 433 CA.

[165] For this timing aspect of the case see paras 9-098 and 39-018, above. Loss of profits was also awarded, but only for a limited period, for inability to use the claimant's premises for a projected business in *U.Y.B. Ltd v British Railways Board* (2001) 81 P. & C.R. DG19 CA. This appears to be a case brought in nuisance although, there being the relation of lessor and lessee between the parties, the claim was also founded in contract: see the facts at para.28-011, above.

CHAPTER 40

TORTS CAUSING PERSONAL INJURY

TABLE OF CONTENTS

I.	**Forms of Award and of Compensation**	. . . .	**40-004**
	1.	INTERIM AWARDS	40-005∎
	2.	PROVISIONAL AWARDS	40-007∎
	3.	PERIODICAL PAYMENTS AWARDS	40-009
	(1)	Introductory	40-009
	(2)	Matters in issue	40-014
II.	**Certainty of Loss**	**40-035**
	1.	CHANGES BEFORE THE DECISION OF THE COURT OF FIRST INSTANCE .	40-038
	2.	CHANGES BEFORE THE DECISION OF THE APPEAL COURT	40-047
	3.	CHANGES AFTER THE LITIGATION HAS ENDED	40-056
III.	**Heads of Damage: Function and Interrelation**	**40-057**
	1.	FUNCTION	40-058
	2.	INTERRELATION	40-060
IV.	**Loss of Earning Capacity and Related Benefits**	**40-063**□
	1.	GENERAL METHOD OF ASSESSMENT	40-067
	2.	CALCULATION OF THE MULTIPLICAND AND OF THE MULTIPLIER . . .	40-076
	(1)	Diminution in earnings: the basic factor for the multiplicand	40-076
	(2)	Earnings of different categories of person	40-080
	(3)	Adjustments for variation in annual earnings loss	40-096
	(4)	Period of years of claimant's disability: the basic factor for the multiplier	40-103
	(5)	Adjustments where life expectancy is cut down by the injury	40-106
	(6)	The appropriate discount rate for the multiplier	40-121
	(7)	Adjustments to the multiplier for contingencies	40-130
	(8)	No specific adjustments for unearned income	40-144
	(9)	No specific adjustments for inflation	40-146
	(10)	Adjustments for taxation	40-148
	3.	THE DEDUCTIBILITY OF COLLATERAL BENEFITS	40-151
	(1)	Insurance moneys	40-152
	(2)	Wages, salary, and sick pay	40-154
	(3)	Pensions	40-156
	(4)	Gratuitous payments privately conferred	40-161
	(5)	Monetary social security benefits	40-164

(6)   The present position 40-167
(7)   Social security benefits other than monetary 40-183

V. Medical and Related Expenses 40-185
  1.   EXPENSES INCLUDED 40-185
    (1)   Medical expenses 40-185
    (2)   Related expenses .... 40-196□
  2.   GENERAL METHOD OF ASSESSMENT 40-213
  3.   THE DEDUCTIBILITY OF COLLATERAL BENEFITS 40-225
    (1)   Insurance moneys 40-226
    (2)   Payments under obligation by private third parties other
           than insurers 40-227
    (3)   Payments made gratuitously by third parties 40-228
    (4)   Care provided gratuitously by relatives and others 40-229
    (5)   Monetary social security benefits 40-242
    (6)   Social security benefits other than monetary 40-250

VI. Non-Pecuniary Damage 40-257
  1.   A CONVENTIONAL AWARD 40-257
  2.   HEADS OF NON-PECUNIARY DAMAGE 40-258
    (1)   Pain and suffering 40-260
    (2)   Loss of amenities of life 40-262
    (3)   Loss of expectation of life 40-266
    (4)   Other possible heads of loss .... 40-268■
  3.   VARIOUS ASPECTS OF THE NON-PECUNIARY AWARD 40-272
    (1)   Unity of past and prospective loss 40-273
    (2)   Relevance of age 40-274
    (3)   Relevance of social and economic position 40-275
    (4)   Relevance of ability to enjoy the damages 40-276
    (5)   Relevance of manner in which injury inflicted 40-277
    (6)   Relevance of receipt of social security benefits 40-278
  4.   LEVEL OF AWARDS .... 40-279■

**VII. ENVOI: The Particular Case of Claims by Parents Arising
     Out of the Birth of their Children** 40-288
  1.   SETTING THE SCENE .... 40-288■
  2.   DEVELOPMENTS BEFORE MCFARLANE V TAYSIDE HEALTH BOARD . 40-291
    (1)   Failure to sterilise 40-292
    (2)   Failure to warn of disability 40-293
  3.   THE NEW THINKING: MCFARLANE V TAYSIDE HEALTH BOARD ... 40-294
  4.   THE NEW THINKING EXTENDED: REES V DARLINGTON MEMORIAL
     HOSPITAL NHS TRUST 40-296
    (1)   The disabled parent equated with the normal parent 40-297
    (2)   The conventional award 40-298
  5.   THE POSITION TODAY 40-302
    (1)   Extra costs of care of the disabled child: the still uncertain
           position 40-303
    (2)   Full costs of care of the disabled child: a possible
           development 40-308
  6.   ISSUES OF AVOIDED LOSS 40-310

I. FORMS OF AWARD AND OF COMPENSATION

1. INTERIM AWARDS

After "… so that there is no risk of overpayment.[26]", add:

Ultimately, this suggestion of a possible limit should not be accepted. The bet- **40-006** ter approach is to recognise that there is no such fixed limit. Provided that a conservative approach is taken, there is no reason that a court should not take into account special damages that are extremely likely to accrue between the date of the interim payment order and the date of the quantum trial.[26a] Nevertheless, the greater the degree of uncertainty, the less weight that the court should give to any such estimate, potentially with no weight at all to such amounts if there is any substantial uncertainty.

[26a] *PAL v Davison* [2021] EWHC 1108 (QB) at [26]–[29]; *Salwin v Shahed* [2022] EWHC 1440 (QB) at [44].

2. PROVISIONAL AWARDS

Replace paragraph with:

The next inroad on the final lump sum award was specifically designed to deal **40-007** with the uncertainties of a claimant's future in their injured condition. A claimant is now entitled, where it is anticipated that their condition may in the future change substantially for the worse, to claim damages on the provisional basis that their condition will remain stable but with the right to return to the court for further damages should this prove not to be the case.[27] More precisely, it is enacted by s.32A of the Senior Courts Act 1981[28] that, where there is a chance that at some time in the future a person will, as a result of their injury, develop a serious disease or suffer a serious deterioration physically or mentally,[29] the court may award them damages assessed on the assumption that they will not develop the disease or suffer the deterioration in their condition, and award further damages at a future date if they develop the disease or suffer the deterioration.[30] If an order for provisional damages is made and the condition deteriorates, but the claimant then dies before the further damages can be awarded, then the right to pursue the application will pass to the claimant's estate under s.1 of the Law Reform (Miscellaneous Provisions) Act 1934.[30a]

[27] In *Kotula v EDF Energy Networks (EDN) Plc* [2011] EWHC 1546 (QB) the claimant was awarded provisional damages allowing him to return for a further lump sum should his condition substantially worsen while retaining the right to seek, in the same eventuality, to have his periodical payments varied upwards. In *Woodward v Leeds Teaching Hospitals Trust* [2012] EWHC 2167 (QB) there was held to be a real risk of the claimant's condition deteriorating disastrously so as to allow an award of provisional damages in respect of part of her personal injury claim. In *Loughlin v Singh* [2013] EWHC 1641 (QB) an order for provisional damages was made where there was a significant risk of post-traumatic epilepsy developing: see at [98].

[28] Introduced by s.6 of the Administration of Justice Act 1982. The equivalent provision for the county court is s.51 of the County Courts Act 1984.

[29] On the interpretation of chance and serious deterioration see *Willson v Ministry of Defence* [1991] 1 All E.R. 638. What was said in *Willson* was approved by the Court of Appeal in *Curi v Colina* unreported 29 July 1998, and was applied so as to make no provisional award in *Davies v Bradshaw* [2008] EWHC 740 (QB). By contrast, *Willson* was applied so as to allow a provisional award to be made in *Kotula v EDF Energy Networks (EDN) Plc* [2011] EWHC 1586 (QB). Provisional damages are not available where the chance is not deterioration in condition but the need for care and accommodation that will no longer be free: *Adan v Securicor Custodial Services Ltd* [2005] P.I.Q.R. P6 at 79.

[30] It is enacted by s.32A(2) that provision was to be made by rules of court for enabling the court to award provisional damages. While the introduction of detailed procedural rules took some time, s.32A

applies to actions whenever commenced: Administration of Justice Act 1982 s.73(2). The procedural rules are now contained in CPR Pt 41.

[30a] *Power v Bernard Hastie & Co Ltd* [2022] EWHC 1927 (QB).

After para.40-007, add new paragraphs:

40-007A   The court should ask three questions[30b]: (i) is there a chance of a serious disease developing or future physical or mental deterioration as a result of the injury? (ii) is the disease or deterioration serious? and (iii) should the court exercise the discretion to award provisional damages? As to the first question, the chance must be more than fanciful but it can include even a very small chance of a serious condition, such as a 0.15%[30c] chance or a 0.1% chance[30d] of serious consequences. As to the second question, the seriousness is a question of fact which will depend on the circumstances of the particular case,[30e] but it does not include a circumstance where the chance is not of deterioration in condition but of a need for care and accommodation that will no longer be free.[30f] As to the third question, it must not be forgotten that the award, and the sacrifice of certainty for defendants, is exceptional and there should usually be a clear threshold which will identify the occurrence of the outcome that was the risk.[30g] Also relevant to the threshold is any potential for injustice to a claimant. For instance, the possibility of a small risk materialising might be a good reason in favour of exercising the discretion to make the award because the very small size of the chance could leave the claimant seriously undercompensated.[30h] These three questions have been answered in favour of an award in cases such as: a small chance of developing epilepsy[30i] or a chance of developing mesothelioma.[30j] The three questions have been answered against an award in cases such as: a fanciful possibility of developing a type of dementia which would not be easily separable from the injury[30k] or the possible development of pleural changes the effect of which on the claimant would be very difficult to assess.[30l]

[30b] *Willson v Ministry of Defence* [1991] 1 All E.R. 638 QBD; [1991] I.C.R. 595 at 598–599; *Mathieu v Hinds* [2022] EWHC 924 (QB); [2022] P.I.Q.R. Q4 at [290].

[30c] *Mitchell v Royal Liverpool and Broadgreen University Hospitals NHS Trust* unreported 17 July 2006 QBD (Manchester), discussed in *Mathieu v Hinds* [2022] EWHC 924 (QB); [2022] P.I.Q.R. Q4 at [292].

[30d] *Kotula v EDF Energy Networks (EPN) Plc* [2011] EWHC 1546 (QB) at [43]–[46]; *Mathieu v Hinds* [2022] EWHC 924 (QB); [2022] P.I.Q.R. Q4 at [292].

[30e] *Mathieu v Hinds* [2022] EWHC 924 (QB); [2022] P.I.Q.R. Q4 at [293].

[30f] *Adan v Securicor Custodial Services Ltd* [2004] EWHC 394 (QB); [2005] P.I.Q.R. P6 at [79].

[30g] *Willson v Ministry of Defence* [1991] 1 All E.R. 638; [1991] I.C.R. 595 QBD at 602; *Mathieu v Hinds* [2022] EWHC 924 (QB); [2022] P.I.Q.R. Q4 at [297].

[30h] *Mathieu v Hinds* [2022] EWHC 924 (QB); [2022] P.I.Q.R. Q4 at [350].

[30i] *Sarwar v Ali* [2007] EWHC 1255 (QB); [2007] LS Law Medical 375 at [10]–[11]; *Loughlin v Singh* [2013] EWHC 1641 (QB); [2013] Med. L.R. 513 at [98]; *Mathieu v Hinds* [2022] EWHC 924 (QB); [2022] P.I.Q.R. Q4 at [311].

[30j] *Patterson v Ministry of Defence* [1987] CLY 1194.

[30k] *Mathieu v Hinds* [2022] EWHC 924 (QB); [2022] P.I.Q.R. Q4 at [342], [358].

[30l] *Patterson v Ministry of Defence* [1987] CLY 1194.

40-007B   A provisional award of damages will inevitably be less than a final award because the final award includes the possibility of further and more serious conditions in the future. By contrast, the claimant who receives provisional damages can return to court if such serious conditions were to materialise.[30m] But other than this difference, the methodology for the calculation of provisional awards should not substantially differ from a full and final award. Hence, although there can be no rigid rule, a sensible methodology for the calculation of provisional awards is to calculate conservatively the full and final award and reduce that award by the amount included for the possibility of further and more serious conditions in the future. This was the approach taken in *Hamilton v NG Bailey Ltd*.[30m] The approach is undertaken conservatively, which usually means that special damages will only be included in the expected final award if they have already been incurred, or are very likely to be awarded and it is reasonably necessary to include them such as for immediately required accommodation.[30o] Conversely, when a full and final award is made after a provisional damages award then the full and final award should involve adding to the provisional damages an amount for the possibility of further and more serious conditions in the future. This was the approach, not questioned on appeal to the House of Lords,[30p] taken by the Court of Appeal in *Rothwell v Chemical and Insulating Co*,[30q] although with the qualification that this methodology might not be appropriate where the claimant had another unrelated morbid condition that was likely to reduce their expectation of life substantially. This approach does, however, present difficulty in the application of the Judicial College's *Guidelines for the Assessment of General Damages in Personal Injury Cases*, the usual operation of which is discussed below.[30r] The difficulty is that although the *Guidelines* are intended to apply to both provisional and final damages, and make reference to both, there is only one set of lower and upper brackets. Plainly, as the Deputy High Court judge observed in *Hamilton v NG Bailey Ltd*,[30s] there would be an unworkable discontinuity between the brackets unless all of the upper and lower limits were taken to refer only to provisional damages or only to full and final damages. Since the *Guidelines* are intended to include the possibility of further and more serious conditions, the best approach is to treat the amounts as concerned with full and final damages but with the recognition, rightly taken in *Hamilton v NG Bailey Ltd*,[30t] that they are guidelines only and are not rigid or fixed.

[30m] *Hamilton v NG Bailey Ltd* [2020] EWHC 2910 (QB); [2021] P.I.Q.R. P8 at [22].

[30n] [2020] EWHC 2910 (QB); [2021] P.I.Q.R. P8 at [22].

[30o] *PAL (a child) v Davison* [2021] EWHC 1108 (QB) at [26]–[27], [38]–[39].

[30p] *Rothwell v Chemical & Insulating Co Ltd* [2008] A.C. 281. See para.40-008 below.

[30q] [2006] EWCA Civ 26; [2006] I.C.R. 1458 at 1507 [174]–1508 [179].

[30r] [2006] EWCA Civ 26; [2006] I.C.R. 1458 at 1507 [174]–1508 [179].

[30s] [2020] EWHC 2910 (QB); [2021] P.I.Q.R. P8 at [33].

[30t] [2020] EWHC 2910 (QB); [2021] P.I.Q.R. P8 at [50].

IV. Loss of Earning Capacity and Related Benefits

Replace the paragraph with:

In *Pickett v British Rail Engineering*,[256] Lord Wilberforce spoke of the claim by **40-064** a living person for loss of earnings during the lost years. That prompted his concern to address the objection that nothing is of value to a person who is not alive to enjoy it. His answer to that objection was that what was lost was the "existing capability to earn well for 14 years". He had been "deprived of his ability to earn". That capability was of value to him because even if the income could not be used it could be left to dependants or causes that the claimant supported.[257] Lord Wilberforce relied in part upon the reasoning of principle of the great Australian judge, Windeyer J, in the High Court of Australia in *Skelton v Collins*.[258] In that case, Windeyer J had described the loss as a loss of "earning capacity", not a loss of earnings. This characterisation was critical in the decision of the High Court of Australia in *Amaca Pty Ltd v Latz*,[259] where the majority said that the loss "has been described as a capital asset—the capacity to earn money from the use of personal skills".[260] This also explains why in *Head v The Culver Heating Co Ltd*,[261] her Honour Judge Melissa Clarke would have been correct to hold that the claimant's earnings of more than £4 million during the lost years were irrecoverable if those earnings comprised dividends from capital that the claimant already owned at the time of death. On appeal, the Court of Appeal accepted the correctness of that underlying proposition, giving the example of a claimant who won the National Lottery after the negligent act and subsequently lived off the investments.[261a] But Bean LJ, with whom Males and Andrews LJJ agreed, considered that the claimant was the driving force within the company from which the dividends were generated and that for reasons of tax efficiency the claimant had drawn only a very modest salary which did not reflect the value of his work.

[256] [1980] A.C. 136 at 148.

[257] [1980] A.C. 136 at 149.

[258] (1966) 115 C.L.R. 94 at 129. See [1980] A.C. 136 at 150–151.

[259] [2018] HCA 22; (2018) 264 C.L.R. 505 at 533 [89].

[260] See also *CSR Ltd v Eddy* (2005) 226 C.L.R. 1 at 16 [30].

[261] [2019] EWHC 1217 (QB); [2020] P.I.Q.R. Q2.

[261a] *Head v The Culver Heating Co Ltd* [2021] EWCA Civ 34; [2021] P.I.Q.R. Q2 at [30].

V. MEDICAL AND RELATED EXPENSES

1. EXPENSES INCLUDED

(2) Related expenses

(e) Special accommodation expenses

Replace paras 40-211 and 40-212 with:

40-211   The problem after 2017, as observed in past editions of this book, was that the application of *Roberts v Johnstone* effectively denied the fundamental principle that compensation be given for reasonable, proven losses caused by wrongdoing. To that extent, the inequity of *Roberts v Johnstone* was ameliorated by the Court of Appeal in *Swift v Carpenter*.[975] In that case, the trial judge found that the additional capital cost of special accommodation was £900,000 but she considered that no award could be made because interest rates were negative. The Court of Appeal concluded, with respect correctly, that it was not bound by *Roberts v Johnstone*. That decision was authoritative guidance which was binding in the circumstances in which it was applied as the means of ensuring that compensation would be fair and reasonable. But since the circumstances had changed, the decision was no longer binding to the new circumstances of negative or low interest rates and long expected lives.[976]

[975] [2020] EWCA Civ 1295; [2021] Q.B. 339. And see also, earlier, *LP v Wye Valley NHS Trust* [2018] EWHC 3039 (QB).

[976] [2020] EWCA Civ 1295; [2021] Q.B. 339 at [80]–[81].

40-212   The solution reached by Irwin LJ, with whom Nicola Davies and Underhill LJJ agreed, in *Swift v Carpenter* was not to replace the *Roberts v Johnstone* approach with payment of a lump sum that would allow the purchase of adapted accommodation. To do so would overcompensate by providing the claimant or their estate with a residual benefit of the increased value of the reversionary interest when the modifications were no longer required, typically after the claimant's death. In the absence of a market for reversionary interests, a calculation of the amount of that overcompensation was made, and the award reduced, by using a cautious discount rate which, on expert evidence, was 5% to calculate the present value of that residual benefit at the likely date it will arise which was the date of the claimant's death.[977] But, as Underhill LJ observed, this solution was still imperfect.[978] One difficulty with it, unfavourable to claimants, was that in the absence of a market for the sale of the residual, reversionary benefit, a claimant would need to use their funds from other heads of damages to purchase the additional accommodation. Another difficulty, which would be favourable to some claimants, would arise if the discount rate were applied from the expected date of death where it is likely that the need for the adapted accommodation would cease at a time well before death. It would be appropriate in such a case for the discount rate to be calculated based upon an earlier date and therefore a shorter period.

[977] [2020] EWCA Civ 1295; [2021] Q.B. 339 at [198]–[201], [224].

[978] [2020] EWCA Civ 1295; [2021] Q.B. 339 at [225]–[229].

VI. NON-PECUNIARY DAMAGE

2. HEADS OF NON-PECUNIARY DAMAGE

(4) Other possible heads of loss

(a) Loss of congenial employment

Replace paragraph with:

In quite recent years it has become a feature of personal injury cases where the **40-269** claimant is no longer able to continue in their former employment to make a separate award under the rubric "loss of congenial employment". One can trace the idea as far back as *Hale v London Underground*,[1286] where it was already being said, at first instance, that loss of congenial employment was "now well recognised ... [as] a separate head of damage"[1287] though no authority for this was cited. Certainly, in the early years of this century this head of damage was being recognised by the Court of Appeal, both in *Willbye v Gibbons*,[1288] and in *Chase International Express Ltd v McRae*.[1289] For some time, however, courts have been very wary of these awards. Two earlier Court of Appeal decisions are instructive. In *Willbye* the first instance award of £15,000 on account of loss of congenial employment was reduced to £5,000, Kennedy LJ saying that it was "important to keep this head of damages in proportion".[1290] In *Chase* the trial judge's award of £2,000 was set aside because the Court of Appeal did not regard the claimant, who worked as a motor cycle courier, as having provided enough evidence to indicate that he enjoyed riding his motor cycle and found his work as a motor cycle courier extremely satisfying. Significantly Kennedy LJ said[1291]:

> "The award can only be made to compensate a claimant for the loss of congenial employment, as the head of damages indicates. Any award for the interference with the satisfaction which a claimant gets, for example, out of the use of a motor cycle in his ordinary

social life has to be compensated for under the head of pain, suffering and loss of amenities."

Yet why should there be a difference in the way of regarding the damages awarded between the joy of work and the joy of play? The professional motor cyclist seems to be no different from the professional violinist whose deprivation of the enjoyment of playing has often been regarded as compensable by way of loss of amenities. On occasion, such as in *Stansfield v BBC*,[1291a] the simple truth is obvious that the joy of work and the joy of play might not be separable without much artificiality. That case involved a television science presenter whose work and career was closely integrated with his family life in terms of the joy that it brought him. A single award was made of £65,000 for pain, suffering and loss of amenity. But although the courts usually regard loss of congenial employment as a different category of non-pecuniary loss from loss of amenities, there remains a need to prove a particular loss of enjoyment of work rather than simply losing a period of employment or being unable to perform the work in exactly the same way. Hence, in *Foreman v Williams*[1292] it was rightly conceded by the claimant, and accepted by the trial judge, that it is not enough that a claimant who remains in current employment cannot undertake their job in exactly the same way as they did in the past. And in *Zeromska-Smith v United Lincolnshire Hospitals NHS Trust*,[1293] where the claimant had not yet established herself in her career, and would be able to return to the career within two years, no award was made under this head.

[1286] [1993] P.I.Q.R. Q30.

[1287] [1993] P.I.Q.R. Q30 at 39.

[1288] [2003] EWCA Civ CA 372.

[1289] [2003] EWCA Civ CA 372.

[1290] [2003] EWCA Civ 372 CA at [11].

[1291] [2003] EWCA Civ 505 CA at [22].

[1291a] [2021] EWHC 2638 (QB).

[1292] [2017] EWHC 3370 (QB) at [45].

[1293] [2019] EWHC 980 (QB) at [111]–[112].

4.   Level of Awards

Replace paragraph with:

40-285   Again in 2012 a further increase was proposed by the courts and then in 2013 put into effect. In its first hearing in *Simmons v Castle*,[1350] which was a case of a minor personal injury, the Court of Appeal declared that in all personal injury claims for which judgment is given after 1 April 2013 the level of general damages for pain, suffering and loss of amenity should be increased by 10 per cent.[1351] In so deciding, the court was adopting the recommendation made in the package of reforms appearing in the *Jackson Report on Civil Litigation Costs*, to the implementation of which recommendation the judiciary was committed,[1352] with 1 April 2013 being the date on which the legislation was to bring certain of the Jackson reforms into effect. Then in a further hearing of *Simmons v Castle*,[1353] the Court of Appeal went much further and decided that the 10 per cent increase would apply to all civil claims and to all heads of non-pecuniary loss, thereby requiring the declaration put forward in the first hearing to be replaced by a declaration which of course included personal injury cases but now in a global context.[1354] The uplift applies to all cases of personal injury and it includes claims for injury to feelings as well as psychiatric harm.[1355] The Court of Appeal gave short shrift to an attempt, a decade later, to argue that the decision in *Simmons v Castle* should not have extended beyond tortious claims to claims such as a contractual claim for disrepair: a claim such as that for general damages for breach of a repairing covenant fell squarely within the purpose of the *Simmons v Castle* uplift.[1355a]

[1350] [2012] 1 W.L.R. 1239 CA; first hearing at 1240.

[1351] See [2012] 1 W.L.R. 1239 CA at [20] of the first hearing.

[1352] See [2012] 1 W.L.R. 1239 CA at [7] of the first hearing.

[1353] [2012] 1 W.L.R. 1239 CA; further hearing at 1243.

[1354] See the replacement of [20] of the first hearing by [50] of the further hearing. For more on the procedural history and reasons for this development see para.40-285, below.

[1355] *Pereira de Souza v Vinci Construction UK Ltd* [2017] EWCA Civ 879 CA at [25]–[35].

[1355a] *Khan v Mehmood* [2022] EWCA Civ 791; [2022] H.L.R. 34 at [58].

VII. ENVOI: THE PARTICULAR CASE OF CLAIMS BY PARENTS ARISING OUT OF THE BIRTH OF THEIR CHILDREN

1. SETTING THE SCENE

Replace paragraph with:

Essentially in issue are claims by the parents. The child injured pre-natally or in **40-289** the course of being born because of a defendant's negligence or other tort will have its own claim—generally under the Congenital Disabilities (Civil Liability) Act 1976 or, as decided by *Burton v Islington Health Authority* and *De Martell v Merton and Sutton Health Authority*,[1373] at common law where the injury predated the coming into force of that Act—but there are no special features of such an injury that call for particular treatment. And no claim here is available to a child where their only complaint against the defendant is that they have allowed them to be born in an injured and handicapped condition; the Court of Appeal held in *McKay v Essex Area Health Authority*[1374] that English law does not recognise an action for what has been called wrongful life. There are, however, limited circumstances where the child's claim under the Congenital Disabilities (Civil Liability) Act 1976, resembles to a limited extent a claim for wrongful life. Sections 1(1) and 1(2)(a) permit recovery by a child for disabilities, defined as damage, arising from a wrongful act which affected either parent of the child in their ability to have a normal, healthy child. The similarity with a claim for wrongful life occurs where the wrongful act arises before conception, such as negligence that causes conception resulting in a disabled child or an alleged failure to advise the mother of a child to take folic acid before conception that results in the child being born disabled. The latter was considered in the trial of the preliminary issue in *Toombes v Mitchell*.[1374a] In those cases recovery is possible even if the child would not otherwise have been born. But the similarity with a wrongful life claim is only superficial because s.1(2)(a) is really concerned with the duty to the parents—the occurrence must be one which "affected either parent"—although the action is brought by the child. This provision thus contrasts with s.1(2)(b) which has the effect that the child must prove that they would have been born without disabilities when a claim is brought for wrongful actions which affected the mother during her pregnancy or affected her or the child during birth.

[1373] [1993] Q.B. 204 CA.

[1374] [1982] Q.B. 1166 CA.

[1374a] [2020] EWHC 3506 (QB); [2021] Q.B. 622. Liability was ultimately found in *Toombes v Mitchell* [2021] EWHC 3234 (QB).

CHAPTER 41

TORTS CAUSING DEATH

TABLE OF CONTENTS

I. Claims for the Benefit of the Deceased's Dependants   41-003
    1.   THE STATUTORY ACTION   41-004
        (1) The entitled dependants   41-005
        (2) The entitlement of the dependants   41-008
    2.   THE STATUTORY MEASURE OF DAMAGES   41-017
        (1) Losses in respect of which damages are not recoverable or
             are recoverable only within limits   . . . . 41-018■
        (2) The value of the dependency   . . . . 41-028□
        (3) The non-deductibility of collateral benefits   41-109

II Claims Surviving the Death for the Benefit of the Deceased's
    Estate   41-123
    1.   PROSPECTIVE LOSSES OF THE DECEASED   41-124
        (1) Pecuniary losses   41-125
        (2) Non-pecuniary losses   41-127
    2.   ACCRUED LOSSES OF THE DECEASED   41-129
        (1) Pecuniary losses   41-130
        (2) Non-pecuniary losses   . . . . 41-131■
        (3) Collateral benefits   41-138
    3.   LOSSES FOR WHICH THE DECEASED COULD NOT HAVE SUED   . . . 41-139

I.   CLAIMS FOR THE BENEFIT OF THE DECEASED'S DEPENDANTS

2.   THE STATUTORY MEASURE OF DAMAGES

(1) Losses in respect of which damages are not recoverable or are recoverable only within limits

(a) Non-pecuniary loss, except to a spouse, civil partner or parent, for bereavement

Replace the paragraph with:

The refusal of the court in *Blake v Midland Ry*[90] to take advantage of the statu-   **41-019**
tory wording which was amply wide enough to allow recovery for non-pecuniary
loss[91] reflects the commonly encountered judicial fear that novel extensions of liability are required to be carefully contained if they are not to get out of control.
And, in the equivalent statutes which throughout the common law world followed

hard upon the heels of the English model, non-pecuniary loss was similarly excluded either again by judicial interpretation or by the express provisions of the particular statutes themselves. After over a century of such legislation, however, this fear has largely abated, and a more sympathetic attitude has developed towards the allowance of damages to at least the closest relatives in respect of their grief and of their loss of the deceased's society, care and comfort.[92] Legislation giving a limited entitlement to a limited class of relatives was eventually introduced by the Administration of Justice Act 1982.[93] Now s.1A of the Fatal Accidents Act 1976, as inserted by s.3(1) of the Administration of Justice Act 1982 and as amended by s.83(7) of the Civil Partnership Act 2004 and arts 1(1) and 2(3) of the Fatal Accidents Act 1976 (Remedial) Order 2020, provides that an action under the Act may consist of or include a claim for damages for bereavement,[94] which claim is, however, restricted to spouses, civil partners, cohabiting partners of two years or longer[95] and parents; more precisely, the claim may only be for the benefit of the deceased's wife or husband, of the deceased's civil partner or co-habiting partner, or of both parents of a legitimate, or the mother of an illegitimate, deceased minor who was never married or a civil partner or co-habiting partner.[95a] However, the omission of a category for bereavement damages for cohabitees of two years or more, unlike a dependency claim in s.1, was declared by the Court of Appeal in *Smith v Lancashire Teaching Hospitals NHS Foundation Trust*[96] to be incompatible with Art.14 in conjunction with Art.8 of the ECHR. The claimant, Ms Smith, had cohabited for more than two years with her partner in a relationship that was equivalent to marriage in every respect. In response to this decision, Parliament approved and the Secretary of State made the Fatal Accidents Act 1976 (Remedial Order) 2020 which makes bereavement damages available to claimants who cohabited with the deceased person for a period of at least two years immediately prior to the death. Where both a qualifying cohabitant and a spouse are eligible, in circumstances such as separation, the award is to be divided equally.

[90] (1852) 18 Q.B. 93.

[91] "Damages ... proportioned to the injury resulting": see para.41-017, above.

[92] In *Preston v Hunting Air Transport* [1956] 1 Q.B. 454, in an action brought on behalf of two infant children in respect of their mother's death under the then Carriage by Air Act 1932 giving effect to provisions of the Warsaw Convention analogous to those of the Fatal Accidents Act, Ormerod J boldly held that the recoverable damage was not limited to the children's purely financial loss, but, as Megaw J later pointed out in *Pevec v Brown* (1964) 108 S.J. 219, it was too late for him to do likewise under the Fatal Accidents Act.

[93] Anticipated a good deal earlier by South Australia (1940) and by Eire (1961).

[94] Section 1A(1).

[95] An addition which was the consequence of the declaration of incompatibility in *Smith v Lancashire Teaching Hospitals NHS Foundation Trust* [2017] EWCA Civ 1916; [2018] Q.B. 804.

[95a] Sections 1A(2), (2A).

[96] [2017] EWCA Civ 1916; [2018] Q.B. 804.

Replace the paragraph with:

41-020   The amount to be awarded under s.1A is specified and started, from the end of 1982, at £3,500,[97] but, the Lord Chancellor having been given the power to vary the amount for the time being specified,[98] it has been raised five times, raised for causes of action accruing on or after 1 April 1991 to £7,500,[99] on or after 1 April 2002 to £10,000,[100] on or after 1 January 2008 to £11,800,[101] on or after 1 April 2013 to £12,980[102] and on or after 1 May 2020 to £15,120.[102a] The latest increase, which was of 10%, has been made on account of the Court of Appeal's final ruling in *Sim-

mons v Castle[103] that damages for non-pecuniary loss in all types of civil claim are to be increased by 10% from 1 April 2013.[104] When the claim is on behalf of both parents the amount awarded is to be divided equally between them.[105] It is also provided that the right of a person to claim for bereavement does not survive to their estate.[106]

[97] Section 1A(3).

[98] Section 1A(5). The power is exercisable by statutory instrument subject to annulment in pursuance of a resolution of either House of Parliament.

[99] By SI 1990/2575.

[100] By SI 2002/644.

[101] By SI 2007/3489.

[102] By SI 2013/510.

[102a] By SI 2020/316.

[103] [2013] 1 W.L.R. 1239 CA; final ruling from 1243.

[104] For the procedural history and reasons for this development, stemming from the package of reforms appearing in the *Jackson Report on Civil Litigation Costs*, see para.40-285, above.

[105] Section 1A(4). The subsection provides that the division is to be made after deducting any costs not recovered from the defendant.

[106] This is achieved through the insertion of a s.1(1A) in the Law Reform (Miscellaneous Provisions) Act 1934 by s.4 of the Administration of Justice Act 1982; see too para.23-011, above.

(c)   Pecuniary loss related to the pecuniary benefit derived from the continuance of the life but not attributable to the family relationship

Replace paragraph with:

On the other hand, when a wife or son renders services to the husband or father **41-026** at less than the market rate, the amount by which the rate falls below the market rate forms a benefit arising from the relationship, the relationship being to that extent the motive of the contract.[143] And in *Feay v Barnwell*,[144] the court allowed recovery to a husband for the loss of the old-age pension which he had received in respect of his wife before her death; this was a benefit derived from the relationship.[145] Somewhat similar is *Malyon v Plummer*.[146] In that case the claimant widow and her deceased husband were the sole directors of a private company carrying on a one-man business, the husband owning all of the shares except one owned by the claimant. The claimant received a substantial salary from the company for part-time, essentially casual work in connection with the business, and the whole of the combined salaries of the claimant and her husband was paid into the husband's bank account from which he paid out moneys for the family expenditure, either by cheques or by cash to the claimant. The claimant claimed that the total amount which she would have received from the husband's banking account for the benefit of herself and her children had the deceased survived represented the amount of the dependency. The defendant contended that so much of this total amount as consisted of the claimant's salary should be excluded. The defendant relied first on *Burgess*, arguing that the claimant's salary should be excluded on the ground that it was not attributable to the husband and wife relationship. The court rejected this argument. Pearson LJ said:

> "It would be inappropriate and unconvincing to say that the wife has lost her salary by being deprived of her co-director or managing-director or travelling salesman. The fact is that she has lost her husband, who was the family bread-winner."[147]

The interposition of the company did not prevent the court from looking at the matter realistically and assessing the wife's true loss. Similarly, in *Welsh Ambulance Services NHS Trust v Williams*,[148] where the deceased had brought his wife and three children into his very successful business he had done so because they were members of his family. It was said that any argument based on *Burgess* was bound to fail.[149] Finally, in *Witham v Steve Hill Ltd*,[150] the claimant was able to recover for loss suffered when she was required to give up her full-time career to replace her deceased husband to provide care for two foster children. The relationship was not merely incidental to the benefit provided by the husband because they would not have decided to foster the children without their relationship. His services were provided because of their relationship. Nor did it matter that the foster children had no dependency claim. The foster children may have suffered loss but this did not preclude the wife also from suffering loss due to the pecuniary benefit of a commercial rate of care that she derived from the husband's free care for their foster children. An appeal was allowed from this decision but not due to any error of principle. Instead, the appeal was allowed because new evidence was led on appeal to show that the foster children were subsequently removed from the claimant's care.[150a] As a matter of principle, Nicola Davies J held, the claimant had lost "the benefit of the service which her husband provided in caring for the children". The decision was not a business decision and hence the continued receipt of foster care payments was irrelevant.[150b] And it was open to value the services at a commercial rate, which was a fact-specific issue, on the basis that it is natural that the claimant would turn to commercial services to achieve the care that had been lost.[150c]

[143] This is how Devlin J in *Burgess v Florence Nightingale Hospital* [1955] 1 Q.B. 349 explained the two Irish cases of *Condon v Gt Southern & Western Ry* (1865) 16 Ir. C.L. Rep. 415 and *Hull v Gt Northern Ry of Ireland* (1890) 26 L. R. Ir. 289.

[144] [1938] 1 All E.R. 31.

[145] So explained on this point in *Burgess v Florence Nightingale Hospital* [1955] 1 Q.B. 349 at 360.

[146] [1964] 1 Q.B. 330 CA.

[147] [1964] 1 Q.B. 330 CA at 345–346.

[148] [2008] EWCA Civ 81 CA; facts at para.41-082, below.

[149] [2008] EWCA Civ 81 CA at [52] and [53]. The Court of Appeal so said while refusing to allow the defendant to put the argument as it had been raised at too late a stage in the proceedings. See, too, *Davies v Whiteways Cyder Co* [1975] Q.B. 262 (facts at footnote to para.41-038, below) where the benefit of moneys given to a wife and son being free of estate duty was held to be a benefit arising from the relationship of husband and wife and of father and son. This surely is incontrovertible.

[150] [2020] EWHC 299 (QB).

[150a] *Steve Hill Ltd v Witham* [2021] EWCA Civ 1312; [2022] P.I.Q.R. P2 at [21]–[34].

[150b] [2021] EWCA Civ 1312; [2022] P.I.Q.R. P2 at [43], [48].

[150c] [2021] EWCA Civ 1312; [2022] P.I.Q.R. P2 at [53]–[54].

(4) Loss of earnings

Replace the paragraph with:

41-027   The general rule is that loss of earnings on the part of the dependant cannot form part of the dependency.[151] As we have seen above, recovery is restricted to damages for the loss of the pecuniary benefit arising from the relationship which would be derived from the continuance of the life. The reason that a loss of earnings claim will usually not fall within that principle is because, as explained by Diplock LJ in *Malyon v Plummer*,[152] a dependant's salary will continue after the death of the deceased. In other words:

"… it would not be a benefit arising out of the relationship of husband and wife which she would lose on his death."[153]

In *Rupasinghe v West Hertfordshire Hospitals NHS Trust*,[154] Jay J considered whether a doctor, who on the death of her husband had decided to return to Sri Lanka where her children would be cared for by family members, could recover for her loss of earnings as a result of having to find less remunerative employment. It was held that the doctor could not recover. Once the separate head of claim for gratuitous care by the doctor for her husband had been valued "there [was] nothing left".[155] It was not a case where the doctor gave up work in order to provide the gratuitous services,[156] nor was it a case where the doctor sought to use her earnings as a proxy measure for the value of those services. Similarly, in *Chouza v Martins*,[156a] the claimant was unable to recover for the lost income of two adult children who gave up their jobs to preserve a company run by the deceased whose income had been earned by the deceased. To have allowed recovery would, in effect, provide double recovery of the lost income of the deceased. In contrast, in *Witham v Steve Hill Ltd*,[157] where the claimant was able to recover for loss suffered when she was required to give up her full-time employment to replace her husband as a carer, that loss was assessed at the commercial replacement rate of a carer rather than her lost earnings from employment.

[151] *Rupasinghe v West Hertfordshire Hospitals NHS Trust* [2016] EWHC 2848 (QB) at [25].

[152] [1964] 1 Q.B. 330 CA.

[153] [1964] 1 Q.B. 330 CA at 351.

[154] [2016] EWHC 2848 (QB).

[155] [2016] EWHC 2848 (QB) at [52].

[156] These services were being provided by her family.

[156a] [2021] EWHC 1669 (QB) at [73].

[157] [2020] EWHC 299 (QB).

(2)   The value of the dependency

(d)   Types of recovery in particular relationships

(i)   Death of husbands, wives, civil partners, with or without children   The title **41-078**
of this sub-paragraph should be changed to "Deaths of husbands, wives, civil partners, with or without children".

Husband, wife or civil partner with children: assessment of value of dependency

After para.41-082, add two new paragraphs:
The three decisions above were considered at first instance and by the Court of **41-082A**
Appeal in *Paramount Shopfitting Co Ltd v Rix*.[373a] After working in the defendant's employment from which the deceased contracted mesothelioma, the deceased spent 46 years building a successful construction, joinery and manufacture business. Although his widow was a shareholder and director, the business success was the result of his skill and effort. Cavanagh J held that it was not possible to distinguish *O'Loughlin* and *Williams* as cases where, in substance, the income of the widow was earned by the deceased rather than from an income generating asset. Although in *Rix* the business was conducted through a company in which the widow was a

director and shareholder, in a passage cited later with approval by the Court of Appeal in a different case,[373b] as well as on appeal from his decision,[373c] Cavanagh J said that the "reality"[373d] was that the income from a director's salary and dividends had been earned by the deceased's skill and effort. As Nicola Davies LJ said in the lead judgment on appeal, "there was no identifiable element of the profits which was not touched by the management of Mr Rix".[373e] By contrast, however, rental income from commercial properties was properly characterised as an income generating asset.[373f]

[373a] [2021] EWCA Civ 1172. At first instance: *Rix v Paramount Shopfitting Co Ltd* [2020] EWHC 2398 (QB).

[373b] *Head v Culver Heating Co Ltd* [2021] EWCA Civ 34; [2021] P.I.Q.R. Q2 at [27].

[373c] [2021] EWCA Civ 1172 at [68].

[373d] See, e.g., the "practical reality" applied in *Malyon v Plummer* [1964] 1 Q.B. 330; [1963] 2. W.L.R. 1213; *Ward v Newalls Insulation Co Ltd* [1998] 1 W.L.R. 1722; [1998] 2 All E.R. 690 CA.

[373e] [2021] EWCA Civ 1172 at [60].

[373f] [2021] EWCA Civ 1172 at [68].

41-082B   A second question, and the heart of the appeal in *Paramount Shopfitting Co Ltd*, is how the value of the claimant's labour should be quantified. Cavanagh J quantified the value on the basis of the widow's lost income because the evidence of that loss was clearer than the cost to the business of employing a replacement for the claimant.[373g] That quantification was upheld by the Court of Appeal, where Nicola Davies LJ observed that it was irrelevant that the business had thrived since the death because the valuation of the dependency needed to be conducted at the date of death.[373h] It is not clear whether the appellant had argued that evidence that the business thrived after death could cast doubt upon the factual assertion that the value of the business was wholly attributable to the deceased. This would not be to value the business at a date after death; it would be solely as evidence to assess how integral the deceased was to the business *before* death. Further, in some cases, the latter method, namely the cost of employing a replacement, will plainly be more appropriate. One example is where there is evidence that the claimant is easily able to be replaced by a person of equal skill and ability and the difference in cost to the business of the replacement can be readily measured. Conversely, another example, given by Underhill LJ in *Paramount Shopfitting Co Ltd*,[373i] is a case like *O'Loughlin* where an estimate of the increase in income from the special skills of the deceased would have been highly speculative.

[373g] [2020] EWHC 2398 (QB); [2021] 2 All E.R. 844 at [103].

[373h] [2021] EWCA Civ 1172; [2020] 4 W.L.R. 123 at [62].

[373i] [2021] EWCA Civ 1172; [2020] 4 W.L.R. 123 at [77].

(e)   Loss of gratuitous services and associated claims

(ii)   Loss of a parent's special care

Replace the paragraph with:

41-105   This head of loss is now firmly established for child claimants and features in nearly every case involving them. It is commonly referred to as the special qualitative factor in *Regan v Williamson*,[519] or even just the *Regan v Williamson* element.[520] It is most profusely to be found in the cases starting with *Spittle v Bunney*,[521] from 1988 and continuing, where the claim was on behalf of the child or children of the family only. It was subject, wrongly, to an exception in *Watson v Wilmott*,[522] because the adoptive mother was now providing the care and in *Stanley v Saddique*,[523] rightly, because of the indifferent quality of the mother. But it was properly confined to minor children and refused for adult children in *Chouza v Martins*,[523a] relying upon this paragraph from the 21st edition.

[519] See *Cresswell v Eaton* [1991] 1 W.L.R. 1113 at 1122H–1123A, per Simon Brown J.

[520] See *Hayden v Hayden* [1992] 1 W.L.R. 986 CA at 990G, per McCowan LJ.

[521] [1988] 1 W.L.R. 847 CA.

[522] [1991] 1 Q.B. 140.

[523] [1992] Q.B. 1 CA.

[523a] [2021] EWHC 1669 (QB) at [88].

(iii)   Non-pecuniary loss arising from arranging alternative provision of services

Replace the paragraph with:

Beyond this additional care that leads to greater pecuniary benefit, however, it **41-108** is difficult to justify a claim for loss of intangible benefits of having services performed by the deceased. One such intangible loss is the inconvenience that arises from having to spend time to find someone to do that which the deceased spouse or deceased partner would have done voluntarily. In *Mosson v Spousal (London) Ltd*,[532] Garnham J said that frustration and inconvenience is the sort of claim that bereavement damages were meant to cover. Again in *Magill v Panel Systems (DB Ltd)*,[533] Judge Gosnell, sitting as a Deputy High Court judge, said that the nature of this type of claim for intangible benefits is the irrecoverable "perceived advantages of having a service performed by a member of the family rather than a commercial provider". Another characterisation of the loss has been said to be the loss of the time itself, irrespective of any inconvenience. In *Grant v The Secretary of State for Transport*,[534] Martin Chamberlain QC, sitting as a Deputy High Court judge, declined to follow the decision in *Mosson*. In his view, the loss was simply the time spent by the wife to make arrangements for a painter, plumber or decorator to perform work that her husband would have done which has a pecuniary value.[535] So too, in *Blake v Mad Max Ltd*[536] a Deputy High Court judge allowed £2,500 for the intangible benefits of a spouse including the loss of household services such as making beds, for which no pecuniary expense would be incurred, and the inconvenience due to time taken to organise the provision of other replacement services. But if the lost intangible benefits do not involve pecuniary loss, and if it cannot be recovered as frustration or inconvenience then it is hard to see how the mere lost "time" is real loss in the sense of some adverse consequence experienced by the plaintiff. The cases continue to award this head of damages, sometimes understandably giving up on any search for principle and relying only upon the increasing weight of authority.[536a] But it has rightly been refused to be extended any further to a claim for services that were thought necessary to maintain "family reputation or honour or name" in the preservation of a company run by the deceased.[536b]

[532] [2016] EWHC 1429 (QB) at [75]. See also *Lugay v Hammersmith and Fulham LBC* [2017] EWHC 1823 (QB) at [76].

[533] [2017] EWHC 1517 (QB) at [66].

[534] [2017] EWHC 1663 (QB).

[535] [2017] EWHC 1663 (QB) at [108].

[536] [2018] EWHC 2134 (QB) at [42].

[536a] Another example is *Jackman v Harold Firth & Son Ltd* [2021] EWHC 1461 (QB) at [26].

[536b] *Chouza v Martins* [2021] EWHC 1669 (QB) at [74].

II   Claims Surviving the Death for the Benefit of the Deceased's Estate

2.   Accrued Losses of the Deceased

(2)   Non-pecuniary losses

(a)   Pain and suffering

Replace paragraph with:

41-131   The decisions have made it clear that damages in an action by the estate may be awarded in respect of the pain and suffering borne by the deceased up to the time of death, although such damages will generally be small as the death so often follows quickly upon the injury and, even where it does not, may be preceded by a period of unconsciousness relieving the victim of any physical pain. In *Bishop v Cunard White Star*,[634] where the circumstances of death and the length of time that the deceased had survived the injury were unknown, it was held that no award should be made "in the absence of clear evidence of reasonably prolonged suffering".[635] Similarly, in *Hicks v Chief Constable of the South Yorkshire Police*,[636] claims by the personal representatives of three young spectators, crushed to death at the stadium in the Hillsborough disaster, for pain and suffering before their deaths were rejected at all levels of adjudication in the absence of clear evidence. In the Court of Appeal Parker LJ said that in his view:

> "... when unconsciousness and death occur in such a short period after the injury which causes death no damages are recoverable. The last few moments of mental agony and pain are in reality part of the death itself."[637]

For rather different reasons, the Court of Appeal in *Kadir v Mistry*,[638] agreed with the trial judge's refusal to award any damages for pain and suffering. Diagnosis of cancer in the deceased had been negligently delayed. Had there been no delay the deceased would have suffered the same symptoms, although somewhat later and in the interim would have been subjected to painful treatment to deal with the cancer. Laws LJ, giving the only reasoned judgment, stressed that there were no special rules for assessing pain and suffering in estate claims; the criterion is, as always, to put the now deceased in the same position as they would have been if the negligence had no occurred.[639] The position now is that some award is almost always made, although in cases of near-instantaneous death the award will not usually be more than several hundred pounds. For instance, in *Chouza v Martins*,[639a] the sum of £500 was awarded for "a maximum of 5 seconds of mental anguish and fear followed by almost instantaneous death".

[634] [1950] P. 240.

[635] [1950] P. 240 at 247.

[636] [1992] 1 All E.R. 690 CA.

[637] [1992] 1 All E.R. 690 CA at 694b. The House of Lords' dismissal of the claimants' appeal is at [1992] 2 All E.R. 65.

[638] [2014] EWCA Civ 1177.

[639] [2014] EWCA Civ 1177 at [11]–[12].

[639a] [2021] EWHC 1669 (QB); [2021] P.I.Q.R. Q4 at [20].

CHAPTER 42

ASSAULT AND FALSE IMPRISONMENT

TABLE OF CONTENTS

I. **Assault** 42-001
   1. HEADS OF DAMAGE 42-001
   2. AGGRAVATION AND MITIGATION 42-002
     (1) Aggravation of damage ....42-002□
     (2) Mitigation of damage 42-009
   3. EXEMPLARY DAMAGES 42-012

II. **False Imprisonment** 42-013
   1. DAMAGES AS OF RIGHT 42-013
   2. HEADS OF DAMAGE ....42-014■
   3. REMOTENESS OF DAMAGE: CONTINUATION OF THE IMPRISONMENT BY
     JUDICIAL ORDER 42-028
   4. AGGRAVATION AND MITIGATION 42-029
   5. EXEMPLARY DAMAGES 42-034

I. ASSAULT

2. AGGRAVATION AND MITIGATION

(1) Aggravation of damage

Replace the paragraph with:

In *Richardson v Howie*,[25] the Court of Appeal heralded a change by holding that **42-004** in cases of assault it is in general inappropriate to award aggravated damages on top of, and in addition to, damages for injured feelings. The assault there took place in this fashion. While a male and female couple described as being in a volatile relationship were holidaying far from home in the Caribbean, the man made a frenzied and spiteful attack on the woman with a glass bottle causing permanent scarring injuries. The trial judge awarded £10,000, which amount included £5,000 by way of aggravated damages. On appeal the defendant contended that any damages for the injury to the claimant's feelings should be encompassed within the award for general damages and that it was wrong in principle to make an award for aggravated damages. The Court of Appeal agreed. Given the substantial overlap between injury to feelings and aggravated damages, subsequent cases have avoided the risk of double recovery by making a single award for injury to feelings (as general damages) and aggravated damages. Hence, in *B v Cager*[25a] Johnson J awarded a combined award for injury to feelings and aggravated damages of

£25,000 for sexual assaults that occurred two to three times per week on average over a six to seven year period.

[25] [2005] P.I.Q.R. Q3 CA at 48.

[25a] [2021] EWHC 540 (QB).

II.   FALSE IMPRISONMENT

2.   HEADS OF DAMAGE

Replace paragraph with:

42-021   The main group of cases tends to involve moderate level consequences with periods of false imprisonment of a month or two with serious effects on the detainee. Here the awards tend to range from £15,000 to £30,000. In *R. (on the application of KG) v Secretary of State for the Home Department*,[108] £17,500 plus £2,000 aggravated damages was awarded for 29 days of wrongful detention which followed 24 hours of lawful detention. As for the unlawful detention for 61 days of an unaccompanied asylum-seeking young person, this led in *AS v Secretary of State for the Home Department*[109] to an award of £23,000, before aggravated damages were brought in.[110] And in *R. (Abulbakr) v Secretary of State for the Home Department*[110a] an unlawful detention for 40 days with some exacerbating features due to COVID-19 restrictions and a period of absence of internet access, an award of £17,500 was again made.

[108] [2018] EWHC 3665 (Admin).

[109] [2015] EWHC 1331 (QB).

[110] For which, see para.42-031, below.

[110a] [2022] EWHC 1183 (Admin).

CHAPTER 43

STATUTORY TORTS: DISCRIMINATION AND HARASSMENT

TABLE OF CONTENTS

I. **Discrimination** 43-002
   1. HEADS OF DAMAGE 43-004
     (1) Non-pecuniary loss ....43-005□
     (2) Pecuniary loss 43-008
     (3) Interest 43-009
   2. AGGRAVATED DAMAGES 43-012
   3. EXEMPLARY DAMAGES 43-016

II. **Harassment** 43-017
   1. HEADS OF DAMAGE 43-018
     (1) Non-pecuniary loss ....43-018■
     (2) Pecuniary loss 43-021
   2. AGGRAVATED DAMAGES 43-022
   3. EXEMPLARY DAMAGES 43-023

I. DISCRIMINATION

1. HEADS OF DAMAGE

(1) Non-pecuniary loss

Replace the paragraph with:

The three bands, as updated, have stood the test of time and the courts continue **43-007** to pay attention to them. For purposes of comparison, however, the most useful cases are likely to be those that postdate the relevant guidelines. One of the earliest examples of the application of the 2017 guidelines was *Durrant v Chief Constable of Avon & Somerset Constabulary*.[18] In that case, the police engaged in racially discriminatory conduct, by subconscious bias, when they had: (i) focused upon arresting the appellant; (ii) handcuffed her hands behind her back causing her to be thrown around in the back of the police van and (unknown to her) laughed at by the police; and (iii) delayed for a significant time in allowing the appellant to go to the toilet at the police station, causing the appellant to urinate on the floor of the holding cell in front of a group of male officers. Applying the *Vento* guidelines,[19] the case was found to fall within the lower part of the middle band. An award of £14,000 was made taking into account all of the circumstances, and following the 2017 Presidential Guidance because, even though the claim was brought before the 2017 Presidential Guidance, this was thought to be the simplest way to take inflation into account. One reason why the award was not higher in the middle band or in the upper band must have been the nature of the discrimination as a single incident. In contrast, the decision of the Court of Appeal in Northern Ireland in *Breslin v Loughrey*,[19a] upheld an award at the very top level of £30,000, applying the *Vento* scale prior to the 2017 guidelines, where the discrimination involved a series of incidents, including in the home of the vulnerable appellant.

[18] [2017] EWCA Civ 1808.

[19] *Vento v Chief Constable of West Yorkshire Police (No.2)* [2003] I.C.R. 318 CA.

[19a] [2020] NICA 39.

II. HARASSMENT

1. HEADS OF DAMAGE

(1) Non-pecuniary loss

Replace paragraph with:

43-019   As to the amounts awarded, variation abounds. This is inevitable as in the cases where damages have been in issue the harassment has come in many forms. While *Majorowski v Guy's and St Thomas's NHS Trust*[61] was not concerned with damages for harassment,[62] it did elicit the comment from Lord Nicholls that "awards of damages for anxiety under the 1997 Act will normally be modest".[63] In *S&D Property Investments Ltd v Nisbet*,[64] also, it was said that awards should probably be modest[65]; an award of £7,000 was made for harassment in pursuance of an unpaid debt. As the conduct gets more serious there can be, exceptionally, higher awards. Three examples can be given. The first, *Maisto v Kyrgiannakis*,[66] was a case of persistent harassment by a 32-year-old man following and contacting a young woman of 21 years wherever she went, both at home and abroad, over a prolonged period, so that she found it difficult to carry on her life of study. The judge awarded £15,000. In the second, *Glenn v Kline*,[67] an award of £25,000 was made where the claimant was subjected to a prolonged attack over several months including threatening his livelihood and professional standing by making unfounded allegations of child abuse and spreading them within his community and in national newspapers. The award for harassment was made for the period in which the claim for libel was statute-barred. In the third, *WXY v Gewanter*,[68] the harassment consisted of the posting on the internet of information about the private life of the claimant causing her much distress and, no doubt, anxiety. The award, before aggravation, was just short of £20,000.[69] This sum in *WXY* is also explained by the fact that the claim was primarily for the misuse of private information with which the harassment was said to be part and parcel, not amounting to a separate claim.[70] And in *Hills v Tabe*[71] a persistent campaign of harassment leading to the claimant's depression and suicidal ideations led to an award of £10,000, which was all the claimant sought but which accorded with the trial judge's view that the amount should be in the middle Vento band (albeit at the bottom end of the band). There is also an increased tendency to combine awards for harassment and defamation. In *Suttle v Walker*,[72] *Triad Group Plc v Makar*,[73] and *Blackledge v Persons Unknown*[74] awards of £40,000 (to the claimant in the first case) and £60,000 and £65,000 (to the claimants in the second case) and £70,000 (in the third case) in general damages, all of which appear vastly beyond the usual range, are explicable because the judges, Nicklin J (in the former) and Saini J (in the latter two), included within the awards amounts for injury to reputation or "vindication of reputation" (as part of a defamation claim) as well as amounts for the seriousness of the harassment. It seems in these cases that the harassment claim is doing little more than adding an additional amount to the injury to feelings head of the claim for defamation. It would be more transparent and better for future judicial development of the law if the awards for defamation and harassment were separated so that any increased amount for injury to feelings could be justified. In *Davies v Carter*,[75] for example, the damages were awarded separately for the claims for libel and harassment although the damages for the libel of £10,000 were made excluding the injury to feelings, presumably on the basis that the damages award for harassment of £25,000 extended to all the consequential injury to feelings from the libel and any additional injury to feelings.

[61] [2007] 1 A.C. 224.

[62] See para.43-017, above.

[63] [2007] 1 A.C. 224 at [29].

[64] [2009] EWHC 1726 (Ch).

[65] [2009] EWHC 1726 (Ch) at [75] and [76].

[66] [2012] EWHC 4084 (QB).

[67] [2021] EWHC 468 (QB).

[68] [2013] EWHC 589 (QB); [2013] E.T.M.R. 33.

[69] Aggravated damages increased it by £5,000.

[70] For the primary aspect of the claim see para.47-011, below.

[71] [2022] EWHC 316 (QB).

[72] [2019] EWHC 396 (QB).

[73] [2020] EWHC 306 (QB).

[74] [2021] EWHC 1994 (QB).

[75] [2021] EWHC 3021 (QB).

Replace the paragraph with:

In harassment cases there are no express guidelines on amounts to award along **43-020** the lines of *Chief Constable of West Yorkshire Police v Vento (No.2)*,[77] with its three bands or brackets of figures for compensation for injured feelings in discrimination claims.[78] The courts have turned to the *Vento* guidelines for assistance by analogy, which may lead to awards going beyond the modest. This indeed was what happened in *Maisto v Kyrgiannakis*,[79] *Suttle v Walker*[80] and *Triad Group Plc v Makar*,[81] which we have just looked at.[82] In the former case, the judge was taken to *Vento* and his award of £15,000 was based on his considering the case before him to be a serious one though not in the highest of the *Vento* brackets. Yet it may be questioned whether the precise application of *Vento*, where the figures now go up to £45,000 with middle-of-the-road cases going up to £27,000, is consistent with damages being modest. There is much to be said for the view expressed by Nicol J in *S&D Property Investments Ltd v Nisbet*.[83] He thought it would be wrong simply to apply the *Vento* bands to harassment cases since compensation for discrimination necessarily involves an award for the humiliation of being treated differently on impermissible grounds, which is not a necessary feature of a harassment claim.[84] Nevertheless, the apparent automatic application of the *Vento* bands continues with the award in *Glenn v Kline*[84a] of £25,000 described as falling at the cusp of the upper *Vento* band.

77 [2003] I.C.R. 318 CA.

78 For which see para.43-006, above.

79 [2012] EWHC 4084 (QB).

80 [2019] EWHC 396 (QB).

81 [2020] EWHC 306 (QB).

82 In the preceding paragraph.

83 [2009] EWHC 1726 (Ch). See the case in the preceding paragraph.

84 [2009] EWHC 1726 (Ch) at [77]. The award in *Saxton v Bayliss* unreported 31 January 2014 Central London County Court, for harassment of an old lady by her very unpleasant neighbours causing her profound distress, the neighbours mounting a prolonged and vicious campaign to get her out of her house and thereby eliminate her right of way over their property, was £25,000. It would have been even higher in the absence of an additional exemplary award of £10,000.

84a [2021] EWHC 468 (QB) at [56].

After para.40-020, add new paragraph:

43-020A   In exceptional cases, it is necessary to avoid double recovery for damages for harassment. Just as we have seen in relation to nuisance,[84b] it would be a double recovery if a claimant were entitled to recover damages for injured feelings consequential upon harassment as non-pecuniary loss, where the claimant is already entitled to damages for a diminution of the capital value of land caused by the same harassment. In *Manson-Smith v Arthurworrey*,[84c] the Deputy Judge held that the defendant's harassment was so prolonged and so significant that it had reduced the capital value of the claimant's property by £210,000. But it would have been double recovery to award the claimant a further sum of £30,000 for distress and anxiety or £13,125 for loss of amenity.

84b Above at paras 39-020 to 39-022A.

84c [2021] EWHC 2137 (QB).

Chapter 44

MALICIOUS INSTITUTION OF LEGAL PROCEEDINGS

TABLE OF CONTENTS

1. Types of Actionable Damage 44-002
2. Particular Torts 44-004
   (1) Malicious criminal prosecutions .... 44-004□
   (2) Malicious bankruptcy and company liquidation
       proceedings 44-009
3. Aggravation and Mitigation 44-013
4. Exemplary Damages .... 44-015□

2. Particular Torts

(1) Malicious criminal prosecutions

Replace the paragraph with:

For appropriate awards in respect of all this non-pecuniary loss there was little **44-005** guidance until the decision of the Court of Appeal in *Thompson v Commissioner of Police of the Metropolis*.[21] For the basic damages, these being described as the damages before any element of aggravation[22] and of course before any pecuniary loss, Lord Woolf MR, delivering the judgment of the court, said:

> "The figure should start at about £2,000 and for prosecution continuing for as long as two years ... about £10,000 could be appropriate. If a malicious prosecution results in a conviction which is only set aside on an appeal this will justify a larger award to reflect the longer period during which the claimant has been in peril and has been caused distress."[23]

The Court of Appeal in *Thompson* also said that the jury, a normal feature of malicious prosecution claims,[24] should be informed of the approximate starting figure and the approximate ceiling figure for the basic award.[25] It was recognised that these guideline figures, which presumably should apply where the malicious prosecution is other than by the police, would need adjustment in the future for inflation.[26] Inflation, however, would not suffice to account for the award of £20,000 in *Clifford v The Chief Constable of the Hertfordshire Constabulary*,[27] where the claimant had been wrongly charged with child pornography offences, leading to his arrest and unsuccessful prosecution, but the award was for the resulting psychological damage[28] as well as for the immense distress suffered,[29] £10,000 for each. Also to be taken into account, in addition to inflation, is the Court of Appeal ruling in *Simmons v Castle*[30] that damages for non-pecuniary loss in all types of civil claim are to be increased by 10%.[31] The implicit increase in the *Thompson* range is also evident in the very substantial award made in *Rees v Commissioner of Police of the Metropolis*.[32] Two claimants were wrongfully imprisoned for 682 days (less an initial period that was held to be lawful) as a consequence of malicious prosecution and misfeasance in public office for which the defendant Commissioner was responsible. They were each awarded damages for distress of £27,000 and aggravated damages of £18,000. Separately, and in an award that is more aptly compared with those for false imprisonment,[33] they were awarded £60,000 for loss of liberty. These awards must be at the very top the range, if not beyond it. Curiously, one claimant appealed from the decision, arguing that the award of £155,000 was manifestly inadequate. The Court of Appeal upheld the award, with Davis LJ in the lead judgment observing that one of the flaws in the appellant's heavy reliance upon *AXD v Home Office*,[33a] was that the award of £80,000 in that case was a global award. Another was the obvious error in creating a range from a single case. A third was the different facts in *AXD*.

[21] [1998] Q.B. 498 CA.

[22] [1998] Q.B. 498 CA at 514G.

[23] [1998] Q.B. 498 CA at 515H.

[24] See para.53-006, below.

[25] [1998] Q.B. 498 CA at 515C.

[26] [1998] Q.B. 498 CA at 517E.

[27] [2011] EWHC 815 (QB).

[28] [2011] EWHC 815 (QB) at [58]–[61].

[29] [2011] EWHC 815 (QB) at [62] and [63].

[30] [2013] 1 W.L.R. 1239 CA.

[31] For the procedural history and reasons for this development, stemming from the package of reforms appearing in the *Jackson Report on Civil Litigation Costs*, see para.40-285, below.

[32] [2019] EWHC 2339 (QB). An appeal is pending before the Court of Appeal, to be heard in December 2020.

[33] See paras 42-020 to 42-023.

[33a] [2016] EWHC 1617 (QB). See para.42-023 above.

4. EXEMPLARY DAMAGES

To the end of the paragraph, add:

44-016   And, as the Court of Appeal has subsequently observed, the suggestion that £50,000 should be regarded as the absolute maximum should not be taken as establishing an arbitrary maximum. In the case where that observation was made, Davis LJ said in the leading judgment that although £50,000, adjusted for inflation, was the modern equivalent of £91,500, it was not excessive to make an award of exemplary damages of £150,000 in an exceptional case of malice involving three claimants.[81] Nevertheless, in the absence of evidence of a greater profit being made, this amount must be close to the top of the potential range.

[81] *Rees v Commissioner of Police of the Metropolis* [2021] EWCA Civ 49 at [53]–[56].

CHAPTER 46

DEFAMATION

TABLE OF CONTENTS

I. **Slanders Actionable Only on Proof of Special Damage** 46-003
  1. MEANING OF SPECIAL DAMAGE 46-003
    (1) What is excluded 46-004
    (2) What is included 46-006
  2. REMOTENESS OF SPECIAL DAMAGE 46-011
    (1) Refusal by third party to, or to continue to, deal or associ-
        ate with the claimant 46-012
    (2) Repetition by third party of the slander 46-016
  3. PLEADING AND PROOF OF SPECIAL DAMAGE 46-021
  4. ADDITIONAL GENERAL DAMAGES 46-023

II **Slanders Actionable Per Se and Libel** 46-024
  1. LEVEL OF AWARDS . . . . .46-024■
  2. HEADS OF DAMAGE 46-031
    (1) Injury to reputation 46-032
    (2) Injury to feelings 46-033
    (3) The references to vindication and the quantification . . . .46-035■
    (4) Injury to health 46-039
    (5) Pecuniary loss 46-040
  3. REMOTENESS OF DAMAGE 46-041
  4. PLEADING AND PROOF OF DAMAGE 46-042
  5. AGGRAVATION AND MITIGATION: RELEVANCE OF THE CONDUCT,
     CHARACTER AND CIRCUMSTANCES OF THE PARTIES 46-045
    (1) The defendant's conduct: malice 46-046
    (2) The claimant's character: bad reputation 46-062
    (3) Other circumstances . . . . .46-070□
    (4) Mitigation: offers to make amends . . . . .46-075□
    (5) Mitigation: actions for damages against others 46-078
  6. EXEMPLARY DAMAGES 46-080

II SLANDERS ACTIONABLE PER SE AND LIBEL

1. LEVEL OF AWARDS

Replace paragraph with:
The tide, however, of cautious judicial awards in trials without a jury remains **46-030**
strong, especially with the desire for consistency with awards for personal injury.

In *Umeyor v Nwakamma*,[179] a libellous publication was published to an unincorporated association of 50–60 members dedicated to the interests and welfare of the Mbaise community of which the claimant was a member. The allegation was of forgery but the claimant proved no financial loss and rumours had already abounded. The claimant was awarded only £2,000 in general damages for injury to reputation and feelings despite the acknowledgement by Jay J[180] that "attribution of forgery to the Claimant's [sic] is not something which may lightly be disregarded". In *Summerfield Browne Ltd v Waymouth*,[180a] and *Aslani v Sobierajska*,[180b] where online comments that respectively described the claimant solicitor as "a total waste of money" and "another scam solicitor" and the claimant surgeon as dishonest, grossly negligent and likely to seriously injure or kill his patients, the awards of general damages were respectively £25,000 and £40,000. And in *Dudley v Phillips*,[180c] allegations of professional incompetency, dishonesty and fraud to several hundred people including those professionally and personally related to the claim would have attracted an award of £30,000 to £40,000 but for the claimant's choice to limit the claim to £10,000.

[179] [2015] EWHC 2980 (QB).

[180] At [92].

[180a] [2021] EWHC 85 (QB).

[180b] [2021] EWHC 2127 (QB).

[180c] [2022] EWHC 930 (QB). And see also *Hills v Tabe* [2022] EWHC 316 (QB).

2. HEADS OF DAMAGE

(3) The references to vindication and the quantification

Replace paragraph with:

46-036 So long as this "vindication" is confined to the amount necessary to eliminate these future consequences to the claimant, enabling the claimant to justify themselves, the award will be true compensation for loss. This head is not independent of future "injury to reputation". Indeed, the more substantial an award of vindication, the less likely it should be that there will be future injury to reputation. Hence, it is not uncommon for the most significant element of a damages award for defamation to be for the element of vindication.[204a] As we saw in Ch.17, the growth of this head of damages described as being "to vindicate" reputation has, ironically, occurred at the same time as the decline, and ultimate rejection in *R. (on the application of Lumba) v Secretary of State for the Home Department*,[205] of the concept of "vindicatory damages". The label "vindication" in these cases can be understood as a shorthand reference for a need to ameliorate the prospect of, and respond to future adverse consequences if the libel "emerges from its lurking place at some future date".[206] In an electronic age involving prolific means of dissemination of information this can be of great importance especially in the absence of a public and widespread apology from the defendant. With the focus of the award upon amelioration of any future adverse consequences, either pecuniary or non-pecuniary, the size of the award under this head will therefore depend on factors such as: (i) the seriousness of the allegation, its likely "sticking power", and the "grapevine effect"; (ii) future publicity including media reports of the trial and judgment; and (iii) any apology made by the defendant and the extent of the publicity or dissemination of the apology.[207]

204a *Hijazi v Yaxley-Lennon* [2021] EWHC 2008 (QB) at [163].

205 [2012] 1 A.C. 245.

206 *Broome v Cassell & Co Ltd* [1972] A.C. 1027 at 1071, per Lord Hailsham.

207 *Dhir v Saddler* [2017] EWHC 3155 (QB); [2018] 4 W.L.R. 1 at [103], [108], [110].

Replace paragraph with:

Vindication can also be awarded primarily to reduce future financial loss. An **46-037** example where the single award seemed to be primarily focused upon vindication to reduce future financial losses is *Unite the Union v Freitas*,[207a] where an award of £50,000 was made principally for vindication for attacks on the reputation of the union where reputation was essential for its ability to attract and to retain members.[207b] Unfortunately, an approach which is not transparent, but which is becoming increasingly common, is for an award to be made which instinctively synthesises *existing* distress as well as the prospect of *future* distress and *future* pecuniary consequences.[208] For instance, in *Oyston v Reed*,[209] the defendant posted material concerning the chairman of Blackpool Football Club on a website which was read by many fans of the football club. His conduct aggravated the distress caused by the posting and the trial judge, Langstaff J, referred to all the factors including a reference to "vindication" and awarded a single sum of £30,000. Matters are further confused by the fact that there is another possible, and legitimate, basis for damages that is sometimes concealed in this language of "vindication", which is that the damages are awarded to deter or to punish. "Vindication" is sometimes used in the sense of "vindictive". As one of the finest Australian defamation lawyers, McHugh J, when sitting on the High Court of Australia, remarked, the anger of the claimant is placated only when they know that the defendant has been punished for the wrong. In this sense the award of damages is "punitive or vindictive".[210] Similarly, Lord Hoffmann remarked in *Gleaner Co Ltd v Abrahams*,[211] defamation actions, unlike those for personal injury, "often serve not only as compensation but also as an effective and necessary deterrent".

207a [2022] EWHC 666 (QB); [2022] I.C.R. D7.

207b [2022] EWHC 666 (QB); [2022] I.C.R. D7 at [14], [19].

208 *Cairns v Modi* [2013] 1 W.L.R. 1015 at [38]; *Woodward v Grice* [2017] EWHC 1292 (QB).

209 [2016] EWHC 1067 (QB).

210 *Carson v John Fairfax & Sons Ltd* (1993) 178 C.L.R. 44 at 105, 107.

211 [2004] 1 A.C. 628 PC at [53].

Replace paragraph with:

The best approach would be for the language of vindication to be abandoned **46-038** altogether in this area. In cases where additional damages are given for the purpose of ensuring that members of the public, in future, are aware that the claimant's reputation should be intact then this can be described as compensatory damages for the protection of future reputation. In cases where additional damages are given to deter or punish then this can be described as exemplary damages. However, at present, many cases treat "vindication" (as mislabelled, and really describing future pecuniary or non-pecuniary losses) as lying at the heart of the damages awarded.[212] Thus a libel on the internet, suggesting that the learning courses for adult students run by the claimant company were a scam, led in *Metropolitan International Schools Ltd v Designtechnica Corp*[213] to a £50,000 award of damages which was primarily for "vindication",[214] there being no present loss of business and no injury to feelings as the claimant was a company. By contrast, the allegation in a later case that the claimant was a "serial scammer" by a newspaper with a circulation in the UK of 500,000 people, mainly people of the claimant's Muslim religion, was held to entitle the claimant, a natural person, to an award of £75,000.[214a] Vindication was also central to the description of the award in *Al-Amoudi v Kifle*,[215] since the claimant, an international businessman of huge wealth who had suffered a most appalling libel suggesting links to murder, terrorism and even the killing of his daughter, was not interested in the finances of a probably unenforceable award but in showing to the world that his reputation was secure.[216] The award came to £175,000. So too in *Farrall v Kordowski*,[217] where defamatory statements about a young solicitor claimant had been published anonymously on the defendant's website, Lloyd Jones J considered that, there being neither retraction nor apology, the vindicatory purpose of damages was much in play.[218] The language of vindication can again be seen, and potentially causing added difficulty, when Tugendhat J said in *ZAM v CFW*,[219] in the course of awarding damages, including aggravated damages, of £140,000 that "the primary object of libel actions is to vindicate a claimant's reputation, not to recover damages".[220] Again, in *Harrath v Stand for Peace Ltd*,[221] Sir David Eady awarded damages of £140,000 for libel including that the claimant was a "terrorist" in a publication with a readership in the hundreds or low thousands. The award was made to ensure that there was "no doubt in the mind of a reasonable onlooker of the Claimant's entitlement to vindication".[222] The words preceding the reference to "vindication" are important. They clarify why this is not an illegitimate application of the impermissible vindicatory damages but is, instead, an unfortunately described head of damages to cover future consequences from a libel which can be widespread and lasting. In *Dhir v Saddler*[223] and *Monir v Wood*,[224] where vindication featured strongly, and in each of which there were a number of matters of mitigation, Nickin J awarded £35,000 and £40,000 respectively for words spoken by the defendant at a church meeting, saying that the claimant had threatened to "slit my throat" and for a tweet that described the claimant as a "suspended child grooming taxi driver" from an account with limited followers where very limited recipients other than his neighbour and people in the local area would have understood that the tweet referred to the claimant. In contrast, in *Suttle v Walker*,[225] where the award of damages for the head of injury to reputation took into account the extent of the grapevine or percolation effect, Nicklin J concluded that there did not need to be much, if any, "uplift in this figure for the purposes of vindication".[226] And in *Glenn v Kline*,[226a] where an award of £65,000 before aggravated damages (of an additional £10,000) was made for unfounded allegations including child abuse, the purpose of vindication again featured as a significant reason, although the reasoning had also focused upon the distress caused and the extent of the harm to the claimant in the future including by accessible tweets, archived webpages and emails. And in *Gale v Scannella*,[226b] the claimant local football coach was substantially disappointed in his claim for £50,000 for four tweets about him sent to 16 football organisations, which led to "modest to moderate" local circulation alleging a "darker secret" for why the claimant had been "kicked out" of a football club and questioning whether he was fit to be trusted around young children. Collins Rice J held that the appropriate award for vindication and injury to feelings was £15,000 which was reduced to £8,000 after taking into account the claimant's conviction for domestic violence and the Offer of Amends procedure adopted by the defendant.[226c] Another instance where a smaller award is justified is where the defamatory remarks are likely to be viewed by many as aggressive ad feminam or ad hominem attacks, as is common in the course of vituperative Twitter exchanges. For instance, in *Riley v Murray*[226d] the defendant responded to a provocative political tweet by the claimant saying that the claimant was "as dangerous as she is stupid. Nobody should engage with her. Ever". The defamatory tweet caused numerous abusive and threatening messages to the claimant, although some were difficult to disentangle from other parts of the exchange. The total award made by Nicklin J was £10,000. By contrast, defamatory statements with the extraordinary power and future effect of allegations that a person is a terrorist have usually led to awards of general damages "well into six figures".[226e] The allegation of association with terrorists was sufficient for an award of £60,000 in *Sahota v Middlesex Broadcasting Corp Ltd*.[226f]

[212] Since judge trials began to supplant jury trials in defamation cases, we have much more information on vindication from the judges' judgments; with jury awards we are rather left in the dark. See the full discussion of this supplanting at para.17-008, above.

[213] [2010] EWHC 2411 (QB).

[214] See [2010] EWHC 2411 (QB) at [35].

[214a] *Mirza v Farooqui* [2021] EWHC 532 (QB).

[215] [2011] EWHC 2037 (QB).

[216] [2011] EWHC 2037 (QB) at [45].

[217] [2011] EWHC 2140 (QB).

[218] Vindication had also been the object of the claimant in *Hays Plc v Hartley* [2010] EWHC 1068 (QB) (see at [44]), but the claim failed. See also *Harrath v Stand for Peace Ltd* [2017] EWHC 653 (QB) at [23].

[219] [2013] EWHC 662 (QB).

[220] [2013] EWHC 662 (QB) at [72]. The vexed question of how far, if at all, a judge sitting alone should reduce an award on account of the vindicatory effect of the reasoned judgment is given full consideration in Ch.17 on vindicatory damages.

[221] [2017] EWHC 653 (QB).

[222] [2017] EWHC 653 (QB) at [23].

[223] [2017] EWHC 3155 (QB); [2018] 4 W.L.R 1.

[224] [2018] EWHC 3525 (QB).

[225] [2019] EWHC 396 (QB).

[226] [2019] EWHC 396 (QB) at [59].

[226a] [2021] EWHC 468 (QB) at [95].

[226b] [2021] EWHC 1225 (QB).

[226c] Compare *Monroe v Hopkins* [2017] EWHC 433 (QB); [2017] 4 W.L.R. 68 at [80] ($24,000 for tweets alleging vandalisation of a war memorial with wide circulation) and *Mirza v Ali* [2021] EWHC 1494 (QB) (£17,500 and £35,000 for allegations of dishonesty on a Facebook page for the claimant's community, one of which—relating to the latter award—was viewed over 1,000 times).

[226d] [2021] EWHC 3437 (QB); [2022] E.M.L.R. 8.

[226e] *Sahota v Middlesex Broadcasting Corp Ltd* [2021] EWHC 3363 (QB) at [42].

[226f] [2021] EWHC 3363 (QB) at [40].

After para.46-038, add new paragraph:

The quantification of damages under the head of vindication thus focuses on **46-038A** avoiding future consequences to the claimant other than the way in which their life will be led (injury to reputation generally) and injury to present feelings and future feelings to the extent that reputation is not vindicated. An example of serious present injury to feelings, but with large potential future effect, described as an award to vindicate, is *Hijazi v Yaxley-Lennon*,[226g] which required payment of £100,000 in damages to compensate for injury to feelings and to vindicate the claimant, a 15-

year-old vulnerable Syrian schoolboy at the time of the defamatory remarks. The defamatory remarks were published widely and persisted at trial, in circumstances where, as was predictable, the claimant became the target of abuse which led to him and his family having to leave their home and him having to abandon his education.[226h]

[226g] [2021] EWHC 2008 (QB).

[226h] [2021] EWHC 2008 (QB) at [162]–[163].

5. AGGRAVATION AND MITIGATION: RELEVANCE OF THE CONDUCT, CHARACTER AND CIRCUMSTANCES OF THE PARTIES

(3) Other circumstances

(a) Social and financial circumstances of the parties

Replace the paragraph with:

46-070   Little consideration has been given in the cases to the effect on damages of the social and financial position of the parties. In principle, social and financial position should be relevant to damages only in so far as it shows the extent of the injury to the claimant's reputation.[391] Thus the word of a defendant in a high position socially is likely to be of more weight and thus more injurious to the claimant than that of a person of humbler status: conversely, the higher the claimant is in the social scheme the more the claimant is likely to be harmed. Relatedly, the role that a person plays in society is likely to affect the impact of a defamatory statement on a person's reputation, for example, where the claimant is a child protection campaigner, and defamatory statements are made to the effect that the claimant has protected child abusers.[392] Similarly, in *Gilham v MGN Ltd*,[392a] a significant factor in the size of the £85,000 award, prior to consideration of mitigation, was the damage to the claimant's professional reputation as a teacher and a children's rugby coach by allegations concerning an incident in which the claimant was described as grabbing a seven-year-old boy "by the scruff of his neck" in an article published both nationally and locally.

[391]   In *Barron v Vines* [2016] EWHC 1226 (QB) at [21], it was said that the impact of a libel on a person's reputation can be affected by their role in society.

[392]   See at [2016] EWHC 1226 at [21], referring to *Rantzen v Mirror Group Newspapers* [1994] Q.B. 670 CA.

[392a]   [2020] EWHC 2217 (QB) at [59].

(b) Extent of the publication

Replace the paragraph with:

46-071   As for the extent of the publication of the defamatory statement as a factor operating in aggravation or mitigation of the damages, it was held in *Gathercole v Miall*,[393] that, in the words of Pollock CB:

> "… in order to show the extent of the mischief that may have been done to the plaintiff by a libel in a newspaper you have a right to give evidence of any place where any copy of that libel has appeared for the purpose of showing the extent of the circulation."[394]

This evidence was allowed for this purpose although, because the claimant could not prove that the defendant publisher had industriously circulated the newspaper, the same evidence was inadmissible to aggravate the damages on the ground of malice.[395] Such evidence, however, is only admissible after it is established that the defendant is liable for the total dissemination of the statement: the rule in *Ward v Weeks*[396] may prevent the defendant from being liable for any re-publication at all. In *KC v MGN Ltd*,[397] where the claimant was falsely accused in the defendant's national newspaper of raping a young girl, the Court of Appeal reduced the trial judge's starting figure[398] of £150,000 to £100,000 because too much attention had been paid by him to the large circulation and readership of the newspaper when it had been possible to keep the claimant anonymous throughout, the newspaper not having named him.[399] And in *Fentiman v Marsh*[399a] and *Ghannouchi v Middle East Online Ltd*[399b] awards of £45,000 were made for, respectively, blog posts involving allegations of cyber-attacks and a newspaper article alleging terrorism but only read, respectively, by around 500 people and several hundred people.

[393] (1846) 15 M. & W. 319.

[394] (1846) 15 M. & W. 319 at 331; see, too, *Plunkett v Cobbett* (1804) 5 Esp. 136. Detailed evidence of the numbers of the circulation of a newspaper well-known to the jury is not admissible: *Whittaker v Scarborough Post Newspaper Co* [1896] 2 Q.B. 148 CA, overruling *Parnell v Walter* (1890) 24 Q.B.D. 441 and, in effect, *Rumney v Walter* (1891) 61 L.J.Q.B. 149.

[395] See (1846) 15 M. & W. 319 at 326, per Parke B.

[396] (1830) 7 Bing. 211; see para.46-016, above.

[397] [2013] 1 W.L.R. 1015 CA.

[398] It was subject to a discount on account of the offer of amends procedure: see the case at para.46-076, below.

[399] See [2013] 1 W.L.R. 1015 CA at [47] and [48].

[399a] [2019] EWHC 2099 (QB). See also *Woodward v Grice* [2017] EWHC 1292 where £18,000 was awarded for postings seen by hundreds rather than thousands of people.

[399b] [2020] EWHC 1992 (QB).

(4) Mitigation: offers to make amends

Replace the paragraph with:

Sections 2 to 4 of the Defamation Act 1996 introduced what was effectively a **46-075** statutory defence by way of an offer to make amends, being in place of the offer of amends provisions of the repealed s.4 of the Defamation Act 1952, the rather complicated requirements of which had caused it to be hardly ever used. By contrast, the new more extensive and streamlined defence of offering to make amends has become popular. By s.2(4) of the 1996 Act an offer to make amends is an offer to make and publish both a correction of the statement and an apology, and to pay to the aggrieved party such compensation as may be agreed or determined. It is specifically provided by s.4(5) that an offer of amends which is not accepted may be relied on in mitigation of damages. As to the giving of compensation, s.3(5) provides that, where the parties are not in agreement on the amount to be paid, the court must determine the amount, applying the same principles of damages as apply in defamation proceedings. Determining the amount to be paid will necessarily involve a discount on what otherwise would have constituted the damages and thus lead effectively to mitigation. In this regard, the assessment of damages proceeds in two stages: (i) identifying the award that would have been made without reference to the offer by consideration of a hypothetical trial and nothing to mitigate the damage, and (ii) discounting that figure to take into account the offer of amends.[417]

[417] *Barron v Collins* [2017] EWHC 162 (QB), citing *KC v MGN* [2012] EWCA Civ 1382; [2013] 1 W.L.R. 1015. See also *Gilham v MGN Ltd* [2020] EWHC 2217 (QB) at [26]–[27].

CHAPTER 47

PRIVACY, CONFIDENCE AND PRIVATE INFORMATION

TABLE OF CONTENTS
1.   HEADS OF DAMAGE   47-002
    (1)   Non-pecuniary loss   .... 47-003■
    (2)   "Right to control information" and licence fee damages   . 47-012■
    (3)   Pecuniary loss   47-016
2.   AGGRAVATION AND MITIGATION   47-018
3.   EXEMPLARY DAMAGES   47-021
4.   ACCOUNT AND DISGORGEMENT OF PROFITS   47-024

1.   HEADS OF DAMAGE

(1)   Non-pecuniary loss

After para.47-010, add a new paragraph:

Unfortunately, in *Sicri v Associated Newspapers Ltd*,[45a] Warby J held that non-pecuniary losses arising from damage to reputation could not be recovered in an action for misuse of private information. In that case, the defendant published an article reporting on the arrest of Mr Sicri in connection with the Manchester Arena terrorist attack. Mr Sicri was later released without charge. Warby J relied upon two arguments. First, authorities concerning the reluctance to extend prior restraint principles beyond defamation to other torts which might not justify such restraint.[45b] But there is a clear difference between restraining defamatory conduct and restraining conduct which involves a misuse of private information. There is no difference between non-pecuniary losses that flow from either. Secondly, Warby J considered that a major obstacle to allowing losses flowing from damage to reputation would arise if a terrorist subject, whose identity was wrongfully disclosed in breach of their privacy rights, was entitled to recover for damages flowing from loss of reputation even if the suspect were later charged and rightly convicted.[45c] But the answer to this concern is surely that any non-pecuniary losses flowing from loss of reputation in such a circumstance would be too remote from the misuse of private information.[45d] It is also difficult, in light of the awards discussed immediately below, to justify the award of £50,000 in general damages to Mr Sicri if those general damages did not include the likely consequences to Mr Sicri consequent upon his damage to reputation. On the other hand, this principle is readily apparent in the award in *Hayden v Duckworth*[45e] of only £1,500 for the claimant's distress from an abusive tweet that misused her private information. In *Bloomberg LP v ZXC*,[45f] Lords Hamblen and Stephens, giving the judgment of the Supreme Court, observed that the trial judge had denied the availability of any element of purely

47-010A

reputational damages and later observed that they had "reservations about the extent to which quantification of damages for the tort of misuse of private information should be affected by the approach adopted in cases of defamation".

[45a] [2020] EWHC 3541 (QB); [2021] 4 W.L.R. 9 at [163]. Applied in *Hayden v Duckworth* [2020] EWHC 1033 (QB) at [28].

[45b] [2020] EWHC 3541 (QB); [2021] 4 W.L.R. 9 at [157].

[45c] [2020] EWHC 3541 (QB); [2021] 4 W.L.R. 9 at [156].

[45d] See above para.8-044.

[45e] [2020] EWHC 1033 (QB) at [28]–[34].

[45f] [2022] UKSC 5; [2022] 2 W.L.R. 424 at [33], [79].

After "… level of damages awarded of £25,000.[60]", add:

47-011   An appeal to the Supreme Court was dismissed with no further comment on the level of damages other than to express reservations about the extent to which quantification of damages should be affected by the approach in defamation.[60a]

[60a] *Bloomberg LP v ZXC* [2022] UKSC 5; [2022] 2 W.L.R. 424 at [79].

(2)   "Right to control information" and licence fee damages

Replace paragraph with:

47-015   The characterisation of the right to control information as a type of "licence fee damages" was at issue in *Lloyd v Google LLC*.[66] The nature of damages for an infringement of private information rights arose in that case in the context of an application for permission to serve proceedings on Google LLC, a foreign corporation. The proceedings alleged a breach by Google of s.4(4) of the Data Protection Act 1998 by secretly tracking, collating, using and selling data concerning the internet activity of Apple iPhone users. The claimant sued on his own behalf and on behalf of a class of other English residents for damage suffered under s.13 of the Act. The case therefore concerned the scope of damages under domestically implemented European law since the Data Protection Act implemented the Data Protection Directive.[67] At first instance, Warby J refused leave to serve out, giving as one reason that the statutory requirement for "damage" suffered in the jurisdiction had not been satisfied. The real issue should have been whether s.13 of the Act requires loss in the conventional sense and does not include licence fee damages.[68] If s.13 were to be understood in such a narrow way it would be enough to say that, following *Murray v Express Newspapers*, the claim should fail because it was not alleged that any financial loss had been suffered or that distress had resulted.[69] As Warby J observed, mere "loss of control" over personal data establishes an infringement but does not establish loss or damage in the conventional sense; some people are "quite happy" to have their personal information collected in order to receive advertising or marketing.[70] The Court of Appeal allowed an appeal. The Chancellor, Sir Geoffrey Vos, with whom Davis LJ and Sharp P agreed, held that a claimant could recover damages for loss of control of their data under s.13 without the need to prove any mental distress.[71] The Supreme Court overturned the decision of the Court of Appeal and restored the decision of Warby J.[71a] In reasons with which the other members of the Supreme Court agreed, Lord Leggatt held that compensation under s.13 required proof of material damage or distress. In other words, loss in a conventional sense. It is noteworthy that Mr Lloyd's representative claim did not seek compensation for misuse of private information. Lord Leggatt observed that such a claim would have been available and he explained *Gulati v MGN* as a decision that should be understood as awarding licence fee damages.[71b] One of the members of the Supreme Court who agreed with Lord Leggatt was Lady Arden, who had delivered the reasons for decision in *Gulati v MGN*. Like the information in *Gulati v MGN*, a person's "browser generated information" is an asset with real economic value, the taking of which should require licence fee damages to rectify or reverse the wrongful act.

[66] [2019] EWCA Civ 1599; [2020] Q.B. 747.

[67] At the relevant time, 95/46/EC of the European Parliament and of the Council of 24 October 1995 on the protection of individuals with regard to the processing of personal data and on the free movement of such data.

[68] *Murray v Express Newspapers* [2007] EWHC 1908 (Ch); [2007] EMLR 22.

[69] [2018] EWHC 2599 (QB); [2019] 1 W.L.R. 1265 at [3].

[70] [2018] EWHC 2599 (QB); [2019] 1 W.L.R. 1265 at [58]–[59], [74].

[71] *Lloyd v Google LLC* [2019] EWCA Civ 1599; [2020] Q.B. 747 at [88].

[71a] *Lloyd v Google LLC* [2021] UKSC 50; [2021] 3 W.L.R. 1268.

[71b] *Lloyd v Google LLC* [2021] UKSC 50; [2021] 3 W.L.R. 1268 at [141].

Chapter 48

ECONOMIC TORTS AND INTELLECTUAL PROPERTY WRONGS

Table of Contents

I.   Inducement of Breach of Contract   . . . . .48-004□

IA.   Intimidation   . . . . 48-008A□

II   Injurious Falsehood   48-009
      1.   Injurious Falsehoods Other than Passing Off   48-009
      (1)   Pecuniary loss   48-011
      (2)   Non-pecuniary loss   48-012
      2.   Passing Off   48-016

III. Conspiracy   48-019
      1.   Pecuniary Loss   48-020
      2.   Non-Pecuniary Loss   48-024

IV   Breach, or Misuse, of Confidential Information   48-026

V.   Infringement of Rights in Intellectual Property   48-034
      1.   The Relevance of the European Union Directive   48-037
      2.   The Present English Law, The Directive Apart   48-041
      (1)   Infringement of patents   48-042
      (2)   Infringement of trade marks   48-049
      (3)   Infringement of copyright and design right   . . . . .48-054■
      3.   The Impact of the European Directive   48-071
      (1)   Range of application   48-072
      (2)   Application by the courts   48-078

I.   Inducement of Breach of Contract

Replace the paragraph with:

Yet although the damages are at large, the only loss which the court is prepared **48-008**
to infer is a pecuniary loss: indeed it seems that even clear proof of a non-
pecuniary loss by way of injury to feelings or to reputation is not sufficient to
ground the action.[31] Thus McCardie J in *Pratt v British Medical Association*[32]
regarded pecuniary loss as necessary to the cause of action, while Nevile J in
Goldsoll v Goldman[33] spoke of the damage which the court could infer as damage
inflicted "in the ordinary course of business". The primary protection afforded by
the tort ushered in by *Lumley v Gye*[34] is against business losses: business people
cannot complain of injured feelings alone. If, however, pecuniary loss is shown,
then *Pratt v British Medical Association*[35] is authority for allowing, in addition,

damages for non-pecuniary loss by way of injured feelings. The defendants, a medical association and members of the association, instituted and pursued a system of professional ostracism and boycott against the claimants, who were medical people, by means of threats and widely extended coercive action, and in the claimants' claim for damages the defendants conceded that they had inflicted pecuniary loss. In these circumstances McCardie J said:

> "The plaintiffs are not limited to actual pecuniary damages suffered by them. The court or jury, once actual financial loss be proved, may award a sum appropriate to the whole circumstances of the tortious wrong inflicted ... I cannot ignore the deliberate and relentless vigour with which the defendants sought to achieve the infliction of complete ruin. I must regard not merely the pecuniary loss sustained by the plaintiffs but the long period for which they respectively suffered humiliation and menace."[36]

The allowable non-pecuniary loss is confined to injury to feelings. In the light of the decisions in *Joyce v Sengupta*[37] and *Lonrho v Fayed (No.5)*,[38] dealing with injurious falsehood and conspiracy respectively, it can fairly be said that the courts have now adopted the firm stance that damages for injury to reputation are not in general to be recoverable outside the tort of defamation.[39] Sometimes, however, the non-pecuniary loss for injury to feelings is awarded as aggravated damages for the manner in which the tort is committed. Hence, in *Antuzis v DJ Houghton Catching Services Ltd*[39a] the claimant chicken catchers who were underpaid their statutory entitlement to wages were awarded a further 20% of their pecuniary losses for the inducement of those breaches of contract by the second and third defendants which involved exploitation, manipulation and abuse causing mental suffering.

[31] It is thought that the damages awarded in *Falconer v ASLEF and NUR* [1986] I.R.L.R. 331 for the inconvenience to the claimant and to the claimant's availability to his business (brief facts five footnotes back) have reference to pecuniary loss.

[32] [1919] 1 K.B. 244 at 281.

[33] [1914] 2 Ch. 603 at 615.

[34] (1853) 2 E. & B. 216.

[35] [1919] 1 K.B. 244.

[36] [1919] 1 K.B. 244 at 281–282. Contrast *British Industrial Plastics v Ferguson* [1938] 4 All E.R. 504 CA at 514, per MacKinnon LJ: "It may well be that the claim ... is not limited to the special damage which he can prove." McCardie J's remarks, however, should not be interpreted, after *Rookes v Barnard* [1964] A.C. 1129, as allowing the awarding of exemplary damages unless the defendant has sought to profit from the tort: see Ch.13, above, especially at para.13-021.

[37] [1993] 1 All E.R. 897 CA.

[38] [1993] 1 W.L.R. 1489 CA.

[39] See below at para.48-014 for injurious falsehood and para.48-025 for conspiracy. The exceptions are false imprisonment (para.42-029, above) and malicious prosecution (para.44-002, above).

[39a] [2021] EWHC 971 (QB).

After para.48-008, insert a new section:

IA. Intimidation

48-008A The tort of intimidation involves a threat by a defendant of an unlawful act which induces a person to act in a way that causes loss to themselves (two-party intimidation) or another person (three-party intimidation). The tort of three-party intimidation was conclusively recognised in *Rookes v Barnard*.[39b] In that case a union, and various defendants, informed an employer corporation that if the claimant was not dismissed then other employees would, in breach of contract, go on strike. The claimant was dismissed in breach of contract. The House of Lords ordered a new trial on damages, including exemplary damages.

The losses that can be recovered for the tort of intimidation include loss of profits, **48-008B** although there are very few such cases. One example is *Morgan v Fry*.[39c] The claimant had been dismissed by his employers from his job as a lockkeeper as a result of being intimidated by the defendant, and he recovered as damages his loss of earnings based on the difference between his former wages as a lockkeeper and his present wages working for one of the gas boards, taking into account the fact that he would probably not have continued in his present employment as a lockkeeper for more than five years.[39d] The Court of Appeal reversed the decision, but only on liability.[39e] There should also be recovery for expenses incurred and for injured feelings in the same way as other economic torts.[39f]

Damages for the tort of intimidation are now also recognised in two-party **48-008C** intimidation cases. These damages should follow the same lines as the damages for deceit where the intimidation is of an economic nature or damages for assault, discrimination or harassment where the intimidation is of a physical or psychological nature. An early example of two-party intimidation is *Godwin v Uzoigwe*,[39g] where the intimidation was of a physical nature—intimidation of a teenage girl by a couple who had trafficked her from Nigeria to England and for two-and-a-half years had exploited and abused her by working her excessive hours without pay and denying her proper food, clothing and social intercourse. The trial judge awarded £25,000 and the Court of Appeal, without giving reasons, substituted £20,000. The depths of such exploitation and the effect upon such a claimant are now properly recognised by more substantial awards. For instance, in *Balogh v Hick Lane Bedding*,[39h] the three claimants were Hungarian nationals who were trafficked to England and put to work in the defendant's factory manufacturing bed frames and mattresses. The defendant failed to provide them with a safe system of work, and intimidated, harassed and exploited them. The claimants were awarded general damages for pain, suffering and loss of amenities consequent upon psychological injury, distress and anxiety and loss of dignity, and exemplary damages. The aggravation was included in the award of damages for injury to feelings and loss of dignity. Master Davison applied the *Vento* guidelines[39i] awarding the claimants amounts of general damages ranging from £50,000 to £65,000, £5,000 exemplary damages and pecuniary losses of up to £190,000.

[39b] [1964] A.C. 1129; [1964] 2 W.L.R. 269.

[39c] [1968] 1 Q.B. 521; [1967] 3 W.L.R. 65.

[39d] [1968] 1 Q.B. 521 at 548–549; [1967] 3 W.L.R. 65.

[39e] [1968] 2 Q.B. 710; [1968] 3 W.L.R. 506, CA.

[39f] See paras 48-008, 48-013 and 48-024, below.

[39g] [1992] T.L.R. 300 CA.

[39h] [2021] EWHC 1140 (QB).

[39i] See paras 43-006 to 43-007 above.

V.   INFRINGEMENT OF RIGHTS IN INTELLECTUAL PROPERTY

2.   THE PRESENT ENGLISH LAW, THE DIRECTIVE APART

(3)   Infringement of copyright and design right

(b)   The provision for additional damages

(iii)   Criteria for assessment

After para.48-070, add new paragraph:

48-070A   Although the quantum of additional damages can vary greatly according to the facts of the case, comparative cases can be useful in establishing a range of awards. But caution should be exercised here because facts can vary so greatly. There can be real dangers in trying to copy a percentage uplift from another case based on different facts. Indeed, there can be real dangers in using a percentage uplift at all because the coincidence of an amount of loss may have no bearing on the underlying punitive and aggravation principles of an award of additional damages. Thus, the percentage uplift amounts have varied greatly. As Mr David Stone observed, while sitting as a Deputy High Court judge in *Original Beauty Technology Co Ltd v G4K Fashion*,[410a] a percentage uplift has varied from 10% to 2100%. In that case, he awarded an amount of £300,000, being an uplift of 200% of the standard damages for a flagrant violation of the claimant's dress designs by more than 15,000 infringing garments. The amount was less than 1% of the defendants' audited turnover for the year.

[410a] [2021] EWHC 3439 (Ch); [2022] F.S.R. 11 at [145]–[147].

CHAPTER 49

MISREPRESENTATION

TABLE OF CONTENTS

I. **Fraudulent Misrepresentation: Deceit** 49-002
   1.   THE TORTIOUS MEASURE OF DAMAGES 49-002
   2.   HEADS OF DAMAGE 49-007
     (1)   Pecuniary loss ....49-007■
     (2)   Non-pecuniary loss 49-046
   3.   EXEMPLARY DAMAGES 49-050
   4.   DISGORGEMENT DAMAGES 49-051

II. **Negligent Misrepresentation** 49-052
   1.   LIABILITY AT COMMON LAW AND UNDER STATUTE 49-052
   2.   THE TORTIOUS MEASURE OF DAMAGES 49-055
   3.   HEADS OF DAMAGE 49-061
     (1)   Pecuniary loss 49-061
     (2)   Non-pecuniary loss 49-072

III. **Innocent Misrepresentation** 49-074

I. FRAUDULENT MISREPRESENTATION: DECEIT

2. HEADS OF DAMAGE

(1) Pecuniary loss

(c) Where the contract is for anything other than shares

(i) Normal measure

After para.49-028, insert new paragraphs:

It is a bold, and usually foolish, claimant who urges a court to depart from this **49-028A** well-established normal measure of damages which is based upon the difference between the price paid and the objective value received. But one case in which the claimant persuaded the judge to adopt a different approach was *Glossop Cartons and Print Ltd v Sidebottom*.[125a] The facts of the case were not unusual, involving a sale of business assets induced by deceit. The claimant paid £300,000 more for the assets than the market value of the business, with that amount being paid for goodwill which did not exist in the loss-making business. In an attempt to recover more than this amount the claimants advocated a measure of damages which started with the price they paid for the assets, a little more than £1.25 million, and then deducted from the cost each amount that the claimants had not subjectively factored into the price that they paid. In the leading judgment in the Court of Appeal, the Master of the Rolls, Sir Geoffrey Vos, said that the claimant's subjective views about what it was paying for the asset acquired was "nothing to the point".[125b] The approach is almost always an objective one.

[125a] [2021] EWCA Civ 639.

[125b] [2021] EWCA Civ 639 at [59].

49-028B   The focus of the normal measure upon undoing the wrongful act means that benefits to the claimant will rarely be taken into account to reduce damages unless the benefit is also received at the time the loss is suffered and has a degree of permanence. In *Tuke v Hood*[125c] the Court of Appeal considered submissions with a "veneer of plausibility" in which a fraudster submitted that in assessing damages for the fraudulent sale of appreciating luxury cars at an undervalue the defrauded seller should bring into account not merely the price received but also the benefit obtained of the opportunity of using the money. In the Court of Appeal, Andrews LJ (with whom Baker and Coulson LJJ agreed) held that the "notional interest to be earned in future is not part of the value he receives for the asset from the purchaser, nor is it properly described as a benefit conferred on him by the sale transaction".[125d] Indeed, even if the opportunity to earn interest or invest the money had actually been taken, and the defrauded claimant had, for example, won £1 million from gambling with the money, that gain would not have been set off, just as any subsequent independent loss would not have been.[125e]

[125c] [2022] EWCA Civ 23; [2022] 2 W.L.R. 983 at 987 [7].

[125d] [2022] EWCA Civ 23; [2022] 2 W.L.R. 983 at 994 [40].

[125e] [2022] EWCA Civ 23; [2022] 2 W.L.R. 983 at 996 [47]. See also *Komercni Banka AS v Stone & Rolls Ltd* [2002] EWHC 2263 (Comm); [2003] 1 Lloyd's Rep. 383.

After para.49-036, insert a new sub-heading and a new paragraph:

49-036A   *(iii) Avoiding double counting*   Since a normal measure and a consequential measure of damages are both available to rectify the wrongful act, it is necessary to avoid double counting. An example of double counting occurred in *Tuke v Hood*.[173a] In that case the claimant was defrauded into selling luxury cars at an undervalue. Jacobs J awarded the claimant the normal measure, which he described as "the base claim", being the difference between the value of the cars at the time of the transaction and the price received for them. But Jacobs J also awarded the claimant consequential losses for the lost investment opportunity as the difference between the greater price of the cars at the later date that they would have been sold and the price received for them. By allowing both heads of loss without adjustment, the double counting meant that the claimant could potentially have been awarded more than the value of the cars, even if they had not been sold. In a subsequent judgment which corrected this error, Jacobs J held that double counting could be avoided by awarding only the additional loss of investment opportunity based upon the market value at the time of the fraudulent transaction.[173b]

[173a] [2020] EWHC 2843 (Comm).

[173b] *Tuke v Hood* [2021] EWHC 74 (Comm) at [2]–[18].

PART 5 HUMAN RIGHTS

CHAPTER 50

DAMAGES UNDER THE HUMAN RIGHTS ACT

TABLE OF CONTENTS

1. INTRODUCTION 50-001
   (1) The turn to Strasbourg 50-005
   (2) A domestic turn? 50-009
2. SCOPE OF THE CAUSE OF ACTION 50-018
   (1) Who can be sued ....50-020□
   (2) Who can sue 50-029
   (3) Appropriate forum and procedural treatment of claims .. 50-040
   (4) Time for bringing claim 50-056
3. CRITERIA FOR DECISION WHETHER TO AWARD DAMAGES 50-062
   (1) General approach 50-062
   (2) Relevant factors 50-084
   (3) Article 13 of the European Convention 50-124
4. THE COURT'S APPROACH TO DETERMINING QUANTUM 50-132
   (1) General approach 50-132
   (2) Causation 50-158
   (3) Loss of a chance 50-173
5. AGGRAVATED AND EXEMPLARY DAMAGES 50-175
6. DAMAGES FOR BREACH OF PARTICULAR RIGHTS 50-181
   (1) Article 2: The right to life 50-182
   (2) Article 3: Prohibition of torture 50-187
   (3) Article 5: Right to liberty and security 50-190
   (4) Article 6: Right to a fair trial 50-194
   (5) Article 8: Right to respect for private and family life ... 50-197

2. SCOPE OF THE CAUSE OF ACTION

(1) Who can be sued

Replace footnote 69 with:

[69] See, for example, the Financial Services and Markets Act 2000 Sch.1 para.19(3)(b). Now, however, **50-028** repealed.

Goff & Jones on Unjust Enrichment, 10th Edition

Editors: *Professor Charles Mitchell QC (Hon) FBA, Professor Paul Mitchell and Professor Stephen Watterson*

ISBN: 978-0-414-10191-3

Forthcoming Publication

Hardback/ProView eBook/Westlaw UK

Goff & Jones is the leading work on the law of unjust enrichment. The new 10th Edition is completely up-to-date and contains detailed discussion of important decisions since the last edition. Several chapters have been wholly or substantially rewritten to take account of significant new cases, and their impact on topics including the recovery of benefits from remote recipients, the recovery of benefits transferred on a condition that fails, the recovery of ultra vires payments by public bodies, the limitation rules governing claims in unjust enrichment and interest awards on such claims.

The new edition contains detailed discussion of the following cases of major importance:

- *Investment Trust Companies (in liq.) v HMRC* [2018] A.C. 275.
- *Swynson Ltd v Lowick Rose LLP* (in liq.) [2018] A.C. 313.
- *Littlewoods Retail Ltd v HMRC (No.2)* [2018] A.C. 869.
- *Prudential Assurance Co Ltd v HMRC* [2019] A.C. 929.
- *Vodafone Ltd v Office of Communications* [2020] Q.B. 857.
- *Test Claimants in the FII Group Litigation v HMRC* [2022] A.C. 1.
- *Test Claimants in the FII Group Litigation v HMRC* [2021] 1 W.L.R. 4354.
- *Pakistan International Airline Corp v Times Travel (UK) Ltd* [2021] 3 W.L.R. 727.
- *School Facility Management Ltd v Christ the King College* [2021] 1 W.L.R. 6129

Charlesworth & Percy on Negligence, 15th Edition

General Editor: *Mark Armitage*

ISBN: 978-0-414-10290-3

June 2022

Hardback/ProView eBook/Westlaw UK

As the foremost guide **Charlesworth & Percy on Negligence** offers unrivalled depth of analysis into the tort of negligence. Building on the excellence of previous editions, the 15th edition focuses on the considerable body of new case law that has emerged since the previous edition and recent legislative changes.

The new edition discusses the following key case law to name a few:

In the Supreme Court

- *Manchester Building Society v Grant Thornton UK LLP* [2021] UKSC 20: examining the fundamental ingredients of the modern tort of negligence and the significance of the scope of a defendant's duty of care in relation to issues of both duty and causation.
- *Khan v Meadows* [2021] UKSC 21: consideration of the principles developed in *Manchester Building Society* in the context of a claim for clinical negligence.

In the Court of Appeal

- *Ford v Seymour-Williams* [2021] EWCA Civ 1848: examining the ingredients required for a finding of liability pursuant to Animals Act 1980 s.2(2).
- *Blackpool Football Club Ltd v DSN* [2021] EWCA Civ 1352: application of the principles of vicarious liability in relation to the actions of an unpaid football scout.

Clerk & Lindsell on Torts, 2nd Supplement to the 23rd Edition

General Editor: *Andrew Tettenborn*

ISBN: 978-0-414-10347-4

June 2022

Paperback/ProView eBook/Westlaw UK

Clerk & Lindsell on Torts, one of our flagship titles and part of the Common Law Library series, is an essential reference tool which is widely referred to by practitioners and cited by the judiciary. It offers the most comprehensive coverage of the subject, providing the end user with indispensable access to current, frequent and unrivalled authoritative information on all aspects of tort law.

The new supplement brings the Main Work fully up to date with the latest developments (including, where appropriate, the fallout from the completion of the Brexit process). These include, among others:

- *ZXC v Bloomberg* on misuse of private information and breach of copyright.
- *Secretary of State for Health v Servier Laboratories Ltd* on the economic torts and unlawful means.
- *McQuillan's Application for Judicial Review* on timing and liability under the Human Rights Act 1998.
- *Bell v Tavistock & Portman NHS Foundation Trust* on young persons and consent to gender reassignment.
- *Barking & Dagenham LBC v Persons Unknown* on property, injunctions, and anonymous trespassers.

Asbestos: Law & Litigation, 2nd Edition

General Editors: *Harry Steinberg QC, Michael Rawlinson QC and James Beeton*

ISBN: 978-0-414-10233-0

June 2022

Hardback/ProView eBook/Westlaw UK

Asbestos: Law & Litigation is the first comprehensive guide to claims for asbestos-related injury in the UK. It has been written by experienced practitioners involved in many of the leading cases on the subject. The scope of the book is wide-ranging; from the development of knowledge, to the law of damages, with all of the legal and practical issues in between.

The new edition discusses the following key case law to name a few:

- *Steve Hill Ltd v Witham, Head v Culver Heating Co Ltd* and *Rix v Paramount Shopfitting Company Ltd*: a recent trilogy of Court of Appeal judgments which clarified the proper approach to the assessment of losses in asbestos disease claims.
- *Bussey v Anglia Heating Ltd*: a key Court of Appeal decision concerning the correct approach to foreseeable risks in tort law and the impact and relevance of important technical guidance documents in asbestos claims.
- *HMG3 LTD v Dunn*: bespoke High Court guidance on the court's approach to the exercise of its discretion to disapply the primary limitation period in cases involving claims for fatal asbestos disease.

Contact us on :   Tel: +44 (0)345 600 9355

Order online: sweetandmaxwell.co.uk